THE GREAT CHIEF JUSTICE

JOHN MARSHALL AND THE RULE OF LAW

CHARLES F. HOBSON

UNIVERSITY PRESS OF KANSAS

Published by the University Press of Kansas (Lawrence, Kansas 66049), which was organized by the Kansas Board of Regents and is operated and funded by Emporia State University, Fort Hays State University, Kansas State University, Pittsburg State University, the
University of Kansas, and Wichita State University

Library of Congress Cataloging-in-Publication Data

Hobson, Charles F.
  The great chief justice: John Marshall and the rule of law / Charles F.
Hobson
    p.   cm. — (American political thought)
  Includes bibliographical references and index.
  ISBN 0-7006-0788-9 (alk. paper)   ISBN 0-7006-1031-6 (pbk.)
  1. Marshall, John, 1755–1835. 2. United States. Supreme Court—
History. 3. United States—Constitutional history. 4. Law—United
States—History. I. Title. II. Series.
KF8745.M3H63 1996
347.73'2634—dc20
[B]
[347.3073534]   96-11195
[B]

British Library Cataloguing in Publication Data is available.

Printed in the United States of America

10 9 8 7 6 5 4

THE GREAT
CHIEF JUSTICE

AMERICAN POLITICAL THOUGHT

EDITED BY
WILSON CAREY MCWILLIAMS & LANCE BANNING

To the memory of my parents
and
to Ann

CONTENTS

PREFACE

The American Revolution's most important contribution to political theory was the location of sovereignty in "the people." The founding generation also gave practical effect to the idea of popular sovereignty in the form of conventions and written constitutions. Theory and practice blended in the framing and ratifying of the United States Constitution. As the permanent embodiment of the people's will, the Constitution was designed to check and control popular government. Precisely how this purpose was to be accomplished, however, was left largely unanswered in 1787. During the next generation Americans formulated an answer that placed major responsibility for safeguarding and interpreting the Constitution in the hands of the judiciary. John Marshall had a pivotal role in this development, making the most of his opportunities for creative judicial statesmanship. His working life spanned the years from the Revolution to the age of Jackson, a period that embraced both the "creation" and the "growth and development" of the American federal republic. Marshall belonged not only to the founding generation but also to the subsequent generation that gave shape and substance to the Constitution that was brought into being in 1787. As chief justice of the United States from 1801 to 1835, he remained on the public stage far longer than his political contemporaries.

Marshall was a man of affairs—soldier, legislator, diplomat, statesman, lawyer, and judge—not a contemplative theorist. He never composed a treatise on government or jurisprudence, though he certainly possessed the intellectual ability and literary talent to produce such a work had he been so inclined. He was capable of deep thought and reflection, but his interest in law and the principles of government was not of a bookish or an academic sort. He was not a scholar-statesman like James Madison, John Adams, or John C. Calhoun; nor was he a legal commentator and publicist like Joseph Story or James Kent. Marshall's learning in government, law, and history, acquired largely through self-tuition, was by no means inconsiderable, but he pursued knowledge to derive assistance or illumination in carrying out particular public and professional tasks. His writings—whether a legislative speech, newspaper essay, diplomatic communication, or judicial opinion—originated in the concrete circumstances of the moment, not out of a conscious design to make an enduring statement of principles.[1]

Yet it was precisely his genius for generalization, for expanding the range and level of discourse beyond the immediate context, that gave Marshall's writings their distinctive quality—and, in the case of his constitutional opinions, their status as important texts of American political thought. His characteristic habit of traveling outside the narrow confines of a particular controversy, his penchant for interweaving "general and abstract doctrine . . . with the decision of the particular case," imparted to his opinions an authoritative, even oracular quality, as if he were unfolding the true meaning of the Constitution.[2] Marshall's importance in the history of American political thought rests on his masterly skill in articulating and applying the leading ideas that emerged from the founding period of the American republic. He was a creative adapter of ideas, not an original thinker who formulated new insights into the nature of government and law.

Chief Justice Marshall was part and parcel of the emergence of the judiciary, "the least dangerous branch" of government, to a status coordinate with the legislative and executive branches. In the United States, judges appointed for life came to be entrusted with power to check and control popularly elected legislatures and executives. Moreover, paradoxical as it seems, this development was justified on the basis of popular sovereignty. The judiciary in America somehow became an institution by which popular sovereignty could restrain popular government. Courts and judges supplied a "republican remedy for the diseases most incident to republican government" that Madison could scarcely have imagined or approved at the time he penned *Federalist* No. 10. "The most dramatic institutional transformation in the early

Republic," writes historian Gordon Wood, "was the rise of what was called an 'independent judiciary.'"[3] John Marshall was both a contributor to and a beneficiary of this transformation.

The emergence of an independent judiciary in the early republic was related to a broader historical trend that scholars have identified as the transition from a "classical republican" political culture of the Revolutionary period to a "liberal" political culture that was more or less in place by 1840. In brief, the essentially patrician, deferential, and communal society of the late eighteenth century evolved into the essentially egalitarian, democratic, and individualistic society of the early nineteenth century. Although historians have pinpointed this change as occurring in the early decades of the nineteenth century, the process was far from complete then or for many years thereafter. In truth, the United States never fully shed its classical republican origins in adopting liberalism as the predominant ideology. Classical values persisted long past the close of the classical era and in some measure continue to permeate our democratic culture and institutions. The Constitution and its institutional guardian, the Supreme Court, are tangible links with our classical past and part of Marshall's legacy as well.

Republicanism was the prevailing ideology of the Revolution, an ideology that was radical, egalitarian, and democratic in its implications. In overthrowing the monarchical regime, however, many American revolutionaries envisioned a republican order that largely retained the ancient distinction between the "few" and the "many." They sincerely believed in "popular" government in the sense of a fairly widespread voting franchise (among white males owning at least some property) but that government itself would continue to be the preserve of the "better sort," gentlemen of sufficient property, education, and leisure to enable them to govern wisely and virtuously. But the radical egalitarianism of the Revolution undermined this patrician republican order almost from its inception. And the Constitution of 1787 was at best a partial and temporary success in its endeavor to shore up and strengthen the classical republic.[4] Throughout his life Marshall steadfastly adhered to the principles, beliefs, and values of the old republic—the balanced government of the Constitution, the wise and virtuous leadership of disinterested statesmen, and the respectful obedience by the citizenry to government and laws. With both chagrin and resignation he witnessed the transformation of the orderly, deferential republic of the founders into the volatile mass democracy of the age of Jackson.

My serious encounter with John Marshall began in 1979, when I assumed the editorship of *The Papers of John Marshall*, a documentary edition sponsored by the College of William and Mary and the Institute of Early American History and Culture. Previously, I had spent seven years with *The Papers of James Madison* project at the University of Virginia. The perspective I bring to the study of Marshall's political and constitutional thought is that of a historian whose calling for more than two decades has been documentary editing. I have had the good fortune to spend my days in the company, so to speak, of two Virginians who profoundly influenced the creation and development of the United States Constitution. That experience has impressed me with the conviction that the constitutional vision that inspired Madison in the 1780s was essentially the same one that animated Marshall as chief justice of the United States.

This book is intended to be a concise yet comprehensive explication of Marshall's jurisprudence. I begin with a biographical sketch and synopsis of his judicial career, emphasizing the decisive influence of the Confederation period in forging his republican political beliefs and nationalist outlook. I next examine the legal culture that shaped Marshall as a lawyer and jurist, namely, the common law tradition as adapted to eighteenth-century Virginia, with a view toward explaining his understanding of judicial discretion. The heart of the book is devoted to his major constitutional opinions, which are grouped around chapters on judicial review, the contract clause, and national supremacy. The doctrine of judicial review as proclaimed in *Marbury* v. *Madison* (1803), I contend, was neither novel nor highly controversial. Marshall understood judicial review as founded in the joining together of the ideas of popular sovereignty and fundamental law in a written constitution. As chief justice he solidified the practice of judicial review by adapting the methods of common law interpretation to the task of expounding the Constitution.

The Marshall Court characteristically employed judicial review to void acts enacted by the state legislatures. In one class of cases, centering on the contract clause, the state law was nullified as unconstitutionally infringing on the private rights of individuals; in another, centering on the supremacy clause, the state legislation was struck down as repugnant to the exercise of a power vested in the federal government. My reading sees the Court as endorsing a limited, essentially defensive form of constitutional nationalism that left ample room for the exercise of state sovereignty. The final two chapters explore more systematically the subject of judicial discretion, drawing upon Marshall's nonconstitutional and private law decisions as well as those expounding the Constitution and public law. The chief justice's continuing endeavor to define the limits of judicial power, to preserve the distinction between law and politics, is evident in some degree in virtually all of his adjudications and forms a unifying theme of his judicial career.

The principal source for this study is the large body of formal opinions that Marshall produced during three decades as a sitting judge. While giving full attention to the "great cases" of constitutional law, I have referred extensively to opinions given in the ordinary cases that composed the bulk of his judicial business. The chief justice revealed the characteristic qualities of his mind as much in disposing of a routine suit for debt as in settling the meaning of the fundamental law. My documentary editing experience has instilled in me the importance of regarding documents in their entirety. I have accordingly devoted ample space to summarizing the major constitutional law opinions in a way that imparts a sense of the logical structure and development of the argument. Synopsis can never be more than a pale reflection of the original, an observation that applies with peculiar force to Marshall's decisions. The rigorous logic and unadorned reasoning that characterize his writing defy easy summary. Marshall read legal texts and wrote his own with exquisite care, with a keen sensitivity to the meaning of words. As Marshall himself examined statutory text to determine legislative intent, so I have searched for the jurist's "intent"—his assumptions, beliefs, ideas, and motives—through a close reading of his judicial writings.

In an important sense I seek to recover a "legal" John Marshall by examining his jurisprudence from the perspective of the common law tradition in which he was bred. Despite some excellent revisionist scholarship during the last thirty years, there is still a prevailing view of Marshall (popularized by biographer Albert J. Beveridge) as a kind of country lawyer unencumbered with much learning, though possessed of a first-rate mind. It is sometimes suggested or implied that his supposed deficiency of law knowledge actually served him well as a jurist, that ignorance of the weight of authority left him freer to practice creative jurisprudence. The chief justice, we are told, did not bother to cite authorities and disdained precedent, as evidenced by his reported remark to Associate Justice Story: "Now, Story, that is the law; you find the precedents for it."[5] This is one apocryphal story that, far from illustrating a truth, perpetuates a myth that needs correcting. The view set forth here is that Marshall was a master of the law and that his mastery of the science was not the least of those attributes which enabled him to achieve eminence as the great chief justice.

I take pleasure in acknowledging those persons who have directly or indirectly influenced the making of this book. Laura S. Gwilliam, my longtime associate on the Marshall Papers, did not live to see publication but was a constant source of encouragement and support during the writing. She was a discerning reader and gentle critic, but more important she was my dear friend. Her radiant personality, charm, and buoyant good humor brightened my days immeasurably. I shall always cherish the memory of her delightful company and shall never forget her courage and self-possession in the face of illness.

Many years ago Robert A. Rutland offered me the opportunity to work on the Madison Papers edition. I am grateful to him not only for extending the invitation but more importantly for entrusting me with major responsibility for particular volumes of that series. In this way he allowed me to develop the experience and qualifications to direct my own editorial project when the opportunity arose. Among the pleasures of directing the Marshall edition has been the opportunity to make acquaintances and develop friendships with scholars, biographers, and others who have used our resources. Over the years L. J. Priestley, judge of the Court of Appeal of New South Wales, Australia, has made several visits to our project. Judge Priestley has a particular interest in Marshall arising from his larger enterprise of exploring the comparative dimensions of United States and Australian law. I have derived incalculable benefit from sharing the company of a working judge who is also a keen student of legal history. Professor Jean Edward Smith of the University of Toronto, author of a major new biography of Marshall, has also been a regular visitor to our offices in recent years. Our many conversations have helped me to refine and solidify my own understanding of the chief justice.

I am grateful to Lance Banning and Carey McWilliams, editors of the

American Political Thought series, for inviting me to participate in this worthy enterprise and for reading the manuscript. Professor Banning, in particular, was a model reader who not only unerringly identified weak points in the argument but also suggested ways I might extricate myself. Kent Newmyer also read the manuscript and offered wise counsel for improving the work. I thank Fred Woodward for his encouragement, patience, and gentle prodding as I ever so slowly carried this project through to completion. An early version of Chapter 2 was presented at the 34th Annual Missouri Valley History Conference, held in Omaha, Nebraska, in March 1991.

This book is dedicated to the memory of my late parents, Richmond P. Hobson and Alice Carey Hobson, and to my wife, Ann Loflin Hobson. For more than a quarter century, Ann has been my loving partner and devoted friend. She has blessed me with her unwavering faith and the precious gift of two exemplary children, Elizabeth and John.

1

REPUBLICAN
REVOLUTIONARY

LIFE AND CAREER TO 1801

John Marshall took the oath of office as chief justice of the United States on February 4, 1801. Then forty-five years of age, he had had a varied career as a soldier, state legislator and executive councillor, lawyer, commissioner to France, member of Congress, and secretary of state. An autobiographical sketch drawn late in life portrays Marshall somewhat misleadingly as an accidental statesman who never aspired to a place in the highest councils of the American republic. In truth, his public career did owe as much to fortuitous circumstances as to conscious design. Although the American Revolution was a powerful attractive force that drew talented and ambitious men into public life, Marshall until the late 1790s largely resisted the call of politics in the face of a more compelling need to make his fortune. Unlike Thomas Jefferson and James Madison, whose inherited wealth allowed them to make statecraft their profession from an early age, the future chief justice first had to concentrate on the mundane business of providing financial security for himself and a growing family. Intermittent though it was prior to 1801, Marshall's participation in public life occurred at times and places that in retrospect appear to have been nicely calculated to prepare him for his high judicial station.

The eldest of fifteen children, Marshall was born September 24, 1755, at Germantown, Virginia, then a part of Prince William County that four years later was incorporated into the new county of Fauquier.

1

His father, Thomas Marshall, was a planter of middling circumstances whose ambition, good marriage, and success in land speculation made him one of the leading men of Fauquier, then a frontier county. His mother, Mary Randolph Keith, was a clergyman's daughter, and through her Marshall was connected with such "first families" of Virginia as the Randolphs and the Lees. The father exerted the stronger influence on young John Marshall's early development. Possessed himself of "a very limited education," Thomas Marshall (his son later recollected)

> was a man to whom nature had been bountiful, and who had assiduously improved her gifts. He superintended my education and gave me an early taste for history and for poetry . . . and to his care I am indebted for anything valuable which I may have acquired in my youth. He was my only intelligent companion; and was both a watchfull parent and an affectionate instructive friend.[1]

At age fourteen Marshall spent a year at the school of the Reverend Archibald Campbell in Westmoreland County (where a future president, James Monroe, was a fellow scholar). Then followed a year of study at home with a Scottish tutor, James Thomson, the local parish priest who temporarily resided with the Marshall family. The two years with Campbell and Thomson constituted the extent of Marshall's formal schooling before the outbreak of the War of Independence. From these two preceptors he acquired the rudiments of a classical education and was beginning to read Horace and Livy by the time Thomson departed. Thereafter young Marshall continued his classical studies "with no other aid than my Dictionary."[2] As important as formal instruction was Marshall's exposure to the informal "curriculum" of the colonial Virginia gentry, that unexcelled practical school for training future American statesmen. In the frontier county of Fauquier, Thomas Marshall enjoyed the free play of his ambition and talent and was able to rise quickly to a position of prominence. He served as surveyor, justice of the peace, sheriff, vestryman, militia leader, and burgess of the county. By observing his father—his close companion—in these various roles, John Marshall acquired the values and habits of a Virginia gentleman and gained admittance to the most famous ruling class America has produced.[3]

At the onset of hostilities with Great Britain, Marshall put aside the classics and Blackstone's *Commentaries* (which he apparently had begun to read before the war) in favor of military exercises and reading political essays. When war broke out, he took up arms, first as an officer of the county militia, then as an officer in the Virginia line of the Continental army. He participated in the battles of Brandywine Creek, Germantown, Monmouth, and Stony Point and also survived the harsh winter's encampment at Valley Forge in 1777 and 1778. During an interlude in the war, in the winter and spring of 1780, Marshall attended a course of lectures on law and natural philosophy at the College of William and Mary. The newly appointed professor of law was George Wythe, who had been Jefferson's law mentor and was then an eminent judge of the Virginia High Court of Chancery. Wythe's lectures occurred twice a week over several months, supplemented by monthly moot court exercises and individual tutorial sessions. The term at William and Mary constituted Marshall's only formal study of law, but at the time formal instruction was not the ordinary means of legal education. Law was a practical profession, for which most aspirants prepared by apprenticeship to a practicing attorney. Marshall's law course with Professor Wythe supplemented his own self-education, which began before and certainly continued after his college attendance. By the standards of the day, Marshall's legal education was equal if not superior to that of his fellow practitioners.

Whatever mastery of the law Marshall had gained by the time he left college in the summer of 1780 was sufficient to qualify him for a law license. The commencement of his law career, however, was postponed until after the British capitulation at Yorktown in October 1781. Full of ambition and talent to match, Marshall rapidly ascended the professional ladder, particularly after moving permanently to Richmond, the state capital, in 1784. Here he joined the small fraternity of lawyers who practiced in the superior courts of the state: the General Court, the High Court of Chancery, and the Court of Appeals. By the end of the 1780s, his reputation placed him at the top of the bar and his income grew commensurately, eventually reaching the tidy sum of five thousand dollars annually. In the meantime he had married, early in 1783, Mary Willis Ambler (known to him throughout his life as "dearest Polly"), daughter of the state treasurer. Ten children were born to the couple, six of whom survived to adulthood.

While building up his law practice, Marshall found time to sit in the Virginia House of Delegates, to which he was first elected as a member from Fauquier in 1782. From November 1782 to April 1784 he served on the Council of State, the executive body of the state government. He then returned to the legislature, serving at the 1784 and 1787 sessions (the latter as delegate from Henrico County). The questions agitating the public mind in those years, the chief justice later recalled, were "paper money, the collection of taxes, the preservation of public faith, and the administration of justice. . . . The state of the Confederacy was also a subject of deep solicitude." On these issues Marshall followed the lead of James Madison, "the enlightened advocate of Union and of an efficient federal government."[4]

All the important questions of the 1780s, whether relating to the internal politics of the states or to the reform of the Confederation, were subsumed in the debate over the Constitution in 1787 and 1788. In no other state was the plan more brilliantly or more fiercely contested, its merits and defects more exhaustively considered, than in Virginia. Marshall actively participated in this debate, most importantly as a delegate to the state ratifying convention of June 1788. Here in the heat of debate he was compelled to reflect on fundamental questions of government, to sharpen and refine the ideas, principles, and beliefs that had been forming in his mind during the previous decade. Nothing could match this assembly in forensic talent arrayed on both sides of the question, with Madison and Edmund Randolph leading the proponents of the Constitution and Patrick Henry and George Mason at the head of the opposition. The very closeness of the contest in Virginia subjected the plan to a searching examination of nearly all its parts, which, with the publication of the debates, became an enduring commentary on the Constitution. But nothing could compare with actual presence at this defining and clarifying moment in the history of the Constitution. To this "ardent and eloquent discussion," Marshall later remarked, "justice never has been and never can be done."[5] He emerged from the convention with a deep conviction that the Constitution marked a decisive break with the past. At the same time, however, he could not fail to recognize the great strength of antifederalism, a political force that he knew would not suddenly die out with ratification but would continue to stand forth as a potential alternative to his own understanding of the Constitution.

Marshall's most important contribution to the cause of ratification was a speech defending the judiciary article, in the course of which he assumed the federal judiciary would have power to pronounce a law invalid that was contrary to the Constitution. If Congress, said Marshall, "were to make a law not warranted by any of the powers enumerated, it would be considered by the Judges as an infringement of the Constitution which they are to guard: They would not consider such a law as coming under their jurisdiction. They would declare it void."[6] Thus did the future chief justice give early expression to the idea that judges should be guardians of the Constitution.

From the time the new government went into effect in 1789 until his judicial appointment twelve years later, Marshall made occasional forays into the public arena that gained him further valuable experience in constitutional dialectics. Pressed to run for Congress or accept a federal office, he resolutely declined all such offers (which included appointments as attorney general and associate justice of the Supreme Court). He could not yet afford to give up his lucrative law practice, which now had expanded to include business in the new federal courts. Politics constantly beckoned during the decade of the 1790s, however, as divisions over financial and foreign policy gave birth to an opposition party, the Republicans, led by Jefferson and Madison. There was never any question that Marshall, whose association (through his father) with George Washington dated from before the Revolution, would remain unswervingly loyal to the president. Although no longer in the state legislature, Marshall assumed responsibility for defending the administration, becoming more or less by default the unofficial leader of the Federalist party in Virginia. This role first became public in the summer of 1793, when at a public meeting in Richmond he drew up a series of resolutions condemning the conduct of French minister Edmond Genêt, who in defiance of American neutrality attempted to outfit privateers in American ports to attack British shipping. Marshall also prepared an address to the president praising him and his administration. For these endeavors Marshall "was attacked with great virulence" in a series of newspaper essays written by James Monroe under the pseudonym of "Agricola." Marshall defended himself and administration policy "with equal vivacity" in four essays under the name of "Aristides" and "Gracchus."[7]

Two years later Marshall again found himself in the midst of partisan warfare, this time over the controversial commercial treaty with Great

Britain negotiated by John Jay. Although ratified by the Senate and signed by President Washington in the summer of 1795, the Jay Treaty provoked such bitter opposition that for a time it appeared the House of Representatives would withhold appropriations to implement it. Once more a member of the Virginia legislature, Marshall at the November 1795 session boldly defended the treaty's constitutionality, and at a public meeting in Richmond in April 1796 he persuaded a majority to adopt resolutions in favor of giving full effect to the treaty. The House subsequently voted the necessary appropriations. These efforts attracted notice beyond the borders of Virginia, as an account of Marshall's speech in the legislature was published widely in newspapers. When, in February 1796, Marshall went to Philadelphia to argue the case of *Ware* v. *Hylton,* Federalist members of Congress received him "with marked attention and favour."[8] Although he lost the only case he ever argued before the Supreme Court, Marshall formed valuable associations with leading northern Federalists, including Fisher Ames, Theodore Sedgwick, and Rufus King.

Having turned down repeated offers of federal appointments, Marshall in June 1797 accepted President John Adams's appointment to a commission (with Charles Cotesworth Pinckney and Elbridge Gerry) to settle outstanding differences with the revolutionary republic of France. In this instance, ambition (along with an erroneous assumption that the mission would require only a brief absence from home) overrode his usual reluctance, as he later explained: "I will confess that the *eclat* which would attend a successful termination of the differences between the two countries had no small influence over a mind in which ambition, though subjected to controul, was not absolutely extinguished."[9] The mission, which kept Marshall abroad for more than a year, was in fact a failure, as the French refused to enter into negotiations until the United States agreed to a loan and payment of a bribe to high officials of the revolutionary government. The mission's failure was nevertheless a personal triumph for Marshall. The dispatches he wrote reporting the commissioners' steadfast refusal to compromise American sovereignty and independence and detailing the intrigues and insulting behavior of the wily French foreign minister Talleyrand and his anonymous agents, "X," "Y," and "Z," created a sensation when published in the newspapers back home. On arriving in New York in June 1798, Marshall was acclaimed a national hero.

Marshall expected to resume full-time practice of law, needing all the income he could command in order to fulfill a contract entered into some years earlier to purchase the Fairfax estate in the Northern Neck of Virginia. These financial considerations, however, yielded to the persuasive powers of General Washington, who urged Marshall to become a candidate for Congress. From December 1799 to May 1800 Marshall served in the Sixth Congress, distinguishing himself in the debates of that notable session as a formidable spokesman for the Adams administration. In March 1800 he delivered the greatest speech (apart from his judicial opinions) of his career, a defense of the president's conduct in the so-called Jonathan Robbins affair. Robbins, who claimed to be an American impressed into British service, had been turned over to British authorities in compliance with the extradition article of the Jay Treaty and was subsequently executed for murder. When Republicans attacked Adams for surrendering Robbins without a trial in American courts, Marshall presented a masterly defense of the president's action as properly within the sphere of the executive's authority to carry out the terms of national treaties.

For this great forensic effort, Adams rewarded Marshall with a place in his cabinet. From May 1800 through the remainder of Adams's term, Marshall was secretary of state. Although he administered that department less than a year, Marshall made a valuable contribution, most notably in forwarding negotiations with Great Britain concerning pre-Revolutionary debts owed to British subjects; this diplomacy bore fruit early in the new administration. Besides carrying out his official duties, Marshall acted as Adams's trusted and confidential adviser. He drafted the president's annual message to Congress and counseled him on the numerous judicial appointments that marked the final days of his presidency. Among these appointments was the chief justiceship of the United States, now vacant by the resignation of Oliver Ellsworth. Adams's first choice, John Jay, who had served as the first chief justice, declined. Not wishing to delay further and risk letting the appointment fall to his Republican successor, Adams tendered the appointment in person to Marshall, who "was pleased as well as surprized, and bowed in silence."[10] He was confirmed by the Senate on January 27, 1801, a little more than a month before he administered the oath of office to President Thomas Jefferson.

A technically sound lawyer and a statesman of broad experience,

John Marshall was a happy choice to fill the highest judicial office in the land. As preparation for his role on the Supreme Court, the knowledge and understanding gained through participation in government were no less essential than the lawyerly skills acquired over nearly twenty years' practice in the state and federal courts. In the area of public law, and constitutional law in particular, his training could not have been better. He came to the bench thoroughly versed in the political processes and workings of the federal and state governments, and he understood as well as anyone the nature and boundaries of legislative, executive, and judicial power. On the state level, he had been a member of the executive council, served in the House of Delegates, and as a lawyer was of course thoroughly familiar with the court system. His federal experience also included legislative and executive service, and again his law practice brought him into regular contact with the judicial branch. "Experience of men and affairs" in these various public offices "doubtless reinforced a temperament to which abstract theorizing was never congenial," wrote a twentieth-century judge who admired Marshall's "hardheaded appreciation of the complexities of government, particularly in a federal system."[11]

THE SUPREME COURT YEARS

At this point the biography of Marshall becomes scarcely distinguishable from the history of the Supreme Court, where he presided for the next thirty-four years. As chief justice, Marshall sat not only on the high court but also on the United States Circuit Courts for Virginia and North Carolina. Over the next three decades he marched to the rhythms of these various court seasons: from February (January, beginning in 1827) to mid-March, he attended the Supreme Court in Washington; from early May to mid-June, and again from early November through mid-December, he held circuit in Raleigh and Richmond. In summertime the chief justice and his family escaped the Richmond heat for extended visits to the mountains, where they often remained until late September or early October. Enjoying unusually good health until late in life, Marshall was present at every Supreme Court term and rarely missed a circuit throughout his long judicial career.

The dominant theme of Marshall's early years on the bench was conflict between the federal judiciary and the new Republican political
majority that controlled the legislative and executive branches.[12]
Among the first acts of the new Congress was the repeal of the Judiciary Act of 1801, which abolished in one stroke the host of new judge-
ships (the so-called "midnight judges") filled by Adams's appointees.
Despite serious reservations about the constitutionality of this action,
Marshall and his fellow Supreme Court justices acquiesced in the repeal. On the other hand, in the case of *Marbury* v. *Madison* (1803),
which arose directly out of the refusal of the Jefferson administration
to deliver a commission to a justice of the peace appointed by Adams,
the Court sternly rebuked the executive for failing to perform its duty.
This case was the first occasion in which the Supreme Court pronounced a law of Congress unconstitutional, though the most controversial aspect of the case at the time was the Court's alleged meddling
in the affairs of the executive department. The *Marbury* opinion was
followed soon after by the impeachment and conviction of a federal
judge and the impeachment of Associate Supreme Court Justice
Samuel Chase, notorious for using his judicial pulpit to air his highly
partisan Federalist views. The Senate's acquittal of Chase, early in
1805, signified a triumph of moderation, however, and introduced a
period of accommodation, if not harmony, between the judicial and
political branches. Conflict did break out anew during the celebrated
treason trial of Aaron Burr, which took place in Marshall's circuit
court at Richmond in the summer of 1807. But by then the concept of
an independent judiciary had more or less gained general acceptance.
Subjected to occasional verbal assaults, the federal judiciary not only
survived intact but in subsequent years also consolidated its independence and expanded its powers.

After 1807 relations between the administration and judiciary im-
proved, reflecting changes in court personnel and a shared commitment to upholding national power. In return for dutifully enforcing the
government's embargo policy, the judiciary received timely and public
support from Madison's administration when the state of Pennsylvania
openly resisted the Supreme Court's decree in *United States* v. *Peters*
(1809). Fortified by this endorsement of federal judicial power against
an assertion of states' rights, the Supreme Court in 1810 for the first
time nullified a state law as repugnant to the Constitution. The same

case, *Fletcher* v. *Peck,* was also the first of a line of decisions interpreting the contract clause of the Constitution.

By 1811 five Republicans had joined Marshall and Bushrod Washington on the Supreme Court, and no further changes occurred until 1823. Party affiliations were virtually meaningless, however, as Marshall enjoyed an unusually harmonious relationship with his brethren. The Court's internal unity—fostered by the chief justice's effective leadership and by fundamental agreement on basic values embodied in the Constitution—was never stronger than during the years from 1812 to 1824. Marshall's greatest constitutional opinions belong to this period: *McCulloch* v. *Maryland* (1819), which in upholding Congress's power to charter a national bank yielded a classic statement of the doctrines of implied powers and national supremacy; *Dartmouth College* v. *Woodward* (1819), which brought corporate charters within the protection of the contract clause; *Cohens* v. *Virginia* (1821), another forceful statement of national supremacy that reaffirmed the Supreme Court's appellate jurisdiction over state judiciaries; and *Gibbons* v. *Ogden* (1824), yet another expansive construction of federal power, this time Congress's power to regulate interstate commerce.

By upholding the exercise of national power, striking down state laws, and asserting a supervisory role over the state courts, the Marshall Court roused the spirit of antifederalism and states' rights, nowhere with greater intensity than in the chief justice's own state, Virginia. The *McCulloch* and *Cohens* opinions, in particular, were subjected to withering denunciation by newspaper essayists, led by Judge Spencer Roane of the Virginia Court of Appeals. Roane and other critics accused the Court of converting a government of limited powers into a "consolidated" government, reducing the states to nullities. These censures so alarmed Marshall that he felt compelled to respond in a series of anonymous newspaper essays. To the chief justice the attacks on the Court were really an attack upon the union, an attempt to reinstate the old Confederation. The aftermath of the *McCulloch* and *Cohens* opinions saw periodic attempts in Congress to curb the powers of the federal judiciary. Bills were introduced, for example, to take away the Supreme Court's appellate jurisdiction in cases where a state chose to become a party, to prevent the Court from hearing appeals from state courts, and to require the concurrence of a supermajority of justices in constitutional cases. That none of these measures succeeded signified an underlying agreement among the American people to preserve the integrity of the institution.

This consensus (clear enough in retrospect, if not to Marshall and his brethren) did not, to be sure, spare the Court from occasional political controversy. During the last decade of his tenure, Marshall continually met with serious challenges to his vision of union and national power and of the role of the Supreme Court as arbiter of the Constitution. Whether by coincidence or for reasons of political expediency, the Supreme Court began to render decisions more favorable to state power. In *Willson* v. *Blackbird Marsh Company* (1829), a commerce clause case, and again in *Providence Bank* v. *Billings* (1830), a contract case, the Court upheld the state law in question. In his last constitutional opinion, *Barron* v. *Baltimore* (1833), Marshall ruled that the Bill of Rights restricted only the federal government, not the state governments.

The internal unity of the Court also began to break down during the last years, a reflection of the chief's diminishing hold over a Court that was also changing with the addition of new members. Not only did separate and dissenting opinions appear more frequently, but after 1830 the justices' communal living arrangements came to an end. In *Ogden* v. *Saunders* (1827), a contract case, Marshall found himself in the minority and registered his only dissent in a constitutional case. Even when the Court did strike down state laws, as in *Craig* v. *Missouri* (1830) and in *Worcester* v. *Georgia* (1832), Marshall was unable to restore the old harmony. The latter case—in which the rights of the Cherokee Indians clashed with the asserted sovereignty of the state of Georgia—underscored the impotence of the Supreme Court to check determined political majorities.

The erosion of the Court's unity coincided with (and seemed to be symptomatic of) a larger crisis of union that overshadowed Marshall's final years on the bench. Nothing portended the mortality of the Constitution and union more ominously than the doctrine of nullification, by which the states claimed the right to declare federal laws unconstitutional and nullify their operation. Marshall regarded this idea as so "extravagant in itself, and so repugnant to the existence of Union between the States" that he could scarcely "believe it was seriously entertained by any person." It was founded on the erroneous assumption that the Constitution was "essentially a LEAGUE and not a GOVERNMENT." If this were the true construction, he asked, what was the point of replacing the Articles of Confederation with the Constitution? "Was it worth the effort of all the wisdom virtue and patriotism of the country meerly to exchange one league for another? Did the convention, did the people, beleive [sic] that they were framing a league and not a government?" At the height of the nullification crisis in 1832, the aging jurist confided that he was yielding "slowly and reluctantly to the conviction that our constitution cannot last." He foresaw the end of a union that had "been prolonged thus far by miracles."[13]

Although his health began to fail after he reached the age of seventy-five, Marshall's intellectual powers remained undiminished until the day he died in Philadelphia, July 6, 1835. The events of his last years, which in his darker moments made him despair for the future of the union and the Constitution and to experience a sense of failure, undoubtedly cast a shadow that obscured from his view the great accomplishments of his judicial statesmanship. Under Marshall's leadership the Supreme Court evolved into a far more powerful institution than it had been in 1801. He laid the foundation whereby the Court could claim fully coordinate status with the executive and legislative branches of government. During the Marshall years the Court successfully assumed its peculiar function as the preeminent interpreter and guardian of the Constitution and as the umpire that made the American federal system more or less workable. In a series of notable opinions Marshall construed the Constitution so as to give full effect to the enumerated powers conferred on the federal government and to the restraints and prohibitions placed on the state governments. This interpretation did not gain full acceptance in his own day, but it has proved to be enduring.

PRIVATE LIFE, PERSONALITY, AND INTELLECT

Marshall's life from 1801 to 1835 was by no means all courts and cases. Attending five relatively short court terms a year still left ample time for other pursuits and avocations. For example, in the midst of the judiciary crisis of his first years in office, Marshall wrote *The Life of George Washington,* a massive life and times of the late general, published in five large volumes between 1804 and 1807. He always regretted having written the *Life* in such great haste and allowing it to be rushed into print without sufficient time for revisions. The preparation of an abridged second edition occupied his attention for much of the rest of his life. He also collaborated with Bushrod Washington in planning an edition of General Washington's correspondence. A historian and writer himself, Marshall was fond of literature and looked forward to a retirement in which he would "read nothing but novels and poetry." He took delight in Jane Austen's novels and recommended them to Brother Story: "Her flights are not lofty, she does not soar on eagle's wings, but she is pleasing, interesting, equable, and yet amusing."[14]

Nor did judicial duties prevent Marshall from answering, on two occasions, a call to public service on behalf of his state. In 1812 the legislature appointed him chairman of a commission to survey a water and land route to connect the eastern and western regions of the state. After leading an expedition to the falls of the Kanawha River (in present-day West Virginia), he prepared a report that became a landmark in the history of internal improvements in Virginia. At the age of seventy-four in 1829, Marshall (in company with two other venerable statesmen, James Madison and James Monroe) participated in the Virginia constitutional convention. There he proved to be an able and impassioned defender of the principle of judicial independence:

> I have grown old in the opinion, that there is nothing more dear to Virginia, or ought to be dearer to her statesmen, and that the best interests of our country are secured by it. Advert, Sir, to the duties of a Judge. He has to pass between the Government and the man whom that Government is prosecuting: between the most powerful individual in the community, and the poorest and most unpopular. It is of the last importance, that in the exercise of these duties, he should observe the utmost fairness. . . . The Judicial Department comes home in its effects to every man's fireside: it passes on his property, his reputation, his life, his all.[15]

In addition to long summer vacations in the mountains, Marshall spent many idle hours of "*laborious relaxation*" at his farm just outside Richmond.[16] In town he enjoyed the company of a close circle of family and friends, regularly hosting lawyers' dinners in his home and attending Saturday meetings of the Barbecue Club, where he liked to imbibe punch laced with brandy, rum, and Madeira and display his skill at pitching quoits. Marshall's fondness for spirits, his relish for sporting games, his utter disregard for his own dignity, were memorably recorded by the portraitist Chester Harding, who attended one such meeting of the club in 1830:

> I watched for the coming of the old chief. He soon approached with his coat on his arm, and hat in his hand, which he was using as a fan. He walked directly up to a large bowl of mint julep . . . and drank off a tumbler full of the liquid, smacked his lips, and then turned to the company with a cheerful "How are you gentlemen?" He was looked upon as the best pitcher of the party, and could throw heavier quoits than any other member of the club. The game began with great animation, there were several ties; and before long I saw the great chief justice of the Supreme Court of the United States, down on his knees, measuring the contested distance with a straw, with as much earnestness as if it had been a point of law; and if he proved to be in the right, the woods would ring with his triumphant shout. What would the dignitaries of the highest court of England have thought, if they had been present.[17]

The "extreme accuracy and justice" of his decisions on these occasions were "so well known" that they were "invariably submitted to without a murmur."[18]

Secure in his place as a member of the Virginia gentry, Marshall exuded warmth and good humor in his personal and social relations. In his unaffected modesty, polite but informal manner, plain attire, and easy familiarity with social inferiors, he fully lived up to the ideal of a republican gentleman. More so than Jefferson, his great democratic rival, he possessed the common touch. "His lax lounging manners," Jefferson once complained (perhaps with a touch of envy), "have made him popular with the bulk of the people of Richmond."[19] A common sight in Richmond was the chief justice, basket in hand, doing the family marketing. Marshall's charm and sociability also served him well as chief justice. During court terms the justices roomed and boarded together, and professional and social life blended into one. In the convivial atmosphere of the dinner table, or in conversation over a glass of Madeira, the chief no doubt achieved a working consensus among his brethren in many a case. The usually ascetic justices were known on occasion to stretch their rule of drinking wine only in wet weather. Marshall would sometimes ask "Brother Story" to "step to the window and see if it does not look like rain." And if Story informed him that the sun was "shining brightly," the chief might reply, "all the better; for our jurisdiction extends over so large a territory that the doctrine of chances makes it certain that it must be raining somewhere."[20]

Along with attractive traits of personality, Marshall was endowed with a mind of the first rank. All who observed him closely attested to his intellectual vigor, the powers of logic, analysis, and generalization that peculiarly fitted him for a life in law while setting him apart from the general mass of the profession. He occupied an intellectual eminence inaccessible to most mortals, which enabled him simultaneously to grasp a subject in its entirety and to analyze its constituent parts and understand their relation to the whole. Contemporaries marveled at his quick and discerning comprehension, his extraordinary ability to extract the essence of law from particular cases—to seize, "as it were by intuition, the very spirit of juridical doctrines."[21] The clear, precise, mathematical quality of his mind was reflected in legal arguments and opinions that moved progressively from premise to conclusion with the logic and rigor of a geometric proof, omitting all superfluous matter. No rhetorical flourishes, "no stopping to weave garlands of flowers, to hang in festoons, around a favourite argument," cluttered his courtroom performances. Critics noted a tendency toward sophistry, toward overly subtle reasoning that yielded conclusions more plausible than true. Even Story, his great admirer, observed that had Marshall possessed "a less practical mind, he would have been the most consummate of metaphysicians and most skillful of sophists." Yet his "love of dialectics" was tempered "by a superior love of truth." He directed his mental powers to the larger goal of mastering the precepts of law.[22]

Native genius compensated for defects in legal learning that admittedly was "not equal to that of many of the great masters in the profession."[23] Yet Marshall's proficiency in the science was worthy of one who occupied his high judicial station. Close associates acknowledged his profound and comprehensive knowledge of English common law and equity jurisprudence, the foundation upon which American law grew and developed. Marshall was a "*common law lawyer* in the best and noblest acceptation of the term," whose particular strength lay in his thorough mastery of principles and doctrines acquired through close study of adjudicated cases. "The original bias, as well as the choice, of his mind was to general principles and comprehensive views, rather than to technical or recondite learning," wrote Story. "He loved to expatiate upon the theory of equity; to gather up the expansive doctrines of commercial jurisprudence; and to give a rational cast even to the most subtile dogmas of the common law."[24] Deficient as he may have been in abstruse knowledge or in familiarity with comparative law, Marshall nevertheless could hold his own with those of greater learning. The chief justiceship, as Story noted, was "the very post where weakness and ignorance and timidity must instantly betray themselves and sink to their natural level."[25]

An engaging intellectual humility enabled Marshall to defer, when necessary, to the superior learning of others. In both courtroom and conference chamber, Marshall was a patient and attentive listener, not merely soliciting but demanding arguments. As much as he commanded respect by his own formidable intellect, the key to his leadership lay in his openness to argument and persuasion, his willingness to subordinate his own views if necessary to obtain a single opinion of the Court. If the Court most often spoke through the chief justice, the opinion was the product of collaborative deliberation, carried out in a spirit of mutual concession and accommodation. Story nicely summed up the qualities Marshall embodied while presiding in court and in private judicial conferences: "Patience, moderation, candor, urbanity, quickness of perception, dignity of deportment, gentleness of manners, genius which commands respect, and learning which justifies confidence."[26]

REPUBLICANISM

The American Revolution, culminating in the adoption of the Constitution, was the defining epoch of Marshall's life, from which the future chief justice forged the political principles and beliefs he was to hold essentially unchanged throughout his days. As a child of the Revolution, he always counted himself among the votaries of republican government. He accepted without question the repudiation of monarchy and of a titled nobility as constituent elements of government and society. He understood and advocated republican government not only negatively as excluding hereditary elements but also positively as "popular" (a term he used interchangeably with "republican") government. Popular government was elective and representative government, in which the right to vote belonged to white male "freeholders," defined in his own state of Virginia as those owning a one-quarter-acre town lot, or twenty-five acres and a dwelling house in the country, or fifty acres of unimproved land. An important tenet of classical republicanism was that responsible and virtuous citizenship required a large measure of personal autonomy. Property, particularly landed property, was believed to confer such autonomy. Nothing better illustrates Marshall's lifelong adherence to classical values than his continuing preference for freehold suffrage long after it had been abandoned in most of the states. He was by no means a diehard defender of the freehold requirement and by 1829 was resigned to its defeat in Virginia. Still, he hoped for a compromise that would retain "a substantial property requirement" for voting.[27]

Marshall was also characteristically republican in his distaste for party politics. Contrary to the modern notion that a party system is essential to a healthy democracy, the founders believed parties undermined social and political stability. Marshall was typical of his generation in bemoaning the existence of "those distinct and visible parties, which, in their long and dubious conflict for power, have since shaken the United States to their centre." Among the worst evils of party politics was its "tendency to abolish all distinction between virtue and vice; and to prostrate those barriers which the wise and good have erected for the protection of morals, and which are defended solely by opinion."[28] Federalist spokesman though he was in the 1790s, Marshall never regarded himself as a "party" man but as a defender of the Constitution and established government against unjustified attacks by partisan factions bent on some selfish or sinister aim. Marshall clung to the classical conception that enlightened statesmen could identify and pursue a single public interest even as he recognized that competing and clashing interests were inevitable concomitants of free and popular governments. The proper goal of politics, he continued to believe, was not to reconcile factional and partial interests but to subordinate them to the common good. With the triumph of party, however, popularly elected legislatures had degenerated into arenas of competing factions pursuing their selfish motives. One important function of courts of law in a republic, Marshall concluded, was to mitigate the pernicious effects of factional politics. As chief justice he consciously sought to create an image of the Supreme Court as a disinterested umpire standing above the partisan fray, a repository of wisdom and virtue acting on behalf of the public interest.

Marshall's ideal republican statesman was George Washington, his friend, mentor, and biographical subject. As delineated by Marshall, Washington's character represented the triumph of patriotism and devotion to the public good over personal aggrandizement and self-interest, of adherence to principle and duty over desire for popularity, of integrity, honesty, and self-discipline over "those selfish passions, which find their nourishment in the conflicts of party."[29] Throughout his life Marshall tried to live up to this code of republican statesmanship. His own self-portrait described a man whose reason controlled his passions and interests, who did not seek office but was called to public life, who entered the public arena out of a sense of duty and at some personal sacrifice, who disdained popularity if it conflicted with principle, and whose conduct and principles were untainted by party motives.

Marshall's self-image as a "republican" captures the essence of his political thought and values. Yet his republicanism, like that of the Revolutionary generation to which he belonged, must be understood in terms of its accommodation to the "modern" world of the eighteenth century. Without explicitly repudiating their classical beliefs, republican theorists throughout Western Europe and North America adopted a modified conception of virtue more in accord with the realities of human nature and better adapted to the rise of commerce and the market, to new institutions such as banks and stock exchanges. This redefined virtue recognized and to some extent gave free play to man's passions and interests. American republican ideology thus accommodated the spirit of commerce, the pursuit of gain, and the notion that private self-interest could serve the public interest. In this respect it assimilated—not always easily, to be sure—beliefs and attitudes characteristic of an emerging "liberal" ideology based on the political philosophy of John Locke and the economic theories of Adam Smith.[30]

Like his fellow revolutionaries, the republican Marshall was a confirmed believer in the idea of the natural rights of the individual and that the object of government was to secure and protect these rights. In certain patterns of behavior as well, Marshall conformed to the "liberal" model. Although born into the Virginia gentry, he did not inherit great wealth, and until he was well into his adult years he had neither the means nor leisure to play the role of disinterested republican statesman. Much of his early life was devoted to private affairs, to earning a living and acquiring a fortune. His principal source of income came from the practice of law, hence indirectly from the commercial endeavors of the planters and merchants who were his clients. Marshall also undertook his own business ventures, most notably in purchasing the manor lands formerly belonging to Lord Fairfax, who during the colonial period had been proprietor of Virginia's Northern Neck. In association with his brothers and close friends, Marshall in 1793 contracted to buy this estate, consisting of more than two-hundred-thousand acres, for twenty-thousand pounds sterling. Financing this scheme commanded all his resources, even to the extent of employing his pen to earn money in writing the life of George Washington. Not until 1806 did the syndicate make final payment on this purchase.

Compelled to enter the market, to pursue his private interests, Marshall nevertheless remained firmly wedded to republican values. Acceptance of the spirit of commerce, belief in the philosophy of individual rights, and recognition of self-interest as a legitimate motive in human affairs did not signify endorsement of an untrammeled acquisitive individualism or an avaricious pursuit of riches. The idea that society was nothing more than a collection of completely self-absorbed individuals and groups and that politics was an arena of scrambling selfish interests was abhorrent to Marshall, as it was to the founders generally. Even as he accepted the reality that society was composed of various and conflicting interests, he never discarded the notion of the public good as a distinct entity in itself. Admitting the impossibility of the Spartan ideal of total self-abnegation, he continued to hold onto a concept of virtue that in some measure required disinterestedness, if not by the whole citizenry then at least by the leadership of the republic. He believed that virtue, fortified by proper constitutional arrangements, could continue to be the animating principle of the American republic. His attachment to the Constitution was based in no small part on the hope that it would preserve and strengthen the career of republican virtue in a society that was becoming increasingly less homogeneous, more factious, and more driven by the imperatives of the market.

Revolutionary republicanism shaped Marshall's political creed and his constitutional jurisprudence. From his experiences as a Continental soldier and postwar Virginia legislator sprang a conviction that the Constitution of 1787 marked a decisive turning point away from a union of confederated states toward a "nation of states" based on the principle of national supremacy. Any attempt to construe the Constitution into a compact resembling the discarded Articles of Confederation was an interpretative heresy that must be combated with all the weapons at his command.

From the vantage point of advanced age, Marshall was inclined to ascribe his early devotion to nationalist principles "at least as much to casual circumstances as to judgement." Nationalism arose naturally from resistance to Great Britain; and his association in the Continental army "with brave men from different states who were risking life and everything valuable in a common cause" confirmed him "in the habit of considering America as my country, and congress as my government."[31] Marshall's partiality to union and nationalism hardened into an unwavering conviction during the 1780s, as the return of peace exposed the dangerous weaknesses of a Confederation government that lacked the power to tax or to impose a uniform commercial policy. He was never an advocate of national power for its own sake, however, but only as a means to preserve and consolidate the newly won independence of the United States and to promote the commercial prosperity of the American people. The impotent Confederation portended political and commercial anarchy, disunion, and eventual loss of independence, as the individual American states would inevitably become subservient to European powers. At the core of his nationalist outlook was a deep-rooted anxiety about the perilous position of the United States in a hostile world. That American security, independence, and, ultimately, liberty required a strong and energetic general government was an axiom Marshall never doubted, and he operated on the assumption that the Constitution conferred the requisite powers to accomplish these objects.

In championing national power, Marshall was not a precursor of modern liberal nationalism or of the positive, interventionist, regulatory state of the twentieth century. Although he and the Court were not infrequently denounced as "consolidationist," the chief justice looked upon the federal government as chronically vulnerable to the aggressive encroachments of the state governments. These internal pressures that undermined the authority of the central government and loosened the bonds of union in turn exposed the United States to external threats—inviting intervention, even invasion, by foreign powers. In the American federal system as Marshall understood it, centrifugal force was much stronger than centripetal. If the republic was to perish, it would not be "by the overwhelming power of the National Government, but by the resisting and counteracting power of the State sovereignties."[32] The Constitution, he believed, was designed to establish an equilibrium between the federal and state governments, an equilibrium that was in constant danger of breaking down in the direction of the states. Marshall's nationalism might properly be described as defensive or negative—resisting the superior force of state sovereignty rather than augmenting federal power.

Instructed by fellow Virginian James Madison, Marshall came to see that the objects of an invigorated national government went beyond enhancing external security and promoting greater commercial prosperity, important as these were. Such a government would also promote internal tranquillity within the states, where the danger to liberty was perhaps more immediately threatening than that posed by external forces. The source of this danger was the American people themselves, a circumstance that cast grave doubts on the long-term prospects for their novel experiment in republican self-government. Madison, indeed, concluded on the eve of the federal convention that the fundamental crisis facing America was the apparent failure of republican government as practiced in the states. Laws enacted by state legislatures far too frequently reflected the selfish interests of popular majorities and trampled upon the private rights of individuals and minorities. Among the most obnoxious and unjust laws were those that authorized the government to issue paper money and make it legal tender, that provided for the payment of debts in installments, and that postponed executions for debts. Madison believed this internal crisis—the evils arising from state legislation—"contributed more to that uneasiness which produced the Convention, and prepared the public mind for a general reform, than those which accrued to our national character and interest from the inadequacy of the Confederation to its immediate objects."[33]

Marshall likewise attributed great influence to this internal crisis in bringing about constitutional reform. It "produced a state of things which alarmed all reflecting men," he wrote, "and demonstrated to many the indispensable necessity of clothing government with powers sufficiently ample for the protection of the rights of the peaceable and quiet, from the invasions of the licentious and turbulent part of the community."[34] As a state legislator himself in the 1780s, he directly witnessed the declining influence of the "wise and virtuous," whose efforts to observe public faith and honor were increasingly challenged by the schemes of self-interested majorities. He and other proponents of court reform, for example, were thwarted by powerful interests—county magistrates and county court lawyers—who resisted this salutary measure. "Indeed," he complained in 1784, "there are many members who really appear to be determined against every Measure which may expedite & facilitate the business of recovering debts & compelling a strict compliance with contracts." Similarly, in 1787, he remarked with disgust that "the debtors as usual are endeavoring to come into the Assembly & as usual I fear they will succeed."[35]

In denouncing "debtors," Marshall did not have in mind the "poor and oppressed" or the "honest and laboring" part of the community but rather those whose selfish greed and delusive hopes led them to purchase beyond their means to pay. Calculating on rising prices for their agricultural produce, an influx of immigrants that would enhance the value of their lands, and a favorable climate for speculation based on a depreciating paper currency, many Americans "found themselves involved in debts they were unable to discharge." Debtors, indeed, formed the core of an increasingly numerous faction that was gaining ascendancy in the legislatures, where under the guise of public law they could mitigate the consequences of private folly. The efforts of this faction "were unceasingly directed" to the debtor's relief by enacting laws for issuing paper money, delaying legal proceedings, and postponing tax collections. If these favorite measures failed at one session, the debtor faction's strength was sufficient "to encourage the hope of succeeding in a future attempt."[36]

This kind of factional politics was symptomatic of a deeper crisis of republicanism, the full dimensions of which were revealed in Shays's Rebellion, an uprising of indebted farmers in western Massachusetts in 1786. Here was one state that, far from indulging the debtor class by suspending tax collections, installing debt payments, or emitting paper money, actually increased taxes in an effort to meet its heavy public obligations. Yet this virtuous attempt to maintain the public faith provoked a civil insurrection that temporarily suspended the authority of government and shut down courts of law. "These violent, I fear bloody, dissentions in a state I had thought inferior in wisdom and virtue to no one in the union," wrote Marshall at the time, "added to the strong tendency which the politics of many eminent characters among ourselves have to promote private and public dishonesty cast a deep shade over that bright prospect which the revolution in America and the establishment of our free governments had opened to the votaries of liberty throughout the globe."[37]

Without question the turbulent and corrupt politics of the postwar years, the disorderly tumults that portended civil anarchy and social chaos, made an indelible impression upon Marshall's mind. In brief, he lost faith in "the wild and enthusiastic democracy" of his youth.[38] He became more pessimistic about the prospects for popular government, more attuned to its excesses and dangers. Human nature, he concluded in 1787, rendered democracy problematic: "I fear . . . that those have truth on their side who say that man is incapable of governing himself." Fifteen years later, after a decade of bitter partisan division at home and of revolution and war abroad, his pessimism had deepened. He now viewed "human nature through a much more gloomy medium than I once thought possible. This new doctrine of the perfectablity of man, added to the practice of its votaries begins to exhibit him I think as an animal much less respectable than he has heretofore been thought."[39]

In commenting on human nature, Marshall characteristically matched "reason and judgment" against the "passions." In this contest the former nearly always yielded to the superior influence of the latter, a fact that did not bode well for popular self-government.[40] There were, to be sure, a few exceptional individuals who rose above the general mass of humanity, distinguished for their ability to subject their ordinary human desires and petty interests to their reason and judgment. In this aristocracy of character, Washington was the shining exemplar. Yet even among the generality of mankind, Marshall recognized that the most vicious passions could be tempered by "interest," a desire for personal security and material well-being. Interest was a hybrid, a kind of low-grade reason or controlled passion. Because it involved rational judgment, interest often allied with reason to check the passions. Merely calculating the costs of following the whims of passion acted as a salutary check upon individual conduct. "Those who know human nature, black as it is," said Marshall in 1788, "must know, that mankind are too well attached to their interest" to indulge in outrageous behavior.[41]

In keeping with a more somber view of human nature, Marshall embraced a chastened and sober republicanism. In place of a "wild and enthusiastic democracy," he advocated a "well regulated Democracy" as embodied in the Constitution, that is, popular government in which there would be "a strict observance of justice and public faith, and a steady adherence to virtue."[42] Republican government could still work tolerably well, Marshall believed, so long as it operated within a system of checks and balances that reinforced the natural moderating effects of self-interest and so long as it produced leaders of excellent character, distinguished for sound and discriminating judgment and disinterested attachment to the public interest. In revising his thinking about republican government, Marshall, like Madison and others, called into question the heretofore superior role enjoyed by legislatures, where much of the obnoxious behavior from which he recoiled in disgust was occurring. His own direct experience with the mischievous, selfish politics of the 1780s left him deeply skeptical of popular assemblies and led him to reflect on the potential role of the judiciary in maintaining a "well regulated Democracy." With the decline of the legislatures into arenas of licentiousness, courts and judges increasingly came to be looked upon as repositories of virtue and wisdom, where reason, reflection, judgment, and disinterestedness continued to hold sway.

From this period as well dates Marshall's lifelong distrust of the state governments and his belief that one of the chief advantages of a reformed and strengthened national government was its capacity to act as a steadying counterweight to those smaller republics. The "general tendency of state politics" had convinced him that "a more efficient and better organized general government" provided the only "safe anchorage ground."[43] In his opinion the most valuable provision of the new Constitution was the restrictions placed upon the states, particularly the prohibition against laws "impairing the Obligation of Contracts." Marshall's later expositions of the Constitution's contract clause were infused with perceptions formed during the post-Revolutionary era. Time and again he recited the evils arising from the state politics of the 1780s, whose vicious and alarming tendency was "not only to impair commercial intercourse, and threaten the existence of credit, but to

sap the morals of the people and destroy the sanctity of private faith."
To remedy these mischiefs was a paramount goal of "all the truly wise,
as well as the virtuous" and "one of the important benefits expected
from a reform of the government."[44] In the hands of Chief Justice Marshall and his "wise and virtuous" brethren, the contract clause emerged
as a potent constitutional remedy for preserving the health of the
American republic.

2

THE COMMON LAW
BACKGROUND

John Marshall's participation in public life outside the courtroom contributed importantly to his formation as a judge, perhaps most significantly in supplying him with the broad principles that underlay his
constitutional jurisprudence. Marshall the jurist cannot be adequately
understood or appreciated without also examining the more specifically "legal" influences and traditions that shaped his judicial statecraft.
Foremost among these was his practice as a lawyer in the superior
courts of Virginia, where his ideas about law and judicial power developed and matured. For more than two decades preceding his appointment to the Supreme Court, Marshall had been a student and
practitioner of English common law and equity. As chief justice he
assimilated the familiar methods of interpreting and adjudicating the
common law to the novel and extraordinary task of creating a constitutional law for the new nation.

Legal commentators in Marshall's day defined common law as "unwritten" law, meaning that its ultimate source was immemorial custom,
reason, or "natural" law. In contrast to "written" law, statutes enacted
by legislative assemblies ("positive" law, in modern terminology), common law was the product of courts and judges in deciding actual cases.
It was, Marshall once said, "human reason applied by courts, not capri-
ciously but in a regular train of decisions, to human affairs according to
the circumstances of the nation, the necessity of the times, and the gen-

eral state of things."[1] Common law as he practiced it was a series of writs, or "forms of action," each with its distinctive pleadings, to prosecute specific legal claims. Although a large body of substantive doctrine had developed from the writ system over the centuries, the common law had not yet transcended its procedural origins. Marshall studied "contracts" and "torts" as offshoots of particular forms of action such as "debt," "assumpsit," and "trespass." Because common law actions sometimes fell short of complete justice or failed to provide any remedy, litigants sought relief in "equity," a system of law that had grown up alongside the common law and supplemented it at many points. Administered by separate courts of chancery, or on the "chancery" side of a single court, equity enjoyed certain procedural advantages and its judges, or chancellors, possessed unique weapons (such as the injunction) to provide remedial justice. By the time Marshall entered the legal profession, equity had shed much of its discretionary character and, like the common law, had evolved into a highly formalized system of law.

In both common law and equity, adjudication was based on precedent and the rule of stare decisis, by which judges were bound by former decisions on the same points. These precedents, formed from an ever expanding body of adjudications, were embodied in voluminous reports of cases dating from the fourteenth century. As Blackstone explained, the rule of abiding by precedent made the law certain instead of variable according to the private opinions and feelings of the individual judge.[2] Yet within this system of precedent, English judges enjoyed a measure of discretion. Common law, sometimes defined as "right reason" or as "natural justice," was conceived of as a body of general principles existing independently of particular decisions. This distinction between law and authority was well stated by the great eighteenth-century English judge Lord Mansfield, who declared that English law "would be a strange science indeed if it were decided upon precedents only. Precedents serve to illustrate principles and give them a fixed certainty." The law, consisted not "in particular cases, but in general principles, which run through the cases and govern the decision of them."[3] Adherence to former adjudications, said Blackstone, did not require a judge to abide by a decision that was evidently contrary to reason, natural justice, or divine law. Judges being fallible, their opinions and the law were not "convertible terms."[4] By appealing to principle, to reason and justice, judges in fact made new law while professing to remain faithful to established legal doctrines. Precedent, in dialectic with principle, was thus not incompatible with slow, piecemeal innovation in the common law, which accordingly proved remarkably resilient and adaptable to new circumstances.

The ways in which the English common law system was adapted to the particular circumstances of colonial Virginia produced a distinctive legal culture that profoundly shaped Marshall's jurisprudence. Perhaps the most obvious contrast with the English model was the rudimentary organization of the colonial court system. In the mother country the administration of justice took place within a highly differentiated system of local, ecclesiastical, merchant, and royal courts. Virginia, until the Revolution, made do with a simple arrangement of county courts and one superior court, the General Court, both of which had legislative and executive functions as well. As courts of law they decided a variety of causes—common law, equity, admiralty, spiritual—that in England would have been heard in distinct courts for those purposes. The "gentlemen justices" who composed these courts—the great landowners and prominent men of affairs—were ill-equipped to perform their diverse judicial duties, few of them possessing more than a veneer of legal learning. Even as late as the mid-nineteenth century, there was "not one in fifty" county court judges who "pretended to any knowledge of the law." As for the colonial General Court, "no legal attainments were required" for appointment to this body, which was first and foremost an executive council. In these circumstances, it was not surprising that legal proceedings were often irregular, with little attention paid to niceties of procedure, forms of action, pleading, or any technicalities that did not seem to go to the merits of a cause.[5]

Particularly neglected in Virginia was the science of pleading, the process of refining various claims and defenses into specific "issues" for decision by court or jury. Technical learning of this sort never took root because it was not essential to success at the bar. An advocate had to state his case with clear and simple reasoning that could be comprehended by lay judges who distrusted "every argument which could not be understood without an effort." Subtle points and fine distinctions were of little avail, and the prudent lawyer avoided them so as not "to discredit his cause." The motives for studying law as a technical science were thus largely absent in Virginia, a situation that remained essentially unchanged despite the appointment of professional judges to newly created state courts during the Revolution. These judges were drawn from the ranks of lawyers trained in the practices and traditions that had become entrenched during the colonial period.[6]

Marshall's schooling in this legal culture reinforced an "original bias" (in Story's phrase) of his mind to general principles rather than to abstruse learning. In a Virginia courtroom, sound practical knowledge of law, assisted by sharp wits and good sense, counted for more than mere learning. The pre-Revolutionary law careers of George Wythe and Edmund Pendleton, later to become eminent judges, illustrate the point. Wythe, whose "active mind found its only enjoyment in profound research," was perhaps the only man in Virginia who could claim to be a learned lawyer. Pendleton's intellectual talents were equal to Wythe's, but were applied only "to the study of so much of the law as the established usages of the country permitted to prevail." Greatly superior to Pendleton in legal erudition, Wythe at the bar found himself more often than not losing to his more versatile rival. Although Wythe excelled in opening a case, "he was not so fortunate in reply. Mr. Pendleton, on the contrary, was always ready both in opening and concluding an argument, and was prompt to meet all exigencies which would arise in the conduct of a cause in court."[7] As a lawyer, Marshall more closely resembled the clever and resourceful Pendleton than he did the scholarly Wythe.

MARSHALL'S LAW PRACTICE

Marshall's law practice coincided with the beginnings of a new state judicial establishment and, after 1789, with the first years of a new federal court system.[8] The Virginia Constitution of 1776 laid the foundation of the first state court system by providing for the appointment of "judges of the Supreme Court of Appeals, and General Court, Judges in Chancery, Judges of Admiralty," and other officers. The General Assembly subsequently enacted legislation establishing a Court of Admiralty, a High Court of Chancery, a General Court, and a Court of Appeals. These courts in essence replaced the old General Court, which had exercised both original and appellate jurisdiction and united the functions of law and equity. The new courts were engrafted upon the existing system of inferior county and corporation courts.

Throughout the 1780s Marshall regularly attended the General Court, which had common law jurisdiction; the High Court of Chancery, which had equity jurisdiction; and the Court of Appeals. In 1789, with the splitting up of the General Court's jurisdiction among numerous district courts, he began attending the courts in nearby Fredericksburg, Petersburg, and perhaps Williamsburg, as well as in Richmond. After 1790 a flourishing chancery and appellate practice, along with a host of clients in the federal circuit court, allowed him to cut back on his state district court cases.

The bulk of Marshall's common law litigation in both the state and federal courts arose from commercial transactions, the buying and selling of goods, wares, and merchandise. Merchants and planters dominated his list of clients, and plaintiffs and defendants in his cases were typically in the relationship of creditor and debtor. The multiplicity of suits founded on bonds and unliquidated accounts was the natural concomitant of an agricultural economy fueled by credit rather than circulating cash. To a large extent the courts functioned as a collection agency of last resort for creditors. In the federal circuit court, where plaintiffs were often merchants residing in London or in the eastern seaboard cities of New York, Philadelphia, and Baltimore, there were more cases founded on negotiable instruments such as promissory notes and bills of exchange. The great majority of Marshall's federal court cases were suits brought by British creditors for the recovery of debts contracted before the Revolution. In all of these (more than a hundred), Marshall represented the Virginia debtors. As counsel in these "British debt" suits, Marshall argued the appeal of the test case of *Ware v. Hylton* in February 1796, his first and only appearance at the bar of the Supreme Court.

Marshall also had numerous cases in the state High Court of Chancery and on the chancery side of the federal circuit court. Many of these fell into the category of property disputes, usually concerning ownership of land and slaves, and involving complicated arrangements embodied in trusts, mortgages, and wills. A substantial portion of Marshall's chancery business arose from disputes over wills, the parties— typically, the heir at law against other descendants, devisees, or legatees—claiming the same property under the instrument. Yet there

were also a number of chancery cases that were essentially suits to recover debts, as when the court was requested to settle complicated business accounts and decree a sale of property to satisfy the outstanding
balance.

Through handling these mundane private disputes, Marshall acquired his most important qualification to be a judge: a mastery of the
principles of the common law and doctrines of equity. His commercial
practice in particular was most directly applicable to his work on the
Court, as attested by the plethora of cases upon bonds, bills of exchange and promissory notes, and open account that came before the
Supreme Court. It was precisely these kinds of cases, not the "great
cases" of constitutional law, that formed the bulk of his business as chief
justice. In this area Marshall's special familiarity with Virginia law and
practice served him well, for a disproportionate number of cases that
came up to the Supreme Court originated in his native state, many of
them by way of the federal court of the District of Columbia.

The most valuable preparation for Marshall's judicial career was his
experience as a counsellor in the Virginia Court of Appeals.[9] As a
member of the elite fraternity of attorneys practicing in this court,
Marshall had numerous opportunities to develop and refine his skills
of stating a case, of applying and distinguishing precedents, and of interpreting statutes. In plying his craft he had one essential task: to
find the rules of law that governed his particular case and to apply
them in a way that was persuasive to the judges. In most instances
these rules were to be found in English common law and equity precedents, which remained the principal foundation, or "substratum" (to
use Marshall's term), of Virginia law. This was formally recognized by
a 1776 statute declaring English common law (along with general acts
of Parliament "made in aid of the common law" enacted prior to
1607) to be "in full force" until altered by the state legislature. After
1776 the legislature began to move toward a comprehensive revision of
the laws, which in some instances radically altered the common law,
notably by the abolition of entailed estates and of the rule of primogeniture (inheritance by the eldest son).[10] Despite the growth of an in-
digenous Virginia law in the form of statutes that consciously departed
from English models and in adjudications of the Court of Appeals, the
number of Virginia precedents remained but a small fraction of those
cited from English sources.

Marshall had to be prepared to adduce, reject, or distinguish cases as the situation demanded. Since no two cases were exactly alike, the advocate had to show that the similarities were strong enough to come within the same rule. One common tactic employed to undermine the authority of a case was to show that its principle was "fully contradicted" by a train of other decisions. If this did not work and the case stood as law, the alternative was to distinguish it by showing that it was "unlike the present." Resourceful lawyers like Marshall found many ways to distinguish cases. He might contend that the main point of a present case had been only "incidentally decided" in a previous case, which therefore should not "be considered as a binding authority."[11] Or he might show that no adjudicated case had "gone so far as the present."[12] Another favorite distinguishing tactic was to justify a departure from English rules and practice by pointing to the different circumstances and customs of that country, which typically were ascribed to its "highly commercial character."[13]

In most of his appellate cases, Marshall applied rules derived from English jurisprudence. Other cases required interpretation of Virginia statute law and consideration of Virginia judicial precedent. Property disputes, mostly originating in the High Court of Chancery, formed the largest class of appeals. These cases typically centered on the distribution of a decedent's estate among heirs, devisees, legatees, and creditors. In this category, will construction cases came before the appellate court in disproportionate numbers owing to their great complexity. They afforded occasions for lawyers to display their mastery of property law and the technical rules for construing wills that had evolved with ever greater refinement in a multitude of cases. Suits for equitable relief after a judgment at law formed another important group of appeals. Such cases raised the perennially vexing question of the relationship between law and equity, forcing the bar and bench continually to define the boundary between these two jurisdictions.

Here in the arena of the Virginia Court of Appeals Marshall perfected the method and style of legal analysis and reasoning that he later employed so effectively on the Supreme Court. In all his cases, whatever their subject, he would invariably begin by resolving the case into two or more points, which he then disposed of in order. Eschewing rhetorical flourishes, he followed the straight and narrow path of logic, presenting his case like a geometric proof. His technique was to state the law in terms of general principles, laying down one or more premises from which he deduced the consequences and conclusion that inevitably followed. On the bench Marshall characteristically remarked that to decide a case, it was "only necessary to recognize certain principles."[14] Words to this effect, which appear like a refrain throughout his judicial opinions, also regularly recur in his reported appellate arguments.

The appeal to principle to resolve legal questions was not peculiar to Marshall or to Virginia legal culture but reflected the common Anglo-American distinction between law as a body of principles and the particular cases that illustrated those principles. Neither Marshall nor his contemporaries at the bar assumed that the most effective case one could make was to pile precedents one upon another. This does not mean that precedents and authorities were unimportant or were ignored in legal arguments and decisions. The printed reports of Marshall's cases are replete with citations to more than two dozen collections of reports of English cases in the courts of King's Bench, Common Pleas, Exchequer, and the High Court of Chancery, dating from the reign of Elizabeth I to his own time. Marshall appears to have been no less attentive than his fellow counsellors in bringing the relevant authorities to bear in support of his arguments. The relative paucity, by modern standards, of citations in their arguments was owing to a shared conviction that principles, not cases, mattered.

JUDICIAL DISCRETION

As a practitioner in the courts of George Wythe and Edmund Pendleton, Marshall was enrolled in the best of schools for judges. These eminent jurists personified qualities of judicial dignity and integrity that Marshall sought to emulate. From them he acquired an understanding of the role of law and courts in the larger scheme of republican government. Pendleton, presiding judge of the Court of Appeals, more clearly than Wythe, chancellor of the High Court of Chancery, was the future chief justice's model. He was "the mind and voice of the Court," whose eminence invited comparisons with Lord Mansfield, the renowned English jurist. Like his English counterpart, with whom he felt "an innate sense of congeniality," Pendleton was impatient with the

technicalities and formalities of the law. His judicial technique was "to
ascertain the very right and justice of every case, that came before him,
and then to hunt up law to support it." He instinctively kept his mind
uncluttered with legal knowledge that might *"defeat* right and justice."
If not learned in law (much inferior to Mansfield in this respect), the
Virginia judge was nevertheless "perfectly acquainted with the statute
and common law, as well as with the doctrines of equity," and possessed
an almost intuitive understanding of "how to apply them to the habits
and exigencies of this country." Give him a case in which justice was indifferent to the outcome, "and nothing could exceed the profundity of
his researches, or the ability with which he collected and applied his authorities."[15] From Pendleton's example the future chief justice learned
a style of leadership in which the court most often spoke through its
presiding judge and a practical approach to the art of judging that emphasized substance over technicalities.

Perhaps the most important lesson Pendleton and Wythe imparted
to Marshall was that judges in the ordinary course of deciding cases had
broad discretion to determine what the law was, compelled as they were
to choose from a variety of sources: English common and statutory law,
acts of the colonial and state legislatures, and a growing body of state
common law emerging from adjudicated cases in the state courts. Judicial discretion as employed in the courts of post-Revolutionary Virginia
was an extension and refinement of an Anglo-American legal practice
originating in the common law method of adjudication. In searching
for the rule or rules that applied to the case before them, judges
turned to the great body of transcendent principles that ran through
and beyond cases. Their discretion lay in being free to follow or reject,
in greater or lesser degree, previous decisions according to their conformity with or departure from the overarching principles of law. This
freedom to choose, to be sure, operated within narrow bounds and was
regarded as the very antithesis of an act of arbitrary will. The notion
that a judge could decide a case according to his private sense of justice
was emphatically denied as introducing uncertainty and anarchy into
the law. Precedents were presumed to be valid expressions of the law
unless proved otherwise. In departing from precedent, judges did not
think of themselves as making new law but merely as declaring or reaf-
firming the ancient law properly understood. Rejected precedents, said
Blackstone, were not declared to be *"bad law"* but simply *"not law."*[16]

Judicial discretion was the means by which the law was adapted to new circumstances. Although precedents served as a great reservoir of doctrine to draw upon in deciding the nearly infinite variety of disputes involving persons and property, adjudicated cases often did not come directly in point and did not supply a clear rule to be mechanically applied. Faced with this situation, a judge had to creatively adapt existing rules and principles, extending and refining them until, in effect, a new rule came into being and was added to the body of doctrine. To the modern mind this process of adaptation can properly be called "legislation," and the common law simply "judge-made law." In Blackstone's terms, however, judges did not make law but merely found a preexisting rule. They did not adapt law to new circumstances; rather, they accommodated novel situations to the law. Adaptability implies growth and change, but law was conceived to be a set of eternal and unvarying standards.

As more and more English law (particularly from the sixteenth century on) came to be embodied in acts of Parliament, another area opened up for the exercise of judicial discretion: statutory construction. Legislative enactments might be ambiguous, even contradictory, and judicial intervention was required to clear up ambiguities, to fill "the open spaces in the law."[17] Judges interpreted statutes in the same way they interpreted the common law. Statutes, like the common law, were supposed to adhere to the great principles of justice and right reason, which guided the judges in their task of discovering the "intention" of the enactment. Judicial glosses upon statutes became part of the law itself, though again, as with common law interpretations, these were not understood to be acts of lawmaking. By the eighteenth century a number of rules for construing statutes had evolved, which aspiring practitioners like Marshall could find conveniently brought together in the pages of Blackstone.[18]

Whether they "made" or merely "discovered" law through interpreting the common law and statutes, judges, in greater or lesser degree, performed acts of intellectual creativity. As long as this creativity was perceived to operate within the confines of legal discretion, judges were not "legislators." Eighteenth-century jurisprudence assumed a strict line between discretion and legislation, between "law" and "politics," although the boundary was not always easily discernible. Because judicial creativity was inherent in the common law method of adjudication, there was a constant danger that a creative, or merely arrogant, judge would stretch or exceed the limits of discretion. Americans today typically associate judicial legislation with an expansive exercise of judicial review, but this problem was of long standing in Anglo-American law, predating the emergence of judicial review.

Among English judges none was more creative than Lord Mansfield, chief judge of the Court of King's Bench in the latter half of the eighteenth century. Over many years on the bench Mansfield carried out a great legal reformation, most notably in rationalizing and systematizing the commercial law and integrating it within the traditional body of English law. He also effected reforms that simplified practice and procedure and that curtailed the powers of juries. In charting new legal territory, Mansfield employed his fertile genius in a variety of ways to hack away at the dense thicket of authority and precedent. Yet he did his work within the traditional methods of common law adjudication, by exploiting the well-founded distinction between the great principles of law and the particular cases that illustrated those principles. Mansfield in this respect differed only in degree from his judicial contemporaries and predecessors. In the recurrent debate about the nature of judging that oscillated between strict submission to precedent and reliance on individual intellectual capacity to discern the true principles of law, Mansfield fell as much within the accepted norm as those judges who occupied the other end of the spectrum. The business of judges, remarked a judicial contemporary of Mansfield, was to declare "how the law stands, not how it ought to be; otherwise each judge would have a distinct tribunal in his own breast, the decisions of which would be as irregular and uncertain and various as the minds and tempers of mankind." Another stated the duty of a judge more starkly: "I cannot legislate, but by my industry I can discover what our predecessors have done, and I will servilely tread in their footsteps." This view, had it prevailed, would have effectively foreclosed the path of legal development.[19]

To many in both England and America, Mansfield was the prime example of judicial discretion run riot, the judge who instead of acting as expositor of existing law assumed the role of lawgiver, one who framed a rule to guide future conduct. Thomas Jefferson, for example, denounced the English jurist for persuading common law courts to revive the practice of "construing their text equitably," that is, of departing from established rules and precedents and wandering into the unsettled and uncertain realm of discretionary justice. "No period of the English law, of whatever length it be taken," complained Jefferson, "can be produced wherein so many of it's [*sic*] settled rules have been reversed as during the time of this judge." Indeed, there was "so much sly poison" in Mansfield that Jefferson wanted to forbid American courts from citing any English decisions rendered since his accession to the bench.[20] Mansfield had his American admirers as well, including John Marshall, who called him "one of the greatest Judges who ever sat on any bench, & who has done more than any other to remove those technical impediments which grew out of a different state of society, & too long continued to obstruct the course of substantial justice." With delicious irony, Marshall delivered this encomium in a case where Jefferson was defendant.[21] Among the various elements composing the deep-seated conflict between these two Virginians, not the least important was Jefferson's concern that an American Mansfield held the chief justiceship of the United States.

As suggested by Jefferson's criticisms of Lord Mansfield, the emergence of republican ideology in Revolutionary America intensified the debate over the proper role of judges. A great legal reformer himself, Jefferson regarded judicial discretion as an abuse to be remedied in constructing a new legal code for Virginia founded on republican principles. In colonial courts, where judges had to select from a confusing compound of English and local law, discretion had flourished to an extraordinary degree. Conditions were so different in America that the divergence between precedent—that is, English common law and English statutes—and principle was even more pronounced than it was in the mother country. Judges in these circumstances were compelled to administer and apply law equitably, according to right reason and justice, on which they increasingly relied as the ultimate authority and foundation of law. Jefferson and other Revolutionary reformers believed that it was possible to maintain a system of laws founded in reason and equity without resorting to judicial discretion. Law in a republican commonwealth would be founded on the consent of the people and at the same time be rational and just.[22]

Jefferson's reform for Virginia aimed not only to purge the laws of all monarchical features but also to reduce much of common law and equity to statute form. He envisioned a code of laws "adopted to our republican form of government . . . with a single eye to reason, and the good of those for whose government it was framed." This republican code would be rational, clearly understood, and easily applied. Deeply distrustful of discretionary judicial power, he frankly admitted that his goal was to confine judges to the strict letter of the law so that they would be mere "machines." Laws properly drawn, he believed, would contain their own equity. "Let mercy be the character of the law-giver," he wrote in 1776, "but let the judge be a mere machine. The mercies of the law will be dispensed equally and impartially to every description of men; those of the judge, or of the executive power, will be the eccentric impulses of whimsical, capricious designing man."[23] Although he later tempered his faith in legislative power, Jefferson continued throughout his life to harbor misgivings about judicial legislation— which inevitably occurred whenever judges were relieved "from the rigour of text law" and permitted "to wander into it's equity." A judge must be kept on a short tether, he insisted, and his "word for what the law is" should go no further than "is warranted by the authorities he appeals to."[24]

Contrary to Jefferson's hopes, republican legislatures did not always enact sensible, rational, and properly drawn laws. The Virginia Assembly never adopted Jefferson's comprehensive reform plan as a single code but instead enacted parts of it in piecemeal fashion, frequently departing from the form in which bills were originally drawn by Jefferson. But this partial revision only seemed to produce perplexity, confusion, and contradiction rather than simplicity and clarification.[25] The result was a luxuriant growth of legislation, a multiplication of laws that were the offspring of earlier defective laws. Instead of preventing or ending litigation, statutes often were the parent of lawsuits, thus making courts increasingly responsible for interpreting the laws and fixing their meaning. Finding "many defects" in the revised laws, Edmund Randolph frankly acknowledged the role of the judiciary in curing these defects: "To say the truth, I absolutely fear, that the new language, which those laws contain, is far, very far, from being fixed by adjudications." Even one of Jefferson's prized republican reforms, the law "directing the course of descents" was "in practice often found to be most unrighteous and difficult of execution."[26]

The emergence of a republican political order, in short, did not establish a system of laws founded on precise legislative enactment, to be mechanically applied by a judiciary bound by the strict letter of the law. The promise of codification was never realized in post-Revolutionary Virginia, and this failure made possible the judicial careers of Pendleton and Wythe—and by extension, that of John Marshall. Because of confusing, contradictory, and, most disturbingly, a growing number of unjust laws, judicial discretion became even more necessary than it had been under the colonial regime. To the traditional task of applying English common law and equity was added that of construing the positive laws of the commonwealth. Each year brought a harvest of new laws, many of them consciously departing from English models, requiring ever increasing adjudications. Virginians got used to the idea that their courts were necessary to prevent or ameliorate mischiefs arising from the laws. They came to accept the notion, which the judges themselves consciously fostered, that judicial discretion in the interpretation of the laws was not the exercise of the arbitrary and capricious will of the judge but, in the deepest sense, giving effect to the will of the law.

In brief, judicial discretion was adapted and assimilated to republicanism. While accepting a newer conception of law as the command of the sovereign—in republican America, "the people"—Americans also retained the ancient belief in law as embodying reason and justice.[27] Republican legislatures, however, as the tumultuous history of the 1780s disclosed, often fell woefully short of these standards in their enactments. The upshot was an emerging distinction between "legislative will" and "justice," a growing perception that statutory law was not necessarily reasonable and just law. This distinction became the foundation of a conception of judicial independence and discretion that was consistent with the republican belief in the sovereignty of the people. In Virginia, under the leadership of Pendleton and Wythe, the judiciary self-consciously assumed the role of interpreter of the laws in the republican commonwealth. Not only were courts ordained to administer justice in disputes between private persons but also to be the peculiar guardians of the rights of individuals against encroachment by government and to be disinterested umpires in disputes between branches of the government. In carrying out these grave responsibilities, judges repeatedly proclaimed the principle of judicial independence and stoutly resisted legislative interference with what they regarded as their peculiar prerogatives.

The opinions and decrees of Pendleton, Wythe, and their brethren evinced a spirit of vigorous independence, even in the most mundane cases, and furnished lawyer Marshall with countless practical lessons in judging. The routine function of applying the common law frequently involved the exercise of discretion, particularly when the occasion called for adjusting the law to suit Virginia circumstances. Although English precedents continued to be the predominant authority relied on in arguing and deciding cases in Virginia courts until well into the nineteenth century, this by no means meant a mechanical deference to such authority. The Court of Appeals judges and Chancellor Wythe regarded their tribunals as equivalent to the superior courts of England and claimed the same privilege enjoyed by their English counterparts of detecting and correcting errors pronounced in earlier cases. A Pendleton or a Wythe no less than a Mansfield was capable of this task. English cases were the starting point for inquiry, but Virginia judges felt free to follow or depart from them as reason dictated. Indeed, the very tradition of English jurisprudence, which posited a clear distinction between law as a body of fixed principles and the application of those principles to particular cases, invited Virginia judges to hold up every precedent to the standard of right reason before it could be considered a controlling authority in the courts of the commonwealth.

Nowhere was this discretionary application of the common law more evident than in will construction cases. Typically the court was required to reconcile the "intention" of the testator with the laws of property and "settled and fixed" rules of construction. Not surprisingly, the string of English citations was longest in such cases, to the point, as Pendleton remarked, of obfuscation. The very proliferation of often contradictory and confusing cases forced judges to be independent and creative. In one such case Chancellor Wythe boldly declared himself "emancipated from a servile obsequiousness to the authority of adjudications in some particular instances." He was unwilling to "wait for leave from english judges . . . to reject an english determination," which he believed was "clumsy, bungling, [and] unfinished."[28] In will cases the court strove to give effect to the testator's intention—this was "the governing rule," said Pendleton, "to which all other rules of construction must yield." Precedents were of limited use in these cases, for his own experience was that they "have more frequently been produced to disappoint, than to illustrate the intention." "Where a testator's intention is apparent to me," said Pendleton, summing up his pragmatic approach to will cases, "cases must be strong, uniform, and apply pointedly, before they will prevail to frustrate that intention."[29]

The explication of statutes enacted by the Virginia General Assembly was another fertile field for the exercise of judicial discretion. One such law, adopted in 1781, declared that paper money should no longer be a legal tender and provided that all subsisting debts and contracts entered into in this currency between 1777 and 1782 should be reduced to their actual specie value according to a scale of depreciation. It set the ratio of paper to specie for each month of paper's circulation. Although the depreciation law furnished a fixed and known standard to settle paper money contracts without the intervention of courts, there were numerous applications to courts for an equitable departure from the scale—indeed, the law itself provided for such legal redress. During the period of Marshall's practice the Court of Appeals interpreted the depreciation law in sixteen reported cases, in most of which the court had to decide whether the circumstances of a contract justified a departure from the legal scale of depreciation. As Pendleton observed, the law furnished a "good *general rule* for scaling paper money contracts, but it was certainly not just in all cases."[30]

Perhaps no judge better epitomized the independent-minded jurist, fearless in the performance of his duty of meting out discretionary justice, than did Chancellor Wythe. At a time when Virginia courts refused to hear cases brought by British subjects for debts incurred before the Revolution, Wythe in May 1793 issued a chancery decree in favor of the legal rights of British creditors. In particular, he declared that payments made by debtors into the state loan office under the sequestration law of 1777 did not discharge the debtor of his individual liability to the British creditor. He so construed that law as to deny that the Virginia legislature meant to confiscate British debts, for confiscation of private debts was contrary to "the law and usages of nations."[31] Not even the federal circuit court, which shortly thereafter heard the case of *Ware* v. *Hylton,* went as far as Wythe in upholding British creditor rights. The Supreme Court eventually adopted Wythe's position on loan office payments in the appeal of *Ware* in 1796. Another of Wythe's notable decrees, given in 1798, reflected his deeply held antislavery convictions. The suit required him to construe the will of John Pleasants, which provided for the manumission of his slaves when they reached the age of thirty, contingent upon Virginia's passing a law allowing private manumission. Such a law was enacted in 1782 (some years after Pleasants's death), but the case was so complex as to raise doubts whether any of the slaves could be freed under the will. The chancellor, however, decreed that not only those slaves aged thirty and above were entitled to immediate freedom but also those under thirty who had been born after the law of 1782, whom he regarded as being free at birth. He went even further and ordered an account of profits, to be awarded to any slaves who had been wrongfully held in bondage—an unprecedented action by a Virginia judge in a suit for freedom. Not surprisingly, the Court of Appeals subsequently restricted the scope of this radical decree.[32]

Virginia judges understood that maintaining their independence required them to keep discretion within proper bounds. To exceed these bounds, to be perceived as invading the "legislative" power, was to invite attacks on judicial power that would bring courts under the strict control of the legislature. Thus Pendleton offered the following assurance to allay fears that a court in professing to give effect to the testator's intention might in fact rewrite the will: "But I would first premise, that we disclaim all legislative power to change the law, and only assume our proper province of declaring what the law is: we disclaim all authority to mould testators' wills into any form which fancy, whim, or worse passions might suggest."[33] This judicial tactic was later employed by Chief Justice Marshall, who learned well the lesson that self-denial (or the appearance of self-denial) could serve to enhance judicial power. "Courts are the mere instruments of the law, and can will nothing," he remarked. "When they are said to exercise a discretion it is a mere legal discretion, a discretion to be exercised in discerning the true course prescribed by law."[34]

Marshall's understanding of judicial discretion, derived from his days in the courts of Pendleton and Wythe, formed an essential underpinning of his jurisprudence. Far from being a disingenuous rationale for judicial lawmaking, the claim that judicial discretion was "a mere legal discretion" reflected the still prevailing assumption that the principles of law had an independent, objective existence apart from particular cases and distinct from the personal bias of the judge. The distinction between principle and precedent compelled judges to exercise discretion, but principles also acted as a check upon discretion. Judging, Marshall believed, consisted of "discovering" and applying legal principles, an activity that he did not doubt could be kept quite distinct from the legislative function of creating new law. At the very outset of his judicial tenure, Marshall announced a characteristic feature of his jurisprudence, the separation of the domain of "law" from that of "politics," by disclaiming "all pretensions" on the part of the judiciary to decide questions "in their nature political." The usefulness of this distinction was that in all matters that could be defined as "legal," judges were free to exercise their discretion.[35]

JUDICIAL REVIEW IN VIRGINIA

Ultimately, in Virginia as elsewhere in the new American states, the discretion of judges to decide what law applied in a given case came to include the power to measure ordinary laws against constitutions and to declare the former void if contrary to the latter. Without question the long habit of judicial discretion, springing from the very nature of common law adjudication, was an essential prerequisite for the emergence of judicial review. As the historian Gordon Wood has shown, acceptance of judicial review became possible as a result of the "massive rethinking" Americans undertook during the 1780s about the nature of republican government. This rethinking was necessitated by manifest signs that the republican experiment was not working out as the revolutionaries had hoped. Popularly elected assemblies enacted a mass of confusing, unwise, and unjust legislation. Legislatures, it turned out, were faction-ridden; public law was the guise by which majorities accomplished their selfish projects, in the process remorselessly sacrificing the private rights of individuals and minorities. In reacting against legislative supremacy, Americans transformed the meaning of "separation of powers" in a way that not only reflected a new appreciation for executive power but, more important, cleared the way for a great "enhancement of the judiciary." The judiciary department, in brief, came to be perceived as the guardian of written, people-made fundamental law, as much the representative or servant of the people as the legislative department. This perception facilitated the emergence of judicial review as one among a variety of "republican" remedies for improving the performance of republican government.[36]

The path from judicial discretion to judicial review was neither easy nor straightforward. In Virginia during the years of Marshall's practice, prominent members of the state judiciary went on record in favor of the idea that courts could annul an act of assembly, though among the people at large judicial review was by no means universally accepted before 1800 (or even after). As early as 1782, the Court of Appeals was obliged to confront this "great constitutional question" in a case that brought into view a seeming conflict between the state constitution and a law concerning treason. In this instance the court was able to reconcile law and constitution and thus avoided having to decide this "deep, important, and . . . awful question."[37] The occasion did, however, bring forth an eloquent statement from Chancellor Wythe on the duty of a judge "to point to the constitution" and say to an overreaching legislature, "Here is the limit of your authority; and, hither, shall you go, but no further."[38] Wythe's dicta revealed how fully he had moved beyond a narrow conception of judicial duty to embrace the idea of the judiciary as an impartial umpire between government and citizen and between different departments of government.

Another bold assertion from the judges occurred in 1788 as a result of the legislature's reorganization of the court system. The first district court law enacted by the assembly required the judges of the Court of Appeals to attend the various district courts. This law brought forth a "respectful remonstrance" drafted by Pendleton, which complained that the act assigned new duties without a commensurate increase in pay and therefore undermined the principle of judicial independence embedded in the constitution. The judges found themselves obliged to declare *"that the constitution and the act are in opposition and cannot exist together; and that the former must control the operation of the latter."* In much the same way he defended judicial discretion to discover a testator's intention in will cases, Pendleton contended that such a declaration was a proper judicial function: "To obviate a possible objection, that the court, while they are maintaining the independency of the judiciary, are countenancing encroachments of that branch upon the department of others, and assuming a right to control the legislature, it may be observed, *that when they decide between an act of the people, and an act of the legislature, they are within the line of their duty, declaring what the law is, and not making a new law."*[39] Marshall likewise later asserted that to decide between a constitution and a law was to "determine which of these conflicting rules, governs the case. This is of the essence of judicial duty."[40]

The judges' remonstrance was later cited to justify the first actual exercise by a Virginia court of the power to declare a legislative act unconstitutional. In 1792 the General Assembly, in an attempt to decentralize chancery jurisdiction, enacted a law empowering the district court judges to grant injunctions and to hear suits commencing by injunction. The following year the district judges, sitting together as the General Court in the case of *Kamper* v. *Hawkins,* declared this act void on the ground that the constitution prohibited General Court judges from exercising chancery jurisdiction.[41] As a precedent for judicial review, *Kamper* shares some common features with *Marbury* v. *Madison.* In both cases the laws brought under constitutional scrutiny were judiciary acts. And on both occasions the judges denied the additional jurisdiction conferred upon them by the legislature.

As in the earlier remonstrance, the judges in *Kamper* defended judicial review as a proper exercise of *legal* discretion, scarcely different from that employed in the routine comparison of two statutes. In cases brought judicially before them, they were as duty bound to pronounce a law void for contravening the constitution as they were to declare a law of no force for being virtually repealed by a subsequent act. One of the judges who sat in *Kamper* was Spencer Roane, later to be chief judge of the Virginia Court of Appeals and an outspoken opponent of his counterpart on the federal Supreme Court. Roane's bitter quarrel with the Marshall Court had nothing to do with judicial review, for these two jurists were in fundamental agreement that it was the duty of courts to pronounce the nullity of laws contrary to the constitution. Roane, indeed, went beyond the other *Kamper* judges in asserting a broad scope for exercising discretion in constitutional cases. The judiciary, he maintained, must void laws not only "plainly repugnant to the letter of the Constitution" but also to the "fundamental principles thereof." The latter he defined as "those great principles growing out of the Constitution, by the aid of which, in dubious cases, the Constitution may be explained and preserved inviolate; those land-marks, which it may be necessary to resort to, on account of the impossibility to foresee or provide for cases within the spirit, but without the letter of the Constitution."[42]

John Marshall was the product of a legal culture in which judicial discretion was firmly entrenched. He repeatedly drew upon this tradition while presiding over the supreme tribunal of the United States. After so many years of direct exposure to the tradition, he had so fully absorbed its content and methods that acting the role of a judge was al-most instinctive to him. By the time he took the oath of office in 1801, he had acquired a keen understanding of the meaning of judicial inde-pendence and a sense of the possibilities open to courts, as well as of the limits placed upon them, in the exercise of judicial power.

3

THE PROVINCE OF
THE JUDICIARY:
MARBURY v. *MADISON*

Chief Justice Marshall delivered his first great opinion in the celebrated case of *Marbury* v. *Madison* in 1803. In deciding this case, the Supreme Court for the first time declared an act of Congress in conflict with the Constitution and, for that reason, void. *Marbury* subsequently became the leading precedent for "judicial review," the Court's power to pass upon the constitutionality of legislative acts. Along the way it has acquired the status of a landmark, perhaps the most prominent, of American constitutional law. The case is no less important for its assertion of the judiciary's claim to inquire into the legality of executive acts in certain instances. Indeed, this aspect of the case provoked far more controversy at the time than did the annulment of a statute. Marshall was less troubled by asserting the doctrine of judicial review than he was by the challenge of discovering and applying a principle for bringing executive acts under judicial scrutiny. This inquiry, to which he devoted the greater part of his opinion, constituted the "peculiar delicacy" and "real difficulty" of the case.[1]

POLITICAL BACKGROUND

The case began in December 1801 with a motion for a rule to Secretary of State James Madison to show cause why a writ of mandamus should not issue commanding him to deliver the commissions of William Marbury and others as justices of the peace for the District of Columbia.[2]

47

Marbury and his co-complainants were "midnight judges," nominated by departing President Adams on March 2, 1801, and confirmed by the Senate the same day. Adams signed the commissions on his last day in office and transmitted them to Secretary of State Marshall to affix the seal and send out. Marbury's commission, however, was one of a number that had not been delivered before the new administration of President Thomas Jefferson assumed office. In considering the application, the Supreme Court affirmed that Marbury had a legal right to his commission and that a mandamus was the proper remedy. But the Court ultimately denied relief on the ground that it lacked jurisdiction to issue the writ. Although the Judiciary Act of 1789 authorized the Supreme Court to issue writs of mandamus to officers of the federal government, the Court declared this provision void as purporting to enlarge the Court's original jurisdiction beyond that prescribed by Article 3 of the Constitution.

From its inception Marbury's case assumed an importance beyond that of a mere legal dispute. It arose directly from the victorious party's resentment of the outgoing administration's eleventh-hour appointments to a host of new judicial offices created by the Judiciary Act of 1801 and the act concerning the District of Columbia. The lame-duck Federalist Congress had enacted both laws during the waning days of Adams's presidency. The very bringing of the action, which coincided with the meeting of the first session of the new Congress under a Republican majority, hastened the repeal of the 1801 act and prompted the accompanying act by which the Supreme Court lost a term and did not meet between December 1801 and February 1803. Although the Court technically ruled in favor of the administration by refusing Marbury's application, the opinion provoked the wrath of Jefferson and the Republicans as a gratuitous lecture to the president for not complying with the law. Particularly galling was the Court's irregular proceeding of affirming the merits of Marbury's claim and then deciding that it had no jurisdiction in the case. Nearly all contemporary criticism of *Marbury* centered on its "dicta," its discussion of matters not essential to the determination of the case. By contrast, the Court's presuming to declare a law of Congress unconstitutional aroused little antagonism.[3]

The mandamus case can scarcely be understood apart from the political context of Jefferson's first administration. Whether denounced by Republicans as a party-inspired attack on the dignity and prerogatives of the executive or praised by Federalists as a bold defense of legal right against executive oppression, *Marbury* was interpreted by contemporaries almost exclusively in partisan terms. Modern commentators likewise are inclined to see more politics than law in Marshall's opinion.[4] Yet to read the opinion solely in the light of the raging party battles of the day is to miss the full significance of the case and to misconstrue the motives behind the opinion. Although the immediate effect of the decision was to embroil the Supreme Court in political controversy, the underlying intent of the opinion was to set forth a principled statement of the federal judiciary's place in the American constitutional system that disavowed any political role for courts and judges. Given the peculiar circumstances of the case, the manifest connection between Marbury's claim to his commission and the defeat of the Federalists, Marshall faced a formidable assignment in writing an opinion that breathed disinterested judicial statesmanship. There was an inherent difficulty in assimilating this highly political case to the realm of legal rights and remedies.

Far from being a bold assertion of judicial power, *Marbury* actually marked a strategic retreat by the judiciary from the aggressive, partisan posture it had lately exhibited under the Adams administration.[5] During the war crisis of 1798 and 1799 in particular, federal courts vigorously supported the government's efforts to suppress internal dissent. Republican newspaper editors were fined and jailed on criminal indictments brought in United States courts. Most of these indictments were based on the notorious Sedition Act, though some were prosecuted at common law on the assumption that federal courts possessed jurisdiction over common law crimes in the absence of a specific statute. This assumption, indeed, lay behind the enactment of the Sedition Act, whose proponents contended that it ameliorated the common law of seditious libel. The idea of a federal common law was anathema to Republicans and revived latent fears of judicial discretion and the old Antifederalist specter of federal consolidation accomplished through construction. As James Madison warned, if the common law—"a law of vast extent and complexity, and embracing almost every possible subject of legislation"— were admitted to fall under federal jurisdiction, federal judges would enjoy "an immense field for judicial discretion" that would in effect make them legislators. Through construction they would "new-model the whole political fabric of the country" by effecting a vast transfer of sovereignty from the states to the general government.[6]

Besides proclaiming the doctrine of a federal common law, federal judges rendered themselves obnoxious by the manner in which they conducted trials under the Sedition Act. Abruptly dismissing arguments that the law was an unconstitutional infringement of free speech and freedom of the press, they not only upheld the act but, displaying scant concern for the rights of the accused, went out of their way to aid federal prosecutors in supporting indictments for sedition. When traveling through the country on their circuits, some judges abandoned all pretense of judicial propriety and descended to overt partisanship. In grand jury charges they intemperately denounced opposition to government and exhorted the citizenry to support the wise and virtuous policies of the administration. Republicans angrily denounced such harangues as "a perversion of the . . . grand jury from a legal to a political engine" and rebuked judges who had been "converted into political partisans."[7]

On assuming office in 1801, Marshall set about to repair the federal judiciary's tarnished reputation, to rein in a judicial discretion that was widely perceived as fostering national aggrandizement and political oppression. The change of administration made such a retreat advisable, and happily for this purpose the new chief justice was a man of prudence and moderate political temperament. He had publicly opposed the Sedition Act (though not on constitutional grounds) and privately dismissed the idea of a federal common law as a "strange & absurd doctrine." On his first circuit as a federal judge, Marshall pointedly confined his grand jury charge to points of law "without the least political intermixture." And he declined a request for publication of his "elegant and learned" charge, having "laid it down as a rule from which he did not intend to depart, not to allow his charges to be published."[8]

That the chief justice and his brethren even attended their first circuits after the repeal of the Judiciary Act of 1801 signaled a more cautious judicial posture. The repeal, which restored circuit duties to Supreme Court justices, presented a serious constitutional question that had to be resolved before the commencement of the fall circuits in 1802. Marshall privately doubted the constitutionality of the repeal, believing the Constitution required distinct commissions for circuit court judges from those of the Supreme Court. At the same time, however, he considered it his duty "in this as in all other cases to be bound by the opinion of the majority of the Judges." After ascertaining that most of his colleagues acquiesced in the repeal, the chief justice accordingly announced "that policy dictates this decision to us all."[9]

The measures taken by the chief justice to withdraw the federal judiciary into a more restricted field of activity did not signify any intention to capitulate to the new political majority. On the one hand Marshall recognized that federal judges had exceeded the proper boundaries of judicial discretion; on the other he was concerned that the political backlash generated by judicial excesses would undermine if not destroy the independence of the judiciary. To strike a balance between deferring to the political branches and upholding the legitimate claims of judicial power was the difficult challenge confronting Marshall at the outset of his chief justiceship. This consideration was uppermost in his mind as he framed his opinion in the mandamus case. As much as he would have preferred to avoid any confrontation with the executive, Marshall could not close his eyes to what he believed to be the illegal act of withholding Marbury's commission. He privately expressed "infinite chagrin" on first learning—in March 1801 (well before Marbury brought his legal action)—that President Jefferson had not sent out the signed and sealed justice of the peace commissions. He would have sent them out himself (in his capacity as secretary of state), he explained, but for the press of time and the unavailability of the clerk. That the new president would withhold them was "an act of which I entertained no suspicion."[10]

THE SEPARATION OF LAW AND POLITICS

Marbury v. *Madison* epitomizes the characteristic rhetorical style and method of Marshall's great judicial pronouncements: a resolution of the case into one or more enumerated points; a statement of the law in terms of abstract general principles; a reformulation of the law derived by logical deduction and analysis so that it could be applied to the case at hand; and, finally, a decision stated in general language that could apply to future cases.[11] The opinion also introduced themes that run through the entire corpus of Marshall's judicial writings. Broadly understood, *Marbury* sought to define the "province of the judiciary," a theme that finds frequent restatement in subsequent opinions. This attempt to define in turn gave rise to the important distinction between the spheres of "law" and "politics," according to which the judiciary refused to take jurisdiction over "questions, in their nature political" and confined itself to deciding upon the legal rights of individuals.[12] The separation of law and politics was perhaps the fundamental proposition underlying Marshall's jurisprudence, a proposition that in attenuated form continues to influence our perception of the Supreme Court as an institution elevated above and insulated from the political arena.

In the first part of *Marbury*, the chief justice defined the scope of judicial power in relation to the executive branch. As a congressman three years earlier Marshall had conducted an exhaustive investigation of this subject in his speech on the extradition of Jonathan Robbins. On that occasion he defended President Adams's action in turning Robbins over to British authorities as a legitimate exercise of executive power. The extradition of Robbins, he contended, was a political question unsuited to disposition by the judiciary, which by the Constitution had no "political power whatsoever." The judicial power extended not to all "questions" arising under the Constitution and laws but only to "cases," that is, to controversies "between parties which had taken a shape for judicial decision."[13]

In the mandamus case Marshall employed the same analysis to show that the act of withholding Marbury's commission raised a question of legal right proper for a court to decide. Building on the constitutional distinction between the appointment and the commission, he concluded that the president's power of appointment ceased the moment he signed the commission. At this point Marbury acquired a property right in the office of justice of the peace that was good for five years. To revoke his appointment by withholding the commission was accordingly "an act . . . not warranted by law, but violative of a vested legal right."[14] Here Marshall introduced another resonant theme of his jurisprudence, namely, the idea that judicial power is peculiarly charged with protecting the "vested rights" of individuals, rights deemed so fundamental as to be beyond the control of government in ordinary circumstances.

But was this a case in which the laws afforded Marbury a remedy that could be pursued in a court of law? The answer to that question depended on the nature of the executive act. Some acts were "political," depending entirely on the discretion of the president or of his subordinate officers. For these the president was "accountable only to his country in his political character and to his own conscience" and the subordinate officer was accountable only to the president. Such political acts "respect the nation, not individual rights, and being intrusted to the executive, the decision of the executive is conclusive."[15] There were other cases, however, where discretion could not be exercised, as when the law imposed a duty on the officer "to perform certain acts" on which individual rights depended. In performing such ministerial acts, he acted not as the organ of the president's will but as "the officer of the law" and could not "at his discretion sport away the vested rights of others."[16] Persons injured by official neglect in these cases could seek redress in the courts. Since neither the president nor his subordinate officer had discretionary authority to revoke the appointment of a magistrate who by law had acquired a vested right to hold the office for five years, Marbury had every right to pursue his remedy in a court of law. "The question whether a right has vested or not," said Marshall, "is, in its nature, judicial, and must be tried by the judicial authority."[17]

In writing this section of *Marbury*, Marshall tried to filter out all partisan aspects of the case, to present Marbury's claim in the neutral, disinterested language of law. From reading the opinion, one would never know that Marbury's commission was signed by one president and withheld by his successor who was of a different political party. But this was precisely the point the chief justice wanted to make: political vicissitudes should not affect legal rights and obligations. Conversely, judicial discretion should never be exercised for political purposes. Sensitive to criticism on this score, Marshall anticipated that the Supreme Court's willingness to hear the motion for a mandamus would be considered "as an attempt to intrude into the cabinet, and to intermeddle with the prerogatives of the executive."[18] To correct this misunderstanding, he maintained that judicial power was exercised not to check executive discretion but to uphold the legal rights of individuals. "The province of the court," reads a famous passage, "is, solely, to decide on the rights of individuals, not to inquire how the executive, or executive officers, perform duties in which they have a discretion. Questions in their nature political, or which are, by the constitution and laws, submitted to the executive, can never be made in this court."[19]

Although these assurances failed to mute criticism of *Marbury* as a partisan assault dressed up in the garb of a judicial decision, a close reading of the opinion reveals a dispassionate inquiry to resolve essentially *legal* questions, to discover a rule of law to bring certain executive acts within judicial cognizance. It is this search for legal principle, not the supposed political bias of the chief justice, that is the key to understanding the deeper meaning of *Marbury*. Notwithstanding the plaintiff's notorious status as a midnight judge appointed by a lame-duck Federalist president, the withholding of his commission constituted a plain violation of legal right that could not be ignored. From Marshall's perspective, to let Marbury's claim go unheard would be to implicate the Court in politics, to expose the Court's complicity in the government's illegal proceedings. This was precisely the situation the federal judiciary had recently found itself in, at the high cost of undermining public confidence in the institution. *Marbury* was a part of Chief Justice Marshall's broader objective to restore the honor and integrity of the judicial branch and to reaffirm the reputation of the United States government as "a government of laws, and not of men."[20]

JUDICIAL REVIEW

After painstakingly demonstrating that Marbury had a legal claim that could be asserted in a court of law, Marshall proceeded to show that a mandamus was the proper remedy to compel delivery of the commission. But could the Supreme Court issue this writ? Section 13 of the Judiciary Act of 1789 did indeed authorize the Court to issue writs of mandamus "in cases warranted by the principles and usages of law, to any courts appointed, or person holding office, under the authority of the United States."[21] This statutory provision, however, was shown to be repugnant to Article 3 of the Constitution, which declared that the Supreme Court shall have original jurisdiction "in all Cases affecting Ambassadors, other public Ministers and Consuls, and those in which a State shall be Party" and appellate jurisdiction "in all the other Cases" belonging to federal judicial power. If the Court were to issue the writ in this case, it would be an exercise of original jurisdiction. The statute, in effect, had enlarged the Court's original jurisdiction by extending it to an additional category of cases. Hence the authority to issue the writ was contrary to the Constitution.

These remarks set the stage for Marshall's celebrated exposition of the doctrine that courts can void acts of legislation that infringe upon the Constitution.[22] This section of *Marbury* was essentially a continuation of the broader inquiry that sought to define the province of the judiciary. The chief justice now turned his attention to the limits of judicial discretion in relation to the acts of the other political branch, the legislature. "The question, whether an act, repugnant to the constitution, can become the law of the land, is a question deeply interesting to the United States," he observed by way of preface to the argument that followed, "but, happily, not of an intricacy proportioned to its interest. It seems only necessary to recognize certain principles, supposed to have been long and well established, to decide it."[23] This passage should not be read as a disingenuous attempt to disarm opposition to a debatable proposition. Contrary to myths that still persist concerning *Marbury,* the Supreme Court did not use this case as an opportunity to assert the doctrine of judicial review, to boldly assume possession of a doubtful power. There was no need to do so, for by 1803 the idea that courts could void laws contravening the Constitution was no longer seriously controverted. Courts, moreover, both state and federal, had implicitly and explicitly exercised this power on a number of occasions prior to 1803. Far from marking out a new path for extending judicial discretion, Marshall was merely restating widely accepted principles and beliefs. At the same time, not unmindful of political considerations, the chief justice shrewdly reckoned that the Supreme Court's first exercise of review would be accepted more easily if presented as an act of judicial self-denial—the law in question being nullified on the ground that it gave the Court unlawful power.

He began with the premise that the American people possessed "an original right" to enact a constitution on "such principles, as . . . shall most conduce to their own happiness" and that these principles, proceeding from sovereign authority, were to be considered fundamental and permanent. One such fundamental principle was that the federal government was a government of defined and limited powers, which were enumerated in a written constitution. The people clearly evinced their intention to keep the government from transcending the limits imposed on it. Otherwise, why establish limits and why commit them to writing? There was no "middle ground" between regarding the Constitution as "a superior paramount law, unchangeable by ordinary means," or as an ordinary act of legislation, alterable at the pleasure of the legislature. The latter alternative was patently false unless one assumed that "written constitutions are absurd attempts, on the part of the people, to limit a power in its own nature illimitable." From the principle of limited government established by a written constitution flowed yet another fundamental principle: the theory "that an act of the legislature, repugnant to the constitution, is void."[24]

So far Marshall had said nothing that was in the slightest degree exceptionable. But now he turned to the heart of the matter: What were courts to do when confronted with an irreconcilable opposition between a law and the Constitution? The chief justice made the case for judicial review by anchoring it to the familiar and routine practice of choosing the applicable law to govern the decision of a case:

> It is emphatically the province and duty of the judicial department to say what the law is. Those who apply the rule to particular cases, must of necessity expound and interpret that rule. If two laws conflict with each other, the courts must decide on the operation of each.[25]

Choosing between a Constitution and a law, where both applied to a given case, was no different from deciding between two statutes. Determining the applicable rule was "of the very essence of judicial duty."[26] But were courts to regard the Constitution as a judicially enforceable paramount law that would override an ordinary statute in cases where both apply? This, of course, was the crucial question, which Marshall answered affirmatively by pointing out the unacceptable consequences of the alternative construction, by which "courts must close their eyes on the constitution, and see only the law":

> This doctrine would subvert the very foundation of all written constitutions. It would declare that an act which, according to the principles and theory of our government, is entirely void, is yet, in practice, completely obligatory. It would declare that if the legislature shall do what is expressly forbidden, such act, notwithstanding the express prohibition, is in reality effectual. It would be giving to the legislature a practical and real omnipotence, with the same breath which professes to restrict their powers within narrow lim-

its. It is prescribing limits, and declaring that those limits may be passed at pleasure.[27]

The case for rejecting such a manifestly absurd construction found support in the language of the Constitution itself. The judicial power, for example, extended to "all cases . . . arising under this Constitution," which surely invited, if it did not compel, judges to examine that instrument. The prohibitions against export duties, bills of attainder, and ex post facto laws also seemed to require judicial inquiry. And the clause requiring two witnesses to convict a person of treason was "addressed especially to courts. It prescribes . . . a rule of evidence not to be departed from." These and other provisions, along with the oath requiring the judges to support the Constitution, showed that the framers "contemplated that instrument as a rule for the government of courts, as well as of the legislature." And to remove any lingering doubts, the chief justice referred to the clause designating first the Constitution and secondly the laws of United States "made in pursuance thereof" as the "supreme law of the land."[28]

Marbury was the only occasion in which Marshall expressed in detail his understanding of the doctrine of judicial review. Some commentators have expressed disappointment that he did not present a stronger case supported by an array of precedents and authorities. His argument has been criticized for glossing over or ignoring weak links in the chain of logic, indeed, for seeming to assume the very point to be proved, namely, that the Constitution is judicially enforceable law. He did not appear to take seriously the contrary proposition that existing institutional arrangements—the division of the legislature into two branches, the qualified veto of the executive, and, most important, the force of public opinion as expressed through elections and by other means—could preserve the Constitution without the necessity of judicial review. Nor did he attempt to explain why the Constitution did not explicitly authorize the judiciary to exercise so substantial a power. His case, in short, was persuasive mainly to those already predisposed to accept the doctrine.

These criticisms are rather beside the point, for Marshall did not intend to lay out an exhaustive "proof" to persuade a skeptical audience. Since there was already a broad consensus among Americans that courts could, in some instances at least, annul a legislative act as repugnant to the Constitution, there was no reason to present an elaborate justification for this practice. The omission of citations to authorities was no doubt deliberate, for Marshall was surely acquainted with the so-called "precedents" for judicial review. From his perspective these cases were not needed to establish the principle of judicial review, however useful they might be as illustrations of the principle. He firmly believed that judicial review was grounded in the very nature of American constitutionalism, if not confirmed by the text of the Constitution itself. A practice that was sanctioned by the highest authority did not require further support. The chief justice's modest objective was merely to reaffirm the doctrine in terms well calculated to command broad public assent. In this respect he rendered a remarkably clear and concise summation of constitutional development during the preceding two decades. *Marbury* represents not the beginning of judicial review but its emergence within the broader historical process of defining the judiciary's role in the American constitutional system. The opinion embodied a particular conception of judicial review that can only be understood in relation to this process.

JUDICIAL REVIEW BEFORE *MARBURY*

The doctrine of judicial review spelled out in *Marbury* was based squarely on the ideas of popular sovereignty and of a written constitution as the positive and permanent expression of that sovereignty. It was inextricably tied to that remarkable development in American political and constitutional thought during the 1780s in which the "sovereignty of the people" was reduced to practice through institutions in such a way that the people became in fact, not merely in theory, the source of all political power. Acceptance of judicial review in America hinged on the perception that it offered a practical means of preserving and enforcing the permanent will of the people. No less important was an emerging understanding of a constitution as a formally enacted "law," which, owing to its method of enactment and ratification by special conventions of the people, was conceived to be superior to an ordinary legislative act.

This conception of a constitution as written fundamental law was not in itself sufficient to account for the emergence of judicial review.

Other countries have had written constitutions without adopting the practice of allowing courts to set aside acts deemed unconstitutional. On the other hand, a written constitution was virtually a sine qua non of the American doctrine of judicial review. Judicial enforcement of unwritten standards of natural or divine law, of the eternal and immutable principles of right and justice, never took firm root in America. Indeed, it is inconceivable that judicial review on this basis could have developed into the powerful institution it became in republican America.

Although some scholars have traced the origins of judicial review to a "higher law" tradition in Western political thought, this influence does not adequately explain the peculiar American practice or its justifying rationale. Indeed, the idea of a fundamental law derived from nonhuman sources (e.g., God, nature) militated against judicial review in important respects. The unwritten principles of natural justice were at once too fundamental and too nebulous to constitute the kind of "law" that can run in the ordinary court system. Revolution, not adjudication, was the ultimate means of bringing human laws into conformity with fundamental principles of justice. And judicial review as a substitute for revolution was not likely to have a promising career, for by definition it would be invoked only on extraordinary occasions, when the violations of basic rights were so flagrant and palpable as to justify judicial intervention. Yet if the situation had become so dire, courts and judges by themselves were not likely to be able to save the nation from itself. Something less than a substitute for revolution, American judicial review was devised to enforce a particular kind of "higher law" enacted by the people themselves.

The ancient idea of fundamental law exerted a powerful influence on the political thought of eighteenth-century Britain and America. Yet in one country the doctrine of legislative sovereignty triumphed, while in the other the doctrine of judicial review prevailed. In both Great Britain and the colonies, fundamental law was recognized as a moral restraint upon lawmakers, a set of basic principles they should adhere to in legislating. Judges, too, frequently invoked the principles of natural justice in construing statutes. A legislative act, according to a well-known canon of construction, could not be presumed to violate natural law, reason, or justice. Fundamental law, in short, was used to expound laws, not to nullify them.

There were, nonetheless, a few ambiguous precedents for judicial prerogative to void acts repugnant to fundamental precepts of reason and justice. The most celebrated of these was the case of Dr. Bonham, decided in 1610, in which the great English jurist Sir Edward Coke declared that "in many cases the common law will control acts of parliament and sometimes adjudge them to be utterly void; for when an act of parliament is against common right or reason, or repugnant or impossible to be performed, the common law will control it, and adjudge such act to be void."[29] But Coke's dictum, resonant as it is to modern ears, should not be read anachronistically as sanctioning judicial review. Probably he meant no more than to state a rule of statutory construction that was substantially in accord with Blackstone's later enunciation of the principle of legislative sovereignty. "I know," said Blackstone, "it is generally laid down . . . that acts of parliament contrary to reason are void. But if the parliament will positively enact a thing to be done which is unreasonable, I know of no power in the ordinary forms of the constitution, that is vested with authority to control it." He denied the right of judges to reject a statute whose "main object" was unreasonable, "for that were to set the judicial power above that of the legislature, which would be subversive of all government." Blackstone went on to explain that if a statute produced some "collateral" and obviously unintended consequence that was absurd or unreasonable, judges could then "expound the statute by equity" so as to avoid that consequence.[30]

Although by the mid-eighteenth century fundamental law in Britain imposed only moral and theoretical limits on the authority of Parliament, in the colonies Coke's notion of a legally binding unwritten higher law enjoyed a longer life. In the 1760s and 1770s American patriots repeatedly invoked the principles of natural justice, reason, and the British Constitution to declare obnoxious acts of Parliament void and of no legal effect. This form of protest was best illustrated by James Otis, who in an attack on the issuing of general search warrants to royal customs officials asserted that an act of Parliament "against the Constitution" or against "natural Equity" was "void" and that courts "must pass such Acts into disuse."[31] Arguments of this kind, contending for the superior legal obligation of unwritten fundamental law, continued to be heard in America after 1776 but ultimately became obsolete with the institutionalizing of popular sovereignty. The traditional idea of fundamental law underwent a radical transformation that made possible a novel conception of judicial review.[32]

Popular sovereignty, not legislative sovereignty, became the underlying principle of republican government in America. Initially, the distinction between the two was blurred, for in the first state constitutions virtually all substantive governmental powers were centered in the legislatures. Within a decade of 1776, however, legislative supremacy was reeling from an attack from which it never recovered. The manifest misbehavior of the state legislatures, the selfish and corrupt politics that sacrificed private rights to the whims of majority factions, the seeming disregard for upholding the public good or maintaining minimum standards of justice, provoked a massive reaction that ultimately caused Americans to revise their republican theories. After the unhappy experience of the 1780s, good republicans could no longer equate their governments with the legislatures, could no longer regard their assemblies as the sole embodiment of the people, and could no longer unquestioningly accept legislative enactments as true expressions of the public will, that is, as law.[33]

This diminution in the authority and prestige of legislative power was part of a larger process of separating sovereignty from government and placing it in the active and organized citizenry. During the troubled and creative decade of the 1780s, Americans employed a variety of means to express their will that bypassed the regular channels of government, acquiring for themselves a new identity as a sovereign people distinct from their governments. Ultimately they devised the institution that became the most important American contribution to political and constitutional theory: conventions of the people to frame and ratify constitutions. In its full flowering the convention method of forming constitutions occurred entirely outside of government. It was an extralegal means of creating a supreme law by which government would henceforth be constituted and limited. Through conventions Americans transformed popular sovereignty from a remote and theoretical ideal into a concrete reality. The people became in fact the constituent power, the supreme lawmaking authority of the state. A constitution formed in this manner became something more than a frame of government; it was also a law imposed upon government, to be obeyed in the same way citizens obeyed ordinary statutes enacted by their legislatures. It was a "higher law" derived not from a source outside the people but from the people themselves and intended to be permanent and unchanging, alterable only by the same power that created it.[34]

The formation of a supreme law as the original and deliberate act of the people was the indispensable basis for a theory of judicial review that was compatible with the principles of popular government. In separating sovereignty from government, Americans also revised their understanding of the doctrine of separation of powers in a way that had great implications for the judiciary. The legislature, executive, and judiciary became joined together in an equality of subordination to the supreme authority of the people. The net effect was to enhance judicial power, particularly in relation to legislative power. The judiciary (and executive as well) came to be perceived as exercising its delegated portion of governmental power in essentially the same way as the legislature; judges were as much the representatives of the people as were assemblymen. No longer an adjunct of the legislature or executive, the judiciary began to lay claim to an equal and independent status within the larger scheme of government.[35] Judges increasingly sought to define the nature and special prerogatives of judicial power and to resist encroachments upon their jurisdiction. Asserting as their peculiar province the right to declare what the law is, they denied at the same time the right of legislatures to exceed their prescribed boundaries of determining what the law shall be. Understood in this way, separation of powers supplied a persuasive rationale for judges to maintain that in declaring a law void they were exercising proper *judicial* authority, not usurping the prerogatives of the legislature.

Even before the adoption of the Constitution, state courts had begun to take the first tentative and controversial steps toward judicial review. Two of these early cases illustrate the seemingly insuperable obstacles to acceptance of judicial review founded on unwritten fundamental law. In *Rutgers* v. *Waddington* (1784), a New York act allowing returning citizens of New York City to sue Tory occupants for trespass was challenged as being contrary to the treaty of peace and to the law of nations. The Mayor's Court of New York did not actually overturn this legislative act but expounded it by equity to avoid an "unreasonable" effect in this particular case. In justifying the court's action, Judge James Duane recited the very passage from Blackstone that proclaimed the doctrine of parliamentary sovereignty but allowed courts to construe statutes by equity in certain instances. Despite this acknowledgment of legislative supremacy, the court's decision was denounced as "subversive of good order and the sovereignty of the state" and as contrary to the "nature and genius of our government."[36]

An even greater controversy arose from the case of *Trevett* v. *Weeden* (1786), which brought into question a Rhode Island law denying a jury trial to persons refusing to accept the state's paper money. Although Rhode Island had no written constitution, the attorney for the defendants contended in an elaborate and widely republished argument that the right to jury trial was a "fundamental, and constitutional right" derived from natural and divine law and embodied in the ancient common law. A majority of justices agreed that the law was "repugnant and unconstitutional." Declaring that this decision was "unprecedented in this state and may tend directly to abolish the legislative authority thereof," the state legislature summoned the judges to appear before that body to explain their reasons. At the next election the offending justices were removed from the bench and replaced by others more amenable to the views of the assembly.[37]

Another early defense of judicial review was formulated by James Iredell, counsel for the plaintiff in the North Carolina case *Bayard* v. *Singleton* (1787). Later a justice of the United States Supreme Court, Iredell strikingly anticipated what became the standard justification of the practice based explicitly on a written constitution and popular sovereignty. "The constitution," so his argument ran, "appears to me to be a fundamental law, limiting the powers of the Legislature, and with which every exercise of those powers must, necessarily be compared." Since the duty of courts was to decide cases according to the laws of the state, judges were bound to enforce this written fundamental law: "It will not be denied . . . that the Constitution is the law of the State, as well as an act of the Assembly, with this difference only, that it is the fundamental law, and unalterable by the legislature, which derives all its power from it." To enforce a law inconsistent with the constitution was to disobey "the superior law to which we were previously and irrevocably bound." To disregard an unconstitutional act, moreover, was "not a usurped or a discretionary power, but one inevitably resulting from the constitution of their office, they being judges for the benefit of the whole people, not mere servants of the Assembly." Indeed, "the exercise of the power is unavoidable, the Constitution not being a mere imaginary thing, about which ten thousand different opinions may be formed, but a written document to which all may have recourse, and to which, therefore, the judges cannot wilfully blind themselves."[38]

Iredell's argument contained the essential elements of the doctrine of judicial review endorsed by Alexander Hamilton in the celebrated *Federalist* No. 78 and reiterated by Marshall in *Marbury* v. *Madison*: the Constitution was a written fundamental law enacted by the people; judges were to enforce this fundamental law in preference to ordinary statutes; courts were the peculiar guardians of the constitution, trustees acting on behalf of the people; the refusal to enforce a law contrary to the constitution did not imply judicial superiority over the legislative power but "only presupposes that the power of the people is superior to both";[39] this refusal, moreover, was an act of judicial discretion no different in kind from that exercised in the ordinary cases of determining between two contradictory statutes and of construing a single statute. This version of the doctrine did not, to be sure, obtain easy acceptance, as many Americans remained firmly wedded to legislative supremacy as the true basis of republican government. Yet compelled as they were to rethink and revise their ideas about sovereignty and the separation of powers, they found it increasingly difficult to resist the persuasiveness of judicial review as a logically sound theory and as a practical device for ensuring that popular government would also be orderly and constitutional government. In the decade following the adoption of the Constitution, the doctrine was asserted with increasing frequency and confidence not only in state and federal courts but also in legislative halls. By the time Marshall invoked it in 1803, judicial review had lost much of its controversial character.[40]

MARSHALL AND JUDICIAL REVIEW

Marshall had accepted this conception of judicial review long before he became chief justice of the United States. At the ratifying convention of 1788, for example, he was already speaking of the judiciary as the guardian of the fundamental law, the department that could best provide "protection from an infringement on the Constitution."[41] In forming his ideas on this subject, the future chief justice did not need to look beyond his own state of Virginia, where judicial review became a more or less established practice at least a decade prior to *Marbury*. Indeed, the various strands of the developing doctrine were discernible as early as 1782, when the "great constitutional question" arose in the case of *Commonwealth* v. *Caton.*[42] One of the lawyers who argued the case was St. George Tucker, whose manuscript brief contained a remarkably prescient defense of judicial review. Tucker's principal line of argument contrasted the unwritten, "constructive" British Constitution, which could be altered by Parliament, with the "express" Virginia Constitution, "framed with all the solemnity of an original Compact between Citizens about to establish a Government most agreeable to themselves." The judiciary, said Tucker, was the "Guardian" of the constitution, which was "the touchstone by which every Act of the Legislative is to be tried."[43]

Significantly, the debate over judicial review in Virginia was provoked in large part by laws pertaining to the organization and jurisdiction of the judiciary. In 1788 the judges of the Court of Appeals protested against a district court act as an unconstitutional invasion of the principle of judicial independence, successfully persuading the legislature to repeal the law. In 1793 the General Court, in *Kamper* v. *Hawkins,* refused to execute a law conferring equity powers upon the district judges, the first occasion in which a Virginia court explicitly exercised judicial review.[44] The opinions of the judges strongly reaffirmed the emerging rationale for judicial review founded on popular sovereignty. Spencer Roane, for example, premised his opinion that judges should refuse to enforce a law repugnant to the constitution on the ground that the people were "the only sovereign power," that the legislature was "not sovereign but subordinate . . . to the great constitutional charter, which the people have established as a fundamental law." Similarly, St. George Tucker, building upon his *Caton* brief, spoke of the Virginia Convention that framed the state constitution as deriving its authority from "a power which can supersede all law, and annul the constitution itself—namely, the *people,* in their *sovereign, unlimited,* and *unlimitable* authority and capacity."[45]

The *Kamper* judges grasped the essential connection between judicial review and a written constitution. Where there was no written constitution, said Tucker, the judiciary "were obliged to *receive* whatever *exposition* of it the legislature might think proper to make. But, with us, the constitution is not an 'ideal thing, but a real existence: it can be produced in a visible form': its principles can be ascertained from the living letter, not from obscure reasoning or deductions only."[46] As Marshall was to do in *Marbury*, the *Kamper* judges assimilated judicial review to the routine duty of judges to declare what the law is, a duty that often required them to decide on the operation of two conflicting ordinary statutes. The only difference between this activity and judicial review, said William Nelson, was that in one case a law "is carried out of existence, by a subsequent act virtually contrary to it, and in the other the prior *fundamental law* has prevented its *coming into existence* as *a law*."[47] Roane similarly brought judicial review within "the province of the judiciary to expound the laws, and to adjudge cases which may be brought before them." Judges had to consider "*every* law which relates to the subject"; they could not "shut their eyes against that law which is of the highest authority of any," he said in language similar to that later employed by Marshall.[48] Tucker described a constitution as "a rule to all the departments of the government, to the judiciary as well as to the legislature," a phrase also echoed in *Marbury*.[49]

Marshall no doubt drew on *Kamper* and other precedents in writing *Marbury*—which does not mean that the published reports or even *Federalist* No. 78 were immediately before him as he was preparing the opinion. The chief justice had no need of these materials, for his mind had already thoroughly absorbed their contents. In some respects Marshall was less assertive on behalf of judicial power than were his predecessors. Roane, for example, explicitly tied judicial review to popular government, contending that judges who uphold the constitution in preference to an ordinary law "actually decide on behalf of the people," even in cases affecting the private interest of judges. Although "a judge is interested privately in preserving his independence, yet it is the right of the people which should govern him, who in their sovereign character have provided that the judges should be independent." Conceived in this way, judicial review should be exercised to annul laws "plainly repugnant" not only to the "letter" but also to "the fundamental principles" of the constitution. Roane clearly perceived the potential of popular sovereignty to enlarge the scope of judicial power, as did Tucker, to whom an independent judiciary was a special guardian of the constitution, "a barrier against the possible usurpation, or abuse of power in the other departments."[50]

Marshall omitted comments of this sort in *Marbury*, in keeping with his aim of presenting the least controversial case for judicial review.

Even his famous declaration that it was "emphatically the province and duty of the judicial department to say what the law is" meant no more than what a judge ordinarily does in finding the rule that governs the case. These words should not be read as implying any claim to judicial supremacy in expounding the Constitution or to exclusive guardianship of the fundamental law. Legislative and executive constructions of the Constitution, he did not deny, must prevail in all cases that did not take the form of a legal dispute to be decided in a court of law. His defense of judicial review fully agreed with the "departmental" theory of constitutional interpretation, according to which each of the three coordinate departments of government had final authority to interpret the Constitution when acting within its own sphere of duties and responsibilities.[51]

An important corollary of the departmental theory was that judges must be persuaded beyond a reasonable doubt before declaring a law void as contrary to the Constitution. This "rule of administration" was contemporaneous with the earliest justifications of judicial review and frequently repeated thereafter by both state and federal judges.[52] The rule underscored the conception of judicial review as an exercise of limited judicial discretion clearly distinct from a political function. Although he did not expressly state the rule in *Marbury*, Marshall did recite it on other occasions. In *Fletcher* v. *Peck* (1810), the chief justice observed: "The question, whether a law be void for its repugnancy to the constitution, is, at all times, a question of much delicacy, which ought seldom, if ever, to be decided in the affirmative in a doubtful case. . . . The opposition between the constitution and the law should be such that the judge feels a clear and strong conviction of their incompatibility with each other." In *Dartmouth College* v. *Woodward* (1819), he reiterated that "in no doubtful case would [the court] pronounce a legislative act to be contrary to the constitution." Again, in *Brown* v. *Maryland* (1827), he remarked: "It has been truly said, that the presumption is in favour of every legislative act, and the whole burthen of proof lies on him who denies its constitutionality."[53] Marshall's strongest, if implicit, endorsement of the rule was the decision in *McCulloch* v. *Maryland* (1819) upholding Congress's power to establish a national bank.

What exactly did this rule mean to Marshall, and did he consistently abide by it? At first glance he appears to have patently disregarded the reasonable doubt test in *Marbury*, ignoring alternative constructions that reconciled the judiciary act and the Constitution. On reflection, however, it is clear that he did adhere to the rule properly understood. His espousal of the rule was not a self-serving, hypocritical expression of courtesy and deference to the legislature but a genuinely operative standard he faithfully employed in constitutional adjudication. Confining review only to instances where the repugnancy between statute and Constitution was plain, clear, and unequivocal did not mean that the infraction had to be so obvious, so palpable, that it could readily be detected by comparing the texts of the two laws. If this were the meaning of the rule, then judicial review would be a trivial, insignificant power that would almost never be invoked, for in this sense there could scarcely be any law that was unconstitutional beyond a reasonable doubt.

To Marshall judicial review was not a mechanical comparison of texts but an arduous and delicate exercise of judgment—indeed, the highest form of judgment a court could undertake. In its true meaning, the reasonable doubt rule imposed on a judge the duty to demonstrate by clear and persuasive reasoning, by painstaking legal investigation and deliberation, that law and Constitution were in fundamental opposition to one another. Employing the distinctive methods of the craft, a judge would on occasion find that a legislature had exceeded its constitutional authority, even though the breach was by no means obvious at the time it happened. Until *Marbury*, it had not occurred to anyone that section 13 of the judiciary law was unconstitutional. Once the question was brought before the Supreme Court, however, and subjected to the probing light of judicial inquiry, the hitherto undetected breach was clearly revealed. There was nothing arbitrary or willful in this determination of constitutional guilt. Nor was it simply a matter of the Court substituting its own construction of the law and the Constitution for that of Congress. Rather, the decision sprang from a profound conviction that Congress had transcended the permissible range of its constitutional discretion.[54]

There was no inconsistency in deferring to legislatures, in presuming that they possessed virtue, sense, and competent knowledge, while at the same time recognizing that they did occasionally enact unconstitutional laws—typically, through inadvertence or inattention rather than deliberate disregard of the fundamental law. In the nature of things, legislatures could not be expected to subject every clause of every bill to rigorous constitutional scrutiny. The two principal framers of the Judiciary Act of 1789, Oliver Ellsworth and William Paterson, were sound lawyers and statesmen of the highest wisdom and virtue; both had attended the Federal Convention and both later served on the Supreme Court. Yet upon judicial investigation even their monumental piece of legislation was found to have flaws.

Marshall, of course, believed that this law was constitutionally defective for another reason besides section 13, namely, in not providing for separate appointments and commissions of Supreme Court and circuit court judges. But he reached this conclusion only after circumstances—the repeal of the act of 1801 and the restoration of the 1789 circuit system—compelled him to examine the law. Writing to Paterson in the spring of 1802, Marshall (who was surely aware of his correspondent's authorship of the 1789 law) gave a revealing glimpse into how he approached constitutional questions with an open mind and a presumption of the law's innocence:

> I hope I need not say that no man in existence respects more than I do, those who passd the original law concerning the courts of the United States, & those who first acted under it. So highly do I respect their opinions that I had not examind them & shoud have proceeded without a doubt on the subject, to perform the duties assignd to me if the late discussions had not unavoidably produced an investigation of the subject which from me it woud not otherwise have receivd. The result of this investigation has been an opinion which I cannot conquer that the constitution requires distinct appointments & commissions for the Judges of the inferior courts from those of the supreme court.[55]

The narrow scope of judicial review set forth in *Marbury* stands in sharp contrast to the expansive reach the doctrine has acquired in the twentieth century. For Marshall, judicial review was primarily a defensive weapon to preserve the independence of the judiciary, to resist encroachments by the states on the national government, and to protect private rights against infringement by acts of government (mainly state). Operating within the constraints of the departmental theory, judicial review left ample discretionary power to Congress and to the state legislatures. Since Marshall's day judicial review has evolved into a sweeping general supervisory power of courts that affects virtually all aspects of modern life. With the obsolescence of the departmental theory and the collapse of the rigid distinction between law and politics, the modern Supreme Court is unabashedly understood to be a political institution whose decisions make policy in a way scarcely distinguishable from legislating.

From a modern perspective, the Marshall Court also has the appearance of being a political tribunal, and the public controversies provoked by the Court's decisions—*Marbury* being a case in point—seem to confirm this perception. But the Marshall Court was not "political" in the same way the modern Court is, and one should not assume a too easy similarity between the two. Only in an indirect sense can *Marbury* be said to have laid the groundwork for modern judicial power. Marshall surely understood that Supreme Court decisions could have broad political and economic consequences. Yet recognizing this reality only reinforced his conviction that the Court should be perceived as confining itself to the sphere of law, acting first and foremost as a tribunal for adjudicating private rights. Whatever public policy consequences might arise from deciding private lawsuits should be seen as the indirect and unintended by-product of impartial legal investigation. What neither Marshall nor anyone else could have foreseen in 1803 was the emergence of a strong American propensity, first noticed by Alexis de Tocqueville in the 1830s, to refer great public questions to the courts. "Scarcely any political question arises in the United States," wrote this perceptive French observer, "that is not resolved, sooner or later, into a judicial question."[56]

Marbury v. *Madison* was the first and only time the Marshall Court set aside a law of the Congress of the United States. In keeping with the departmental theory, the Court deferred to Congress, allowing that body broad discretion in the exercise of its powers. Yet if the doctrine is understood to include sustaining as well as nullifying legislation, then coordinate judicial review was by no means an insignificant power in the Marshall era. Indeed, many of the Marshall Court's most important contributions to constitutional law occurred in the process of upholding federal acts. In this regard, *McCulloch* v. *Mary-*

land (1819) stands out as one of Marshall's greatest opinions. Aside from *Marbury*, the Marshall Court's exercise of judicial review to void legislation was employed exclusively against state laws. These cases demonstrated the great potential of judicial review as an instrument to protect private rights and to preserve federalism.

4

PROPERTY RIGHTS AND
THE CONTRACT CLAUSE

Federal judicial review of state laws rested on reasonably solid textual ground: the prohibitions and restraints recited in Article 1, section 10, together with the clause of Article 6 declaring the Constitution, laws, and treaties of the United States to be "the Supreme law of the Land." Chief Justice Marshall made ample use of these provisions to restrict state sovereignty in two broad categories of cases. In one category the state law was challenged as incompatible with a power vested in the federal government. Notable "federalism" cases included *McCulloch* v. *Maryland* (1819), which invalidated a Maryland law laying a tax on the Second Bank of the United States, and *Gibbons* v. *Ogden* (1824), which struck down a New York law creating a monopoly over steamboat navigation on the state's waters.

In the other class of decisions the state law was nullified as unconstitutionally violating the rights of individuals. All of these cases came within Article 1, section 10, which among other things declares that no state shall "emit Bills of Credit; make any Thing but gold and silver Coin a Tender in Payment of Debts; pass any . . . ex post facto Law, or Law impairing the Obligation of Contracts." These clauses of the Constitution spoke directly to the framers' overriding concern to protect private rights—most importantly, the security of property— against infringement by the states. Of the prohibitions recited in Article 1, section 10, the one against impairing the obligation of contracts supplied the Marshall Court with its principal weapon to invalidate state laws, and in a celebrated series of cases the chief justice invoked the contract clause to restrain state interference with property rights.

To Marshall the contract clause epitomized a Constitution whose true character lay less in its grant of powers to the federal government than in its abridgment of state powers. Under his guidance of the Supreme Court, this provision performed a function similar to that later undertaken by the Fourteenth Amendment, which was adopted after the Civil War. That amendment—which declared that no state could "deprive any person of life, liberty, or property, without due process of law; nor deny to any person within its jurisdiction the equal protection of the laws"—in turn during the twentieth century became the Supreme Court's instrument for applying the Bill of Rights amendments to the states. Prior to this development the guarantees of those amendments were held to restrain only the federal government, as Marshall himself declared in one of his last opinions, *Barron* v. *Baltimore* (1833). Yet to a remarkable degree Marshall succeeded in making the original Constitution, via the contract clause, serve as a charter of rights that protected the American people from the acts of their state governments. He expressly recognized this broader constitutional purpose in *Fletcher* v. *Peck* (1810), when he observed (in reference to Article 1, section 10) that "the constitution of the United States contains what may be deemed a bill of rights for the people of each state."[1]

The prevailing view of Marshall's contract clause jurisprudence is that he substantially enlarged the meaning of the clause beyond the intention of its framers. Some contend that the jurist deliberately ignored the original meaning in order to read into it his own political and economic attitudes, notably, his strong attachment to property rights and creditor interests. Given Marshall's "ardent desire to secure further protection for the rights of property," noted one commentator, "it is not surprising that the Supreme Court under his domination should have given to the clause a meaning far broader than any which its framers ever attached to it."[2] Others admire the creativity of Marshall's contract clause opinions, praising the chief justice for carrying out his duty to interpret the Constitution without being tied down to some supposed original and fixed meaning of that instrument.[3]

To explain Marshall's contract decisions as the product of his undeniable sympathy for the rights of property is simplistic and reductionist. Was there a framer or member of a state ratifying convention who did not regard property as sacred and who did not believe that its protection was one of the fundamental purposes of the Constitution? Whatever Marshall's personal beliefs, security for property was indisputably a constitutional value that as chief justice he was bound to uphold. Without question his interests as a property owner and supporter of business enterprise, along with his experience as a lawyer representing merchants, planters, creditors, and debtors, shaped his thinking about the relationship between law and the economy. From the time he began practicing law in the 1780s, Marshall had a lifelong identification with the urban, commercial interests of Richmond. He regularly invested in companies chartered by the Virginia legislature to improve river navigation, construct canals, and build turnpikes, and also subscribed to stock in banks and insurance companies. As a direct participant in these projects, he acquired knowledge of Virginia's political economy and gained an appreciation of the role of corporations in promoting commercial prosperity. Respect for rights conferred by corporate charters was a central tenet of the Virginia system with which he was conversant. That a corporate charter was a kind of contract, perhaps one that was constitutionally protected, was perfectly consistent with Marshall's Virginia experience.[4]

Marshall was familiar with public contracts in an even more direct sense than as a stockholder in chartered business enterprises. The security of his own large-scale investment in purchasing the Fairfax estate rested on an agreement he entered into with the Commonwealth of Virginia that was enacted into law in 1796. To resolve a dispute over title to lands in the Northern Neck of Virginia (which the Fairfax family had held as proprietors before the Revolution), Marshall and others claiming under the Fairfax title relinquished all claim to those lands in the former proprietary that were "waste and ungranted," and the commonwealth relinquished its claim to those lands that had been specifically appropriated by the proprietor. The latter were the so-called "manor lands" that Marshall and his associates had contracted to purchase.[5] Although a state was a party to this contract, the future chief justice might well have assumed that its obligation was as fully protected against impairment as a contract between private parties.

Did Marshall's perception of his self-interest predispose him to accept the idea that the Constitution afforded broad protection for property and contractual rights? A more accurate appraisal of his motives would argue that his adoption of this idea arose less from narrow self-interest than from a reasoned conviction, based on his knowledge and experience of Virginia's political economy, that strong constitutional protection for property and investment capital would promote national prosperity. A better question to ask is whether his supposed bias caused him to distort the meaning of the Constitution, to misread the intention of the framers. This question cuts to the heart of the problem of interpretation. Can a jurist perform the act of interpretation without imposing his own personal beliefs and prejudices? Marshall, of course, held the virtually universal assumption of the day that a judge's subjective will could be effectively kept in check by rigorous application of the time-tested principles and methods of interpretation passed down through centuries of common law adjudication.

In reading the contract clause expansively, Marshall believed he was faithfully adhering to the letter and spirit of the Constitution. He understood "intention of the framers" to mean that intention as expressed in the words of the Constitution, not the private intentions individual framers may have expressed in speeches, debates, essays, and letters at the time the Constitution was under consideration. He interpreted the Constitution by employing traditional methods of statutory construction that looked to the language of the document itself rather than to "extrinsic" sources. The latter were regarded as either useless or dangerously misleading in resolving ambiguities.[6] The process of discovering the intent of the Constitution or of a statute was analogous to that of discerning a testator's intent from his words as recorded in his last will. The general rule was that "parol" evidence could not be admitted to explain that intention. Throughout all his contract clause cases, Marshall took great pains to read the Constitution literally, striving at the same time to reconcile its words with the general spirit of the Constitution as revealed in the great objects it was designed to accomplish. If his exercise of judicial discretion brought cases within the contract clause not contemplated or foreseen in 1787, he would not have regarded this result as an enlargement of the original meaning.

ORIGIN OF THE CONTRACT CLAUSE

There is in fact precious little evidence of what the contract clause meant to the founders other than the text itself. Introduced late in the

Federal Convention, the clause was adopted and ratified without much discussion either at Philadelphia or in the state ratifying conventions. As originally proposed, the text of the clause was taken from a provision in the recently enacted Northwest Ordinance, which read in part: "And, in the just preservation of rights and property, it is understood and declared, that no law ought ever to be made, or have force in the said territory, that shall, in any manner whatever, interfere with or affect private contracts or engagements, *bona fide*, and without fraud, previously formed."[7] If this wording had been retained, it is difficult to conceive how Marshall could have made this clause the basis for some of his most important constitutional decisions. As finally approved, the prohibition was expressed in general terms, omitting such qualifying words as "private" and "previously formed."

Among the handful who uttered thoughts on the subject, the prevailing assumption appears to have been that the clause was intended to embrace only private contracts. But the record is so scanty as to be inconclusive. Even if more evidence could be adduced to show that individual founders believed private contracts alone were to be protected from impairment, how much would be needed to outweigh the alternative conclusion: that the final draft of the clause reflected the collective and deliberate intention of the convention to broaden the scope of the prohibition beyond the terms in which it was originally proposed?[8]

The absence of discussion or controversy surrounding the adoption of the contract clause in 1787 and 1788 should not imply that the framers of the Constitution regarded this provision as trivial or innocuous, having only a restricted applicability to state legislation. Indeed, it more readily implies a broad consensus about one of the principal objects of constitutional reform: the protection of private rights against invasion by the states. What the contract clause meant to the framers can only be understood in relation to this overarching purpose. If this broader context is kept in view, there can be little doubt that Marshall accurately read the mind of the convention in attaching great importance to the contract clause. Although the clause was not proposed until near the close of the convention, the problem it addressed had been recurrent throughout the proceedings. For James Madison in particular the security of private rights was a primary goal of a reformed federal government, perhaps even more important than those of providing for adequate defense and revenue. The "evils" arising from the state politics of the 1780s, he remarked, "contributed more to that uneasiness which produced the Convention, and prepared the public mind for a general reform, than those which accrued to our national character and interest from the inadequacy of the confederation to its immediate objects."[9]

Madison's remedy for preventing the faction-ridden states from trampling upon individual rights was to arm the federal Congress with a "negative," or veto, over the acts of the state legislatures. This proposal was included in the Virginia Plan submitted at the beginning of the convention. In one early vote the veto won approval, though ultimately it was rejected. In defeating the negative, however, the convention rejected only a means of implementing a principle, not the principle itself. The essential idea behind the negative was embodied in the Constitution in the form of the supremacy clause of Article 6, the judiciary article, and the restrictions and prohibitions on the state legislatures—which together constituted a judicial substitute for a legislative negative on state laws. Instead of a prior legislative veto, the framers chose subsequent judicial review as a more practical means of protecting individual rights from the injurious acts of the states.[10]

The real origin of the contract clause, then, was not its formal introduction late in the convention but can be traced to Madison's efforts to secure adoption of a federal veto on state laws. Of all the provisions in the Constitution restraining state sovereignty, the prohibition against impairing the obligation of contracts came closest to embodying the principle of Madison's negative. Soon after the convention, Madison as "Publius" defended the utility of the contract clause in precisely the same terms as he had earlier advocated the negative:

> Bills of attainder, *ex post facto* laws, and laws impairing the obligation of contracts, are contrary to the first principles of the social compact and to every principle of sound legislation. . . . Very properly, therefore, have the convention added this constitutional bulwark in favor of personal security and private rights. . . . The sober people of America are weary of the fluctuating policy which has directed the public councils. They have seen with regret and indignation that sudden changes and legislative interferences, in cases affecting personal rights, become jobs in the hands of enterprising and influential speculators, and snares to the more industrious and

less informed part of the community. They have seen, too, that one legislative interference is but the first link of a long chain of repetitions, every subsequent interference being naturally produced by the effects of the preceding. They very rightly infer, therefore, that some thorough reform is wanting, which will banish speculations on public measures, inspire a general prudence and industry, and give a regular course to the business of society.[11]

Marshall interpreted the contract clause in the spirit of Madison's negative on state laws and brought within its purview a larger class of state legislation than was contemplated by anyone at the time the Constitution was adopted. Yet he believed the framers purposely adopted general language to ensure that the contract clause, like the negative, would embrace not only past and present evils but also guard against unforeseen cases that might arise in consequence of state legislative ingenuity.

THE CONTRACT CLAUSE, VESTED RIGHTS, AND JUDICIAL REVIEW

Chief Justice Marshall set forth his interpretation of the contract clause in four notable opinions: *Fletcher* v. *Peck* (1810), *Dartmouth College* v. *Woodward* (1819), *Sturges* v. *Crowninshield* (1819), and *Ogden* v. *Saunders* (1827). The cumulative effect of these decisions was to solidify the American doctrine of judicial review based on written fundamental law enacted by the people themselves. To be sure, Marshall and his fellow jurists on the federal and state courts continued to invoke unwritten natural law and natural rights in their opinions, as signified by such expressions as the "general principles which are common to our free institutions," "the principles of reason, justice, and moral rectitude," the "vital principles in our free Republican governments, and "the great first principles of the social compact."[12] According to the chief justice's understanding of the developing American doctrine of judicial review, however, unwritten general principles could never provide a satisfactory rationale for judges to annul a law. As a judge he strove to reconcile text-based judicial review with natural law, testing statutes against the standard of a written constitution while finding in that text ample protection for fundamental rights.

The appeal to natural rights and the fundamental principles of the social compact occurred most frequently in cases where a party sought protection for vested contract and property rights against legislative impairment. If the principal function of constitutional law is to set limits on governmental power, especially legislative power, then, in the words of one eminent scholar, the doctrine of vested rights became "the basic doctrine of American constitutional law."[13] Vested rights were rights acquired by individuals under the law, foremost of which was the right to the security and free enjoyment of property. Vested rights were deemed so fundamental as to be beyond the reach of government. An act that impaired or took away a vested right was regarded as exceeding the just bounds of legislative power. As Justice Paterson stated on circuit in 1795, "the right of acquiring and possessing property and having it protected, is one of the natural inherent and unalienable rights of man." A legislature "had no authority to make an act divesting one citizen of his freehold, and vesting it in another, without a just compensation. It is inconsistent with the principles of reason, justice, and moral rectitude; it is incompatible with the comfort, peace, and happiness of mankind; it is contrary to the principles of social alliance in every free government; and lastly, it is contrary both to letter and spirit of the constitution."[14]

A more emphatic articulation of the doctrine was set forth by Justice Chase in a 1798 Supreme Court case:

There are acts which the federal or state legislature cannot do, without exceeding their authority. There are certain vital principles in our free republican governments, which will determine and overrule an apparent and flagrant abuse of legislative power; as to authorize manifest injustice by positive law; or take away that security for personal liberty, or private property, for the protection whereof the government was established. An act of the legislature (for I cannot call it a law) contrary to the great first principles of the social compact cannot be considered a rightful exercise of legislative authority.[15]

According to vested rights doctrine, there were inherent limits to legislative power arising from the very nature of republican and constitutional government. In some statements of the doctrine—by judges in dicta and lawyers in arguments—it was asserted or strongly implied that courts could declare laws void even in the absence of an express constitutional provision. When actually setting aside laws, however, judges invariably brought the offending legislation within some particular prohibition found in a state constitution or the federal Constitution. Even Chase for all his vehement denial of "the omnipotence of a state legislature, . . . although its authority should not be expressly restrained by the constitution, or fundamental law of the State," never maintained that the "vital principles" of republican government supplied the judiciary with an independent standard for nullifying laws. His position, in fact, was scarcely different from that of Justice Iredell, whose views are usually cited as stating the opposing case. If, said Iredell, Congress or a state legislature "shall pass a law, within the general scope of their constitutional power, the court cannot pronounce it to be void, merely because it is, in their judgment, contrary to the principles of natural justice. The ideas of natural justice are regulated by no fixed standard; the ablest and the purest of men have differed upon the subject."[16]

If not in itself a sufficient basis for invalidating laws, vested rights doctrine nonetheless served an important purpose in reinforcing judicial review based on a written constitution. It was particularly useful in explicating the text in terms that reconciled a constitution with the fundamental maxims of good government. In most instances a judge who censured an act as contrary to reason, justice, and morality also found the law to be in violation of an express constitutional prohibition.[17] To Chief Justice Marshall no part of the federal Constitution more clearly expressed the framers' intention to protect vested rights than did the contract clause. His opinions expounding this clause can be read as variations on a single theme: the conformity of the Constitution to the fundamental principles of society and government. By firmly anchoring vested rights to the text of the Constitution, Marshall helped to make judicial review a more acceptable device in a republic for reconciling majority will with the ends of justice.

Although Marshall and his fellow jurists on the federal bench clearly adhered to a theory of judicial review founded on a written constitution, procedural constraints in bringing cases up from state courts to the Supreme Court served to reinforce text-based review. In these cases, arising under section 25 of the Judiciary Act of 1789, the Court was confined to deciding "federal" questions, such as whether a state law was in conflict with the Constitution or with a federal statute or treaty. This restriction did not apply to cases originating in the federal courts, such as those based on diversity of citizenship. Contract clause cases came up via both routes. *Fletcher* v. *Peck*, for example, was a diversity suit that began in the United States Circuit Court at Boston. The Supreme Court in this case considered the validity of a Georgia law on the broad ground of the "general principles" of vested rights as well as on the narrower ground of impairing the obligation of contract. In *Dartmouth College* v. *Woodward*, a section 25 case originating in a New Hampshire court, the single question before the Court was whether a state law violated the Constitution's contract clause. To promote uniformity of decision, Marshall and his brethren increasingly relied on the Constitutional text as the sole basis for adjudicating cases involving vested property and contract rights, no matter whether the case began in a state or federal court.[18]

Before *Fletcher* v. *Peck* in 1810, Marshall had given brief judicial attention to the contract clause in an 1803 circuit court case involving the validity of a North Carolina law. To remove doubts whether an act of 1789 had repealed a 1715 act of limitations, the North Carolina legislature in 1799 enacted a statute declaring the 1715 act to be in force. Marshall's principal objection to the 1799 act was that it violated the principle of separation of powers, which was explicitly declared to be part of the North Carolina constitution:

And the question here is, does it belong to the judiciary to decide upon laws when made, and the extent and operation of them; or to the legislature? If it belongs to the judiciary, then the matter decided by this act, namely, whether the act of 1789 be a repeal of the 9th section of 1715, is a judicial matter, and not a legislative one. The determination is made by a branch of government, not authorised by the constitution to make it; and is therefore in my judgment, void.

He then suggested, as an afterthought, that the law "seems also to be void" on the ground of impairing the obligation of contract.[19]

In this early case Marshall did not yet recognize the full potential of the contract clause in exercising judicial review, placing greater reliance on separation of powers as textual support for the judicial annulment of state laws violating vested rights. By 1810, however, he appears to have concluded that separation of powers was too vague a standard to be applied by courts as a constitutional limitation on state legislatures, especially in view of the long-sanctioned practice by some legislatures of assuming judicial functions.[20]

PUBLIC GRANTS AS CONTRACTS: *FLETCHER* V. *PECK*

Marshall's first major contract clause decision also marked the first time the Supreme Court pronounced a state law void as repugnant to the Constitution. The case was *Fletcher* v. *Peck*, which grew out of the notorious Yazoo land sales by the state of Georgia. In January 1795 the Georgia legislature passed an act disposing of thirty-five million acres of its western lands—constituting most of present-day Alabama and Mississippi—to four land companies at a price of less than two cents an acre. The sale was accompanied by obvious bribery, the legislators exchanging their votes for shares of stock in the companies. In response to widespread popular denunciation of the Yazoo fraud, a newly elected legislature in 1796 repealed the 1795 sale act, declaring it and all subsequent sales made under it null and void. Land claims in this region remained embroiled in politics during the next fifteen years.

Yazoo might have remained a local affair had the original purchasing land companies not in turn hastily sold the lands to third parties throughout the country. A large number of Yazoo purchasers were centered in New England, organized as the New England Mississippi Land Company, one of whose directors was John Peck of Boston. Claiming ignorance of the fraud attending the original sale and of Georgia's intention to revoke it, the New England speculators set about to recoup their investments by petitioning Congress. The Yazoo claimants grounded their petitions on the invalidity of Georgia's rescinding act, which they insisted could not take away rights acquired by innocent purchasers. Unable to obtain legislative relief, they turned to the courts for redress—a tactic that aggrieved groups have frequently adopted throughout American history. *Fletcher* v. *Peck* illustrates the peculiarly American penchant (noted by Tocqueville) of resolving political questions into judicial questions.

Peck, an extensive purchaser of Yazoo lands, in turn sold a tract to

Robert Fletcher, then a New Hampshire resident, in 1803. Fletcher then sued Peck in the federal circuit court at Boston for recovery of the purchase price, alleging that Peck's title was unsound. After losing on circuit, Fletcher took his case to the Supreme Court, where it was argued in 1809 and again in 1810. The circumstances strongly indicate that this suit was an arranged case between friendly parties, brought to obtain a decision by the highest court in the land on the validity of the Yazoo titles. At first reluctant to decide a seemingly collusive case, the Supreme Court justices ultimately satisfied themselves that Fletcher's suit presented a sufficiently "real" controversy to deserve a decision on its merits.[21]

Chief Justice Marshall's opinion for the Court gave due consideration to all the issues arising from the complicated pleadings submitted by the parties. The first question was whether the Georgia legislature had authority under the state's constitution to dispose of the Yazoo lands by means of the 1795 sale act. Finding nothing in the Georgia constitution restraining the legislature from granting the land in question, Marshall took this opportunity to restate the familiar "reasonable doubt" rule that courts should follow in considering the constitutionality of legislative acts:

> The question, whether a law be void for its repugnancy to the constitution is, at all times, a question of much delicacy, which ought seldom, if ever, to be decided in the affirmative, in a doubtful case. . . . The opposition between the constitution and the law should be such that the judge feels a clear and strong conviction of their incompatibility with each other.[22]

A more troublesome point was whether the sale was void on the ground that the act was obtained by bribery of the Georgia legislators. Marshall declined the invitation to inquire into the motives of the legislature as a matter beyond judicial competence. Even if the state itself had brought suit to annul the sale contract, the Court's competence "to vacate a contract thus formed, and to annul rights acquired" by innocent third parties, was highly doubtful. What degree of corruption, for instance, was necessary before a court could intervene? Such an inquiry, Marshall astutely perceived, would draw the Court beyond the line that separated law from politics. In any event, this question could not "be brought thus collaterally and incidentally before the court. It would be indecent, in the extreme, upon a private contract, between two individuals, to enter into an inquiry respecting the corruption of the sovereign power of a state."[23]

Having thus far relied on judicial deference to avoid examining the legitimacy of the 1795 sale, Marshall next took up the central question posed by the case: the validity of the 1796 act revoking the Yazoo grants and subsequent sales. He first considered this point independently of the contract clause, treating it as a case of legislative deprivation of vested rights. In repealing the 1795 act and voiding all sales under it, the Georgia legislature, said Marshall, was in effect assuming judicial power, deciding a question of title. Significantly, he did not invoke separation of powers to deny the right of the legislature to act in this capacity. Yet in so acting, the legislature should have respected "certain great principles of justice" and been governed "by those rules which would have regulated the decision of a judicial tribunal." A court might well have set aside the 1795 sale as fraudulent but only as between the original parties; it could not disregard "the rights of third persons, who are purchasers without notice, for a valuable consideration." That innocent third parties were protected in such situations was a principle of equity. "All titles would be insecure, and the intercourse between man and man would be very seriously obstructed, if this principle be overturned," the chief justice observed.[24]

Could the Georgia legislature, then, dispense with the rules of equity—was its power "competent to the annihilation of such title, and to a resumption of the property thus held"? Conceding a legislature's power to repeal its former acts, Marshall denied that a repeal of a law "in its nature a contract" could divest rights acquired under that contract. "It may well be doubted," he continued, "whether the nature of society and government does not prescribe some limits to the legislative power." Although indicating that the Georgia legislature had transcended its powers, he stopped short of relying on inherent limits to legislative power as a basis for voiding the rescinding law. He merely suggested that the act's validity "might well be doubted, were Georgia a single sovereign power."[25]

Marshall was not compelled to answer this question, however, for Georgia was part of a union of states bound by a Constitution imposing limits upon their legislatures. It remained only to inquire if this case came within the prohibition against impairing the obligation of contracts. He then proceeded to show that Georgia's grant to the land companies met the definition of a contract as set forth by Blackstone. A grant, according to this definition, was a "contract executed" with an implied and continuing obligation on the part of the grantor not to reassert his right to the property conveyed. If a grant was a contract, did the Constitution distinguish between grants between private individuals and grants made by a state? Neither the general language of the contract clause nor its manifest intention to abridge state sovereignty so far as to protect individual rights, the chief justice maintained, could support such a distinction. "Whatever respect might have been felt for the state sovereignties," he said, "it is not to be disguised that the framers of the constitution viewed, with some apprehension, the violent acts which might grow out of the feelings of the moment; and that the people of the United States, in adopting that instrument, have manifested a determination to shield themselves and their property from the effects of those sudden and strong passions to which men are exposed."[26]

Marshall concluded by declaring the Court's "unanimous opinion" that Georgia "was restrained, either by general principles which are common to our free institutions, or by the particular provisions of the constitution of the United States" from passing the 1796 rescinding law.[27] Did this statement imply that "general principles" were equally sufficient with the constitutional text to nullify the law? Marshall's language is sufficiently ambiguous to invite speculation as to the ultimate basis of the Court's disposition of *Fletcher* v. *Peck*; not surprisingly, the opinion has given rise to differing interpretations.

Some commentators contend that Marshall invoked vested rights doctrine merely to give "moral sanction" to his exposition of the contract clause and that he had no intention of deciding the case on the "frail legal basis" of general restraints upon legislative power arising from the "nature of society and government."[28] Others portray Marshall as poised hesitantly between general principles and text, though somewhat more comfortable with deciding the case on the positive law of the Constitution.[29] One scholar suggests that the chief justice brought in the contract clause not so much to decide *Fletcher* as to lay the groundwork for relying on that clause in future cases that might come up from a state court by means of section 25 of the Judiciary Act.[30] Another argues that Marshall conceived of the case essentially in terms of vested rights but that being obliged to base judicial review on "the visible world of text," he constructively altered the meaning of the contract clause in order to accomplish the desired result.[31]

It should be borne in mind that the chief justice's equivocal language may have reflected not his own uncertainty but that of the Court for whom he spoke. At least one of his colleagues, Justice Johnson, preferred to dispose of the case as an unauthorized "taking" of private property rather than as an impairment of the obligation of contract. In a concurring opinion, Johnson declared "that a state does not possess the power of revoking its own grants. But I do this on a general principle, on the reason and nature of things: a principle which will impose laws even on the deity." He wanted to make clear that his opinion was "not founded on the provision in the constitution . . . relative to laws impairing the obligation of contracts."[32] Marshall himself, it seems fair to say, had by this time shed whatever doubts he may have entertained that judicial review must be confined to cases where the law was shown to be in direct conflict with an express constitutional provision. His adherence to a positive law conception of judicial review was not inconsistent with employing the general principles of vested rights doctrine—not merely as window dressing, as a rhetorical tactic, but as a way of explaining a legal decision in terms of orthodox political philosophy. It was typical of jurists of that era to integrate political philosophy with legal analysis, and few excelled Marshall in mastery of this skill.

In assimilating this case into the realm of contractual obligation, Marshall did not distort the meaning of the contract clause. Indeed, the essence of his argument in this part of the opinion had been previously set forth in various writings, though he was the first to employ it as the basis of a legal adjudication. A careful study of this subject has shown that Marshall's classification of a grant or conveyance as a contract with a subsisting obligation was fully in accord with the writings of eminent authorities on natural law (such as Pufendorf) and on the common law (such as Blackstone).[33] There was also considerable weight of authority behind the notion that a grant by a state was a contract whose obligation was no less binding than that arising from a private contract. This view was expressed in the United States as early as 1785 by James Wilson, a prominent member of the Convention of 1787 who was subsequently appointed an associate justice of the Supreme Court.

On circuit in 1795 Judge Paterson described a Pennsylvania law confirming titles to land as "a contract between the legislature of Pennsylvania and the Connecticut settlers."[34] More directly in point was a legal opinion drawn by Alexander Hamilton in 1796 on behalf of the Yazoo claimants. Declaring the Georgia rescinding act contrary to "the first principles of natural justice and social policy," Hamilton proceeded to bring the act within the prohibitory clause of the Constitution. "Every grant from one to another," he said, "whether the grantor be a state or an individual, is virtually a contract that the grantee shall hold and enjoy the thing granted against the grantor, and his representatives." He accordingly was of the opinion that "taking the terms of the Constitution in their large sense, and giving them effect according to the general spirit and policy of the provisions," the act was unconstitutional and that the Supreme Court would declare it so.[35] Like Hamilton, Marshall construed the words of the contract clause "in their large sense," not doubting that this broad reading was consonant with the intention of the framers of the Constitution.

Fletcher established the principle that public as well as private contracts were protected against impairment by the contract clause. Marshall reaffirmed this principle two years later in the case of *New Jersey* v. *Wilson.* The law challenged in this case was an 1804 New Jersey statute repealing a tax exemption on land formerly held by the Delaware Indians, who had sold the land in 1803 and moved to New York. This exemption had been granted by virtue of an act adopted by the colonial legislature in 1758 setting aside certain lands for the Indians. After the New Jersey high court in 1809 upheld an assessment for taxes on the land, the purchasers appealed to the Supreme Court under section 25 of the Judiciary Act. The case was submitted without argument, and the only question was whether the 1804 law repealing the exemption impaired the obligation of contract.

In a brief opinion, devoid of any reference to natural law or vested rights, Chief Justice Marshall disposed of the case with little difficulty. Citing *Fletcher* as authority for extending the contract clause to contracts in which a state is a party, he proceeded to show that the proceedings between New Jersey and the Indians contained "every requisite to the formation of a contract." Although the tax exemption was for the benefit of Indians, this privilege was annexed to the land itself, and the purchasers succeeded to this right. The 1804 repeal accordingly constituted an impairment of contract. This decision did not significantly undermine state sovereignty with respect to the taxing power, however, for Marshall admitted that the state of New Jersey could have insisted upon a surrender of the exemption as a condition for the sale of the land.[36]

CORPORATE CHARTERS AS CONTRACTS: *DARTMOUTH COLLEGE* v. *WOODWARD*

Marshall's next major exposition of the contract clause occurred in 1819 in *Dartmouth College* v. *Woodward.* In an elaborate and closely reasoned opinion, the chief justice held that the charter incorporating Dartmouth College was a contract protected by the Constitution from legislative infringement. Before taking the form of a judicial dispute, the Dartmouth College controversy was mired in the political and religious factionalism of early nineteenth-century New Hampshire. The college was incorporated by royal charter in 1769, largely through the efforts of the Reverend Eleazar Wheelock, who served as first president until his death in 1779. The charter established a trust fund that was to be administered by a self-perpetuating board of trustees. During the administration of John Wheelock (who had succeeded his father as president in 1779), petty quarrels between the president and trustees eventually thrust the college into partisan politics, with Federalists and Congregationalists supporting the trustees and Republicans siding with the Presbyterian president. The college issue dominated the 1816 state elections, which gave Republicans control of the legislature and governorship. In the same year the legislature adopted statutes that radically revised the Dartmouth charter, in effect transforming the college into a state institution. Not only was the number of trustees increased from twelve to twenty-one, with new members appointed by the governor, but the trustees were placed under the control of a board of overseers also appointed by the governor. Henceforth, the institution was to be known as Dartmouth University.[37]

Claiming that this legislation was an unlawful deprivation of property rights, the college trustees sought redress in the state courts, bringing a common law action of trover for recovery of the college records, books, and seal and seeking damages of $50,000.[38] Counsel for the trustees carefully adopted a legal strategy of contending that the state laws were invalid not only as beyond the scope of legislative power and against the New Hampshire constitution and bill of rights but also as contrary to the contract clause of the United States Constitution. In this way, a loss in the state court (which was anticipated) could be appealed under section 25 of the Judiciary Act to the federal Supreme Court.

In the state court, lawyers for the college trustees presented their case as essentially an unlawful deprivation of vested rights, with the contract clause playing a distinctly subordinate role. They contended that the New Hampshire legislature, even without specific constitutional restrictions on its powers, was incompetent to abolish private vested rights of property. Whether the New Hampshire laws were challenged as violations of vested rights or as contrary to specific restrictions contained in the state and federal constitutions, the case for the trustees depended on the classification of the Dartmouth College corporation. Was it a private institution immune from state interference, or was it a public institution subject to legislative control? The trustees argued that Dartmouth College belonged to the class of "eleemosynary"—charitable and benevolent—corporations that originated in private bounty and whose privileges were granted for the purpose of perpetuating and securing the application of the bounty to its charitable objects. Such corporations were always private, having no concern with the civil government of the state, and possessed rights entitled to the same protection as those of individuals. This argument failed to persuade the court, which held that Dartmouth was a public corporation and that no question of private right was involved in the case. The contract clause was not intended, said the court, "to limit the states, in relation to their own public officers and servants, or to their own civil institutions."[39]

Once the case came to the Supreme Court, the single issue was whether the New Hampshire acts violated the contract clause. Virtually ignoring the jurisdictional restriction to the constitutional question, Daniel Webster, representing the college in the appeal, launched a broad-based attack on the New Hampshire acts as an unlawful deprivation of vested rights, similar to the argument presented in the state court. Webster clearly believed the case for the college would be stronger by emphasizing the inviolability of vested rights than by framing the issue as an impairment of the obligation of contract. He devoted the greater part of his argument to showing that the New Hampshire legislature was prohibited from passing the acts in question either by general limitations on legislative power or by specific restrictions found in the state constitution.[40]

After hearing the appeal argued at the 1818 term, the Court was unable to agree on an opinion and ordered the cause continued to the next term. This lack of agreement may have reflected doubts among some justices about the appropriateness of bringing the case within the contract clause. It was expected that a reargument of the case at the next term would also include appeals from new actions commenced on behalf of the college in the federal circuit court. Thus freed from the jurisdictional limits imposed on appeals from a state court, the Supreme Court, said Webster, could consider the broader question of "whether, by the general principles of our government, the state legislatures be not restrained from divesting vested rights."[41] Chief Justice Marshall confounded this expectation, however, when he announced at the beginning of the 1819 term that the Court had come to a decision in the college case. By a vote of five to one, the justices upheld the Dartmouth trustees.[42] In coming to this decision, the justices signified their acceptance of Marshall's resolution of the case under the contract clause.

Unlike his *Fletcher* opinion, which in structure consisted of two virtually independent arguments, one drawing on general principles of vested rights, the other on the constitutional text, Marshall's opinion in *Dartmouth* presented a single, integrated argument stated exclusively in terms of the contract clause. Here the chief justice displayed in its full maturity his method of constitutional exegesis, of adjudging the validity of legislative acts by expounding the constitutional text. Without denying that the Constitution rested on a broad foundation of natural law and common law, Marshall now consciously refrained from making an express appeal to those extraconstitutional sources to explicate the text. Instead of beginning with external principles and then proceeding to the text, his constitutional analysis in *Dartmouth* remained strictly internal, beginning and ending with the words of the Constitution. The results of that analysis so thoroughly demonstrated the comprehensive reach of the contract clause that henceforth there would be no need to resort to the language of vested rights as auxiliary support for voiding a law. The contract clause as construed by Marshall was by no means the exact equivalent of a constitutional guarantee of the inviolability of vested rights; not every law divesting a vested right could be said to impair the obligation of contract. Yet the practical effect of his reading was to discover in that text broad protection for the vested rights of property.[43]

For his part, Webster, who in arguing on behalf of the Dartmouth trustees had relied so heavily on the language of vested rights, was pleased with the result: "The Chief Justice's opinion was in his own peculiar way. He reasoned along from step to step; and not referring to the cases, adopted the principle of them, and worked the whole into a close, connected and very able argument." So, too, was Joseph Hopkinson, Webster's cocounsel, who praised the opinion for placing the college's case "upon principles broad and deep, and which secure corporations of this description from legislative despotism and party violence for the future."[44]

As in *Fletcher*, Marshall began by restating the rule of reasonable doubt in pronouncing a law contrary to the Constitution, this time coupling it with an equally emphatic assertion of the "high and solemn duty" imposed on judges "of protecting, from even legislative violation, those contracts which the constitution of our country has placed beyond legislative control."[45] He assumed without argument that the circumstances giving rise to the 1769 charter incorporating Dartmouth College constituted a "contract." This assumption was scarcely controversial in 1819, for it accorded with natural and common law principles that a grant of property was a contract and with the holding in *Fletcher* v. *Peck* that a grant by the state was as much a contract as a grant between private individuals. And because corporations were classified by the common law as franchises, that is, as a kind of private property, it reasonably followed that a corporate charter granted by the state was as much a contract as a grant of land.[46] This point, indeed, was not seriously disputed by opponents of the college. Their principal contention was that the Dartmouth charter was a grant of political power, not of private property rights, and therefore not a contract meant to be protected by the Constitution.

Marshall agreed with the New Hampshire court that the contract clause was not to be construed in its broadest sense as a general abridgment of state power, that it was never intended "to restrain the states in the regulation of their civil institutions, adopted for internal government." He likewise believed the clause was restricted to contracts that concern private property and that "confer rights which may be asserted in a court of justice."[47] One pivotal issue, then, was the nature of the 1769 charter. If it created a civil institution of government, or if it granted powers or property in trust to be administered for purely public purposes, then the charter was a proper subject for state legislation of the kind enacted by New Hampshire. If, however, the charter created a private, eleemosynary institution, then the question presented itself whether the rights conferred by the charter were of a kind that came within the protection of the contract clause.

Examining the charter, the chief justice had no difficulty in concluding that Dartmouth College in both its origins and funds was an eleemosynary and private corporation and that it retained this character despite the application of those funds to broad public purposes such as education. Merely because Dartmouth was an educational institution did not mean that it had "become a public institution, and its trustees public officers, exercising powers conferred by the public for public objects." Moreover, the fact of incorporation was immaterial in determining an institution's character. A charter of incorporation was merely a legal device that enabled a perpetual succession of individuals to act "like one immortal being" for the promotion of some object.[48] But such an act did not transform a private institution into a public one and did not confer any political power or character upon this artificial being. "The character of civil institutions does not grow out of their incorporation," Marshall observed, "but out of the manner in which they are formed, and the objects for which they are created." Institutions created for the purposes of government, whether incorporated or not, were subject to legislative control; an incorporating act neither gave nor prevented this control. Did the circumstance that the people of New Hampshire were beneficiaries of Dartmouth College make it a public institution? Marshall could find nothing in the charter to support this conclusion:

> The particular interests of New Hampshire never entered into the minds of the donors, never constituted a motive for their donation. The propagation of the Christian religion among the savages, and the dissemination of useful knowledge among the youth of the country, were the avowed and the sole objects of their contributions. In these, New Hampshire would participate; but nothing particular or exclusive was intended for her.[49]

If the 1769 Dartmouth charter was truly a contract with an obligation protected against impairment, Marshall still had to confront the
difficult issue of determining who had a beneficial interest, or vested
right, in this contract. Opponents of the college insisted, and the
chief justice did not deny, that only those contracts in which the parties "have a vested beneficial interest" came within the Constitution's
protection.[50] The founders, donors, and their descendants could not
claim that the alteration of the charter personally injured them; neither could the students, none of whom had "a vested interest in
the institution, which can be asserted in a court of justice."[51] While
strongly implying that the trustees, who alone complained, did have a
personal vested interest, the chief justice avoided deciding this point
by advancing the novel proposition that the corporation itself possessed private, contractual rights deserving of constitutional protection in this case. The corporation was the "assignee" of the rights of
the original founders and donors; it "stands in their place, and distrib-
utes their bounty, as they would themselves have distributed it, had
they been immortal." The charter, in short, was a continuing contract
with a continuing obligation, the same in 1819 as it was in 1769. According to Marshall,

> This is plainly a contract to which the donors, the trustees, and
> the crown (to whose rights and obligations New Hampshire suc-
> ceeds) were the original parties. It is a contract made on a valu-
> able consideration. It is a contract for the security and disposition
> of property. It is a contract, on the faith of which real and per-
> sonal estate has been conveyed to the corporation.[52]

Although such a contract was clearly "within the letter of the constitution," the chief justice admitted that the protection of corporate
rights was probably not contemplated by the framers of the contract
clause. But if a rare or unforeseen case had no part in establishing the
constitutional rule concerning the inviolability of contracts, was such a
case to be excepted from the operation of the rule? As he did on other
occasions, Marshall insisted that courts had to be governed by the intention as manifested by the words of the Constitution, not by the particular intentions that motivated the framers in 1787 and 1788: "It is
not enough to say that this particular case was not in the mind of the

convention when the article was framed, nor of the American people when it was adopted. It is necessary to go farther, and to say that, had this particular case been suggested, the language would have been so varied, as to exclude it, or it would have been made a special exception."[53]

Such a rule of construction obviously permitted great latitude in expounding the contract clause and placed the burden of proof on those who would restrict its reach. Yet if, as Marshall emphatically believed, the framers and the American people intended to establish a Constitution embodying enduring principles that could be applied to changing circumstances, then the only sound judicial course was to abide by its words—unless, of course, such literal construction produced a result "so obviously absurd, or mischievous, or repugnant to the general spirit of the instrument." The chief justice could find no authority, either in the Constitution or "its contemporaneous expounders" or anything "in the nature and reason of the case itself," to justify a construction that would ignore the "plain import" of the contract clause and exclude the Dartmouth charter—and those of all eleemosynary corporations established for the promotion of religion, charity, and education—from its protection.[54] The framers, Marshall reasoned, could not have been unmindful of the universal human desire to ensure the perpetuation and security of charitable gifts. Why, then, would they have left contracts for this purpose—charters of incorporation—subject to the whims of legislative caprice?

Having found the Dartmouth charter to be a contract protected by the Constitution, Marshall had little trouble in showing that the New Hampshire acts did impair that contract. The immediate effect of the ruling was that Dartmouth University once again became Dartmouth College. The *Dartmouth* decision, to be sure, affected more than just the fate of a small New England college. It announced a principle of constitutional law that applied not only to eleemosynary corporations but to business corporations as well. By creating a wide scope for unfettered entrepreneurial activity, this principle facilitated the development of the business corporation and stimulated the economic growth of the new nation. In effect, if not deliberately intended, Marshall's constitutional law suited the requirements of a burgeoning capitalist economy.[55] Yet the case had broader significance than the carving out of a spacious zone of legal immunity for corporations. In essence,

Dartmouth was a statement about the inviolability of private rights in the exercise of state power and a reassertion of the duty of judges under the Constitution to prevent these rights from being sacrificed to the fluctuating policies of legislative majorities. This larger concern, rather than the welfare of corporations as such, was foremost in Marshall's mind at the time he wrote the opinion.[56]

Marshall's argument in *Dartmouth*, as Webster noted, proceeded upon principle rather than authority. Indeed, except for a couple of citations to Blackstone and a brief allusion to the Court's previous contract decisions, the opinion was remarkably uncluttered with references to cases and precedents. In a case where the arguments of counsel and the concurring opinions of Washington and Story were replete with citations to the English common law of corporations, the conspicuous omission of such references is to be attributed not to ignorance or carelessness but to deliberate intention. Marshall relied on that law only to the extent of identifying Dartmouth College as a private, eleemosynary institution. He did not get bogged down in a discussion of such technical doctrines as the visitatorial power, though he was conversant with the cases on this subject, having cited them as a lawyer in a 1790 case.[57] These cases, he concluded, were of dubious precedential value, for the doctrine of visitation was not strictly relevant to the circumstances of the Dartmouth case. Moreover, the cases could be manipulated to support either of two contradictory results, neither of which was consistent with American practice: that all corporate charters, whether public and private, were immune from legislative interference; or that the state had a superintending power over both public and private corporations.[58] The omission of English precedents enabled Marshall to make a stronger case for the college than did either Washington or Story for all their learning and splendid array of citations. The chief justice's colleagues recognized the superior strength of his argument by adopting it as the opinion of the Court.

BANKRUPTCY, INSOLVENCY, AND THE CONTRACT CLAUSE

Two weeks after the *Dartmouth* decision, Marshall expounded the contract clause yet again in the case of *Sturges* v. *Crowninshield*, which brought into question the power of the states to enact bankruptcy legislation. The contract in this case, unlike those in *Fletcher* and *Dartmouth*, was a private contract between two individuals—the very kind of contract that there could be no doubt the Constitution was intended to protect. Until 1819, however, there had been no Supreme Court pronouncement as to whether the contract clause was intended to embrace bankruptcy laws. Coinciding with a financial and business panic and the onset of a severe economic depression, the case attracted great public interest, for the extent to which the states could respond to the crisis hinged on the Court's decision.

In *Sturges* and in earlier cases heard in federal circuit courts, state bankruptcy laws were challenged as repugnant not only to the contract clause but also to the clause empowering Congress to establish "uniform laws on the subject of Bankruptcies."[59] The circuit cases revealed sharply opposing opinions among Supreme Court justices as to the applicability of these provisions to state legislation. Judge Washington in 1814 applied the contract clause to void a Pennsylvania statute that operated retrospectively upon an existing contract. At the same time, he declared that a prospective law, enacted before the parties entered into the contract, "would be clearly constitutional," a position that ultimately became the law of the land in 1827. Washington also set forth his "unhesitating opinion" that the Constitution vested Congress with exclusive power to pass bankruptcy laws, effectively withdrawing this subject from the state governments.[60] Judge Livingston in 1817 emphatically rejected the exclusive power doctrine in upholding a New York statute subsequently overturned in *Sturges*. Livingston also denied that bankruptcy or insolvency laws that discharged a debtor from future liability, whether retrospective or prospective, were intended to be embraced by the contract clause. Such laws, he contended, must be presumed constitutional from the long practice of enacting them in New York and in other states without any complaints that they violated the obligation of contract.[61]

An underlying difficulty presented by these cases was the proper definition of a "bankrupt" law as distinct from an "insolvent" law. In America these terms were employed more or less interchangeably in referring to debtor-relief legislation, resulting in much confusion. The distinguishing feature of an insolvent law was said to be the liberation of the debtor from imprisonment on assignment of his assets to creditors, leaving future assets still liable for his debts. Laws of this kind had routinely been adopted in the American states since the colonial period. The defining characteristic of a bankrupt law, on the other hand, was said to be the release not only of the person of the debtor but also of liability for his debts, enabling him to get a fresh start free from the crushing burden of past obligations. Such laws were not unknown in the colonial period, and since the adoption of the Constitution several states had passed laws discharging debts.[62] Although lawyers could point out other differences between bankruptcy and insolvency legislation, "the line of partition between them," Marshall astutely observed in *Sturges*, "is not so distinctly marked as to enable any person to say, with positive precision, what belongs exclusively to the one, and not to the other class of laws."[63] The New York and Pennsylvania laws discharging debtors from future liability were entitled acts "for the relief of insolvent debtors."

In an 1814 letter to Judge Washington, Marshall privately doubted that the bankruptcy clause conferred exclusive power on Congress, a position he judicially adopted five years later. As for the contract clause, he leaned to the opinion that "on a fair & necessary construction" its words would apply to bankruptcy laws, though such laws were probably not among the obnoxious and mischievous legislative acts the framers had specifically in mind in restricting state power—again foreshadowing his 1819 ruling. As of 1814 Marshall doubted that a general prospective bankruptcy law could "fairly be termed a law impairing the obligation of contracts" and was inclined to accept the validity of such a law. Yet he acknowledged "very great doubts whether I shall retain that opinion."[64] He did not consider this question judicially until 1827, when he held that the contract clause prohibited both prospective and retrospective bankruptcy laws—a conclusion that in all probability he had reached by 1819.

The contract giving rise to the 1819 case consisted of two promissory notes given by Richard Crowninshield to Josiah Sturgis (misspelled "Sturges" on the official record of the case) in New York City in March 1811. A member of a prominent Massachusetts family, Crowninshield was then a resident of New York, having earlier moved his shipping business to that city. By November 1811 he had become insolvent and submitted a petition under a New York statute enacted in April 1811 enabling debtors to be discharged from their debts on assigning their property for the benefit of creditors. Crowninshield obtained his dis-

charge in February 1812 over Sturgis's protest and subsequently returned to Massachusetts, where he established a prosperous textile business. In 1816 Sturgis filed suit to recover his debt in the United States
Circuit Court at Boston. The case was subsequently certified to the
Supreme Court, with Chief Justice Marshall delivering the opinion of
the Court eight days after hearing arguments.[65]

Marshall decided the case under the contract clause, not the bankruptcy clause, holding that the New York law impaired the obligation of
contract. He agreed with counsel for the debtor that the states possessed concurrent power with Congress over the subject of bankruptcies. A grant of power to Congress did not necessarily amount to a
prohibition on the states to exercise that power. If the terms of the
grant or the nature of the power required its exclusive exercise by Congress, then "the subject is as completely taken from the State Legislatures, as if they had been expressly forbidden to act on it."[66] Applied to
bankruptcy, however, the exclusive power construction would produce
"much inconvenience," particularly in view of the difficulty of marking
a clear line of distinction between bankruptcy and insolvency laws.
Were the states to be entirely prohibited from enacting traditional insolvency legislation? "It does not appear to be a violent construction of
the constitution, and is certainly a convenient one," the chief justice observed, "to consider the power of the states as existing over such cases
as the laws of the Union may not reach." In any event, if Congress
chose not to exercise its power, it would be unreasonable to prevent
state legislation on this subject. "It is not the mere existence of the
power, but its exercise," he said, "which is incompatible with the exercise of the same power by the states."[67]

This concession to state power has been called "remarkable" given
the nationalizing tenor of Marshall's other decisions and his general
disapproval of state legislation concerning debtor-creditor relations.
The explanation of this apparent inconsistency is that the chief justice
sacrificed his personal opinion in favor of federal plenary power over
bankruptcy in order to placate other justices and thereby achieve una-
nimity on a badly divided court.[68] Yet Marshall's construction of the
bankruptcy clause in *Sturges* was essentially the same one he had privately advanced in his 1814 letter. Moreover, his opposition to state legislation on this subject did not extend to insolvency laws discharging
the person of the debtor.

Marshall, indeed, saw no reason to forbid the states from passing bankruptcy acts, so long as they did not impair the obligation of contract—this was the "great question on which the cause must depend."[69] On this point Marshall fashioned another characteristically broad reading of the contract clause that also included his most elaborate statement to date of the rule of construction he had employed in earlier cases. As in *Dartmouth*, Marshall had to meet the objection that the contract clause did not cover the particular case—corporate charters in the one and bankruptcy and insolvency laws in the other. If such cases seemed to come within the plain meaning of the words, yet it was objected that the framers never contemplated such cases and therefore to include them within the prohibition would violate the spirit of the Constitution. Insolvency and bankruptcy laws provoked no outcry during the 1780s and were not on the framers' minds when drafting the Constitution. Marshall agreed that "although the spirit of an instrument, especially of a constitution, is to be respected not less than its letter, yet the spirit is to be collected chiefly from its words. It would be dangerous in the extreme to infer from extrinsic circumstances, that a case for which the words of an instrument expressly provide, shall be exempted from its operation."[70] The intention of the Constitution was embodied in its words, which had to be interpreted literally, unless such a construction produced a manifestly absurd or unjust result.

The chief justice then proceeded to show that in this case to depart from the plain meaning of the words, to restrict the contract clause only to those laws complained of at the time, would be a gross misreading of the framers' true intention. Paper money laws, laws enabling debtors to tender specific property in payment of debts, and laws permitting executions for debt to be levied in installments were the particular mischiefs the framers wished to remedy. Since paper money and tender laws were specifically prohibited by other clauses of Article 1, section 10, was the contract clause intended to embrace only the "single case" of installment laws? Such a conclusion defied common sense and insulted the framers' intelligence: "No men would use terms embracing a whole class of laws, for the purpose of designating a single individual of that class." The framers, Marshall explained, were careful not only to prohibit particular means by which contracts could be evaded but also "to prohibit the use of any means by which the same mischief might be produced." The contract clause, then, was not directed at particular laws but "intended to establish a great principle, that contracts should be inviolable." Consistent with this intention, "those rules of construction, which have been consecrated by the wisdom of ages, compel us to say that these words, prohibit the passage of any law discharging a contract without performance."[71]

Although Marshall wrote for a purportedly unanimous Court, the justices remained divided over the reach of the contract clause with respect to bankruptcy legislation. As Johnson later remarked, the *Sturges* judgment partook "as much of a compromise, as of a legal adjudication."[72] He characterized the compromise as one in which the minority acquiesced in the voiding of the New York law only so long as the decision was understood to embrace laws applying to prior contracts. Nowhere did Marshall himself expressly limit the reach of the contract clause to retrospective bankruptcy laws, though he did say that the Court's decision was "confined to the case actually under consideration."[73] Since in this case the New York law had been enacted after the contract, the authority of *Sturges* was restricted to retrospective legislation. It left open the question whether a state law discharging a debtor from a subsequent contract made within the same state was constitutional.

This question finally came directly in issue with the case of *Ogden* v. *Saunders*, decided in 1827. Saunders had sued Ogden for payment on bills of exchange drawn on Ogden in New York City in 1806. Ogden pleaded a discharge under a New York insolvent law of 1801, but a lower federal court gave judgment for Saunders. The appeal was argued in 1824 and again in 1827 by a distinguished array of learned counsel, a measure of the high importance and difficulty of the case and of the Supreme Court's inability to reach a consensus. The Court's ultimate decision upholding prospective state bankruptcy laws—by a vote of four to three—exposed to full light its internal divisions on this perplexing subject. Each of the four justices in the majority—Bushrod Washington, William Johnson, Smith Thompson, and Robert Trimble—delivered their opinions seriatim. For the first and only time in his judicial career Chief Justice Marshall, joined by Joseph Story and Gabriel Duvall, dissented in a constitutional case.[74] In explaining his disagreement with the majority's decision, Marshall penned an elegantly reasoned treatise that embodied his most deeply held convictions about the meaning of the contract clause and the principles of constitutional interpretation. This exercise in constitutional exegesis in turn brought forth reflections on the extent to which natural rights—the right to contract, the right to acquire property—could be modified and controlled by civil society.

In upholding the validity of New York's bankruptcy statute, the majority invoked the Court's reasonable doubt rule of deciding constitutional questions, quoting the chief justice's statement of the rule in *Fletcher*.[75] Except for briefly reiterating the Court's attitude "of profound and respectful reverence" in approaching such questions, Marshall dispensed with another full-blown pronouncement of the rule in *Ogden*. This seemingly perfunctory bow to judicial deference was immediately followed by a reaffirmation of the Court's power to preserve "the constitution from legislative infraction."[76] These remarks did not signify any weakening of his commitment to the rule in guiding the Court's deliberations in difficult constitutional cases. Indeed, the whole thrust of his opinion was to present the case in terms that did not admit of any doubt on his part that the New York law was unconstitutional. For Marshall the reasonable doubt test was to be applied only after subjecting the case to rigorous judicial analysis and reasoning. If uncertainty remained after performing this arduous intellectual labor, then he would agree that a judge should defer to the legislature's construction. In the case at hand, however, reasoning did not leave a mind vacillating between upholding or rejecting the law.[77]

Marshall prefaced his opinion by restating the Court's principles of construction in constitutional cases:

that the intention of the instrument must prevail; that this intention must be collected from its words; that its words are to be understood in that sense in which they are generally used by those for whom the instrument was intended; that its provisions are neither to be restricted into insignificance, nor extended to objects not comprehended in them nor contemplated by its framers.[78]

These rules, uncontroversial in themselves, produced sharp disagreement in their application to the contract clause. Where Marshall parted company with the majority was in adhering to "a severe literal construction" of its words.[79] If, as he readily conceded, a literal reading was not always a reliable guide to intention, yet the burden of proof was on those who would depart from the strict sense of the words and substitute another meaning. In *Ogden* none of the various arguments employed by counsel persuaded the chief justice that the prohibition against laws impairing the obligation of contract did not embrace prospective as well as retrospective bankruptcy laws.

For example, no distinction between retrospective and prospective laws could be inferred from the nature of the American union, which was "intended to make us, in a great measure, one people, as to commercial objects." In order to facilitate free commercial intercourse, the framers not surprisingly contemplated a great if not entire abridgment of state legislation "on the delicate subject of contracts once formed."[80] Nor could such a distinction be maintained on a reading of the whole paragraph of Article 1, section 10, of which the contract clause formed a part. The prohibitions in this paragraph were "complete and total," no matter whether they concerned powers that were essentially political or those that affected individual rights. "A State is as entirely forbidden to pass laws impairing the obligation of contracts," said Marshall, "as to make treaties, or coin money."[81]

The majority justices pointed to the immediate association of ex post facto laws and bills of attainder with laws impairing the obligation of contract as indicating the retrospective intent of the contract clause. Since the prohibitions on the two former classes of laws were manifestly directed at retrospective legislation, so too was the prohibition on laws impairing the obligation of contract. The chief justice stood this argument on its head, discovering instead a clear intention to distinguish between laws punishing criminal offenses (attainders and ex post facto laws) and those relating "to the civil transactions of individuals." Precisely because the prohibitions on the former were expressly confined to retroactive laws, the contract clause must be understood to have a more comprehensive application. This and other clauses concerned with civil transactions, such as that forbidding the passage of tender laws, were "expressed in more general terms; in terms which comprehend, in their ordinary signification, cases which occur after, as well as those which occur before, the passage of the act."[82] There was no discernible difference in principle between a tender law, which was entirely prohibited, and a law that discharged a debt.

If the Constitution contemplated a complete and total prohibition of laws impairing the obligation of contracts, Marshall still had to meet the objection that a prospective bankruptcy law did not impair that obligation. *Ogden* accordingly elicited a probing inquiry into the meaning of "obligation of contract." All the justices believed that the Constitution was intended to enforce the legal, not the moral, obligation of contract, but what precisely was the legal obligation and whence did it arise—from the positive law of the state or from natural law?

One argument urged at the bar insisted that the "municipal," or local, law of the state entered into and formed a constituent part of the contract. A contract was more than an explicit agreement between two parties but consisted as well of all the laws in force to regulate and control contracts. In the contract between Ogden and Saunders, for example, the extant New York bankruptcy statute was to be understood as forming an express stipulation that on the debtor's insolvency a surrender of his property would discharge the debt. Since this municipal law was engrafted onto the contract, it could not therefore impair the obligation of that contract. Not even the majority justices were prepared to accept this principle in its full extent, for it would lead to unacceptable consequences. If a bankruptcy or any other statute relating to contracts formed part of the contract and its obligation, the legislature could not repeal those laws so as to affect existing contracts. "The effect of such a principle," Marshall pointed out, "would be a mischievous abridgment" of legitimate state legislative powers—much more drastic than that resulting from his own construction of the contract clause.[83]

The true principle, according to the chief justice, was "that laws act upon a contract, not that they enter into it, and become a stipulation of the parties. . . . The external action of law upon contracts, by administering the remedy for their breach, or otherwise, is the usual exercise of legislative power."[84] For example, laws providing for the recovery of interest not expressly stipulated for by the parties did not introduce new conditions into a contract. They merely provided a remedy for the breach of an implied contract arising from the act of the parties. Accompanying an express contract, such as a bond, to pay a certain principal sum was an implied contract to pay interest. The stipulation for interest did not become part of the contract through legislation but grew out of the original agreement between the parties. Yet, if the law did not enter into a contract but only acted externally upon it by affording the means of enforcing it, did not this admitted sovereign

power to regulate and enforce contracts embrace the power to prescribe their obligation? Was a bankruptcy law different in principle
from statutes of frauds, acts against usury, and acts of limitation? Did
not such a law enter into the views of parties to contracts in the same
way as these remedial laws—laws that had never been regarded as impairing the obligation of contract? If the Constitution prohibited
prospective bankruptcy laws, so the argument ran, it would also sweep
away a mass of legislation hitherto within the proper jurisdiction of
state authority.

The chief justice took great pains to deny this conflation of remedy
with obligation, and it was on this point that he failed to persuade a majority of his colleagues. The state's power to regulate the remedy, to enforce the obligation of contracts, he contended, was distinct from the
obligation itself. The latter did not originate in municipal law; it did
not derive from some supposed supreme power of the state to declare
what constitutes the performance of a contract. Indeed, so far back as
one could trace legislation, laws concerning contracts "evince the idea
of a pre-existing obligation which human law enforces." The right to
contract and its attendant obligation, in short, existed "anterior to and
independent of society."[85] This right originated in a state of nature and
was brought by individuals with them into society. Obligation arose not
from the law of society but was intrinsic to the contract itself and "was
conferred by the act of the parties. This results from the right which
every man retains to acquire property, to dispose of that property according to his own judgment, and to pledge himself for a future act.
These rights are not given by society, but are brought into it."[86] In forming society and establishing government, individuals did not surrender
their right to contract but only the right of enforcement. In support of
these observations, Marshall referred to "those writers on natural and
national law whose opinions have been viewed with profound respect
by the wisest men of the present and of past ages."[87]

The majority justices did not deny that the obligation of contract was
founded in natural law but insisted that a state had authority to regulate, modify, or control the operation of universal law within its jurisdiction. State law created a civil obligation that, at least as to private
contracts, superseded natural law, and it was this civil obligation of contract that the Constitution was meant to protect. To concede a state's
power to outlaw usury and gambling contracts, to adopt statutes of

frauds and of limitation, was to "surrender" the whole argument, said Johnson, for it admitted "the right of the government to limit and define the power of contracting, and the extent of the creditor's remedy against his debtor."[88]

In vain the chief justice attempted to meet this objection by asserting a material distinction between such laws, which were clearly constitutional, and a bankruptcy law that discharged a debt. Statutes of frauds prescribed "regulations which must precede the obligation of contract," and usury laws declared a contract void from the beginning, denying "it all original obligation." Acts of limitation presented more difficulty, for they did void a once obligatory contract and therefore seemed "to partake of the character" of laws impairing the obligation.[89] Indeed, so strong was the resemblance between acts of limitation and the bankruptcy law under consideration that Johnson professed to "have seen no distinction between the cases that can bear examination."[90] Marshall's position was that acts of limitation did not impair the obligation but only presumed "that a certain length of time, unexplained by circumstances, is reasonable evidence of a performance."[91]

This was a fine point, one that ultimately rested on the distinction between obligation and remedy. To the majority this distinction, whatever its validity in an abstract or theoretical sense, could not be sustained in practice, for the power to control the remedy necessarily affected the obligation. Did not withholding the remedy effectually destroy the obligation? Marshall held that the obligation remained intact in this case, which "like all other cases of misgovernment" left "the debtor still liable to his creditor, should he be found, where the laws afford a remedy."[92] There was no absurdity in leaving the states in full possession of the power over the remedy while prohibiting them from impairing the obligation of contracts. The Constitution presumed these governments would act responsibly and in good faith to enforce remedies on broken contracts. Obligation and remedy, then, were not identical. The former originated in the act of the parties; the latter was provided by the act of government.

Marshall concluded by returning to the matter of intention and construction, reiterating his view that both the "history of the times" and the language of the Constitution made plain the framers' intention to establish the great principle of the inviolability of contracts. "In framing an instrument which was intended to be perpetual," he observed, "the presumption is strong that every important principle introduced into it is intended to be perpetual also; that a principle expressed in terms to operate in all future time is intended so to operate."[93] This intention would be defeated by a construction that restricted the operation of the contract clause to retrospective laws. Careful draftsmen that they were, the framers surely would have inserted "retrospective" or other appropriate language to convey this particular intention. Instead, they stated the prohibition in general terms, reflecting a general intent to protect future as well as previously formed contracts. With respect to contract clause, the surest guide to intent was to interpret the words in their literal sense.

In composing his *Ogden* dissent, Chief Justice Marshall was in full command of his powers of legal reasoning and analysis. His arguments were relentless in their rigor and logic, tenacious in their attempt to meet every objection that could be raised against them. Despite the controversial nature of bankruptcy legislation, he maintained throughout the tone of a dispassionate legal inquiry, revealing a mind actively grappling with the difficult intellectual problem of discerning the meaning of the Constitution. He approached the question openly, willing to abide by whatever result impartial judicial examination might yield, and produced an answer that seemed to emerge from inside the document itself. In this case intensive investigation of the subject compelled him to abandon an initial predisposition in favor of the constitutional validity of a prospective bankruptcy act. Having employed "all the acumen which controversy can give to the human mind . . . in scanning" the whole of the paragraph containing the contract clause "and every word of it," Marshall came to the unshakable conclusion that the Constitution prohibited all state laws impairing the obligation of contracts, no matter whether they operated retrospectively or prospectively.[94] Construing the words of the contract clause in their strict literal sense, he painstakingly sought to demonstrate that this construction accorded with the true spirit of the Constitution.

Apart from the constitutional issue, Marshall is presumed to have disapproved of state bankruptcy laws on the ground of policy as well, though there is no conclusive evidence on this point. No doubt he would have preferred a bankruptcy system established under the auspices of the federal Congress rather than leave this subject in the hands of the individual state legislatures. In view of Congress's failure to pass a national bankruptcy statute, however, he might well have decided that state laws could have beneficial results. In providing relief for "honest debtors" along with reasonable protection for creditors, bankruptcy legislation would have the effect of encouraging commercial enterprise and promoting economic expansion—goals that certainly had the chief justice's blessing. The easier course, then, and surely the more popular, would have been to adopt the majority's construction of the Constitution. In other circumstances and cases the chief justice had not been unwilling to bow to political expediency. That he refused to do so in this instance underscored his conviction that the contract clause, or rather the principle it embodied, contained the vital essence of the Constitution.

Perhaps more successfully than any other of his major opinions, *Ogden* exemplifies the ideals Marshall strove to uphold in constitutional adjudication. His duty, as he conceived it, was to exercise judgment based on the objective legal standard of the Constitution, to keep judicial discretion within its proper bounds of interpreting the law—in short, to dispel any notion that he was imposing his own subjective will. He did not doubt that judges could attain these ideals, however illusory the attempt might appear to modern legal realists.

THE BILL OF RIGHTS: *BARRON V. BALTIMORE*

Ogden v. *Saunders* was the last of Marshall's major contract clause opinions. Until that decision the Supreme Court had upheld the offending state law or local ordinance in just one case brought under the contract clause.[95] Between 1827 and 1835 the Supreme Court decided nine more cases under this clause, sustaining the state legislation in each instance. Although this trend apparently reflected a new posture by the Court of limiting the reach of the contract clause to allow greater state activity, none of these cases was of great importance and probably would have been decided the same way even if Marshall had prevailed in *Ogden*.

In the only contract clause opinion he wrote after *Ogden*, Marshall upheld the right of a state to tax a bank chartered by the state. This was the case of *Providence Bank* v. *Billings*, decided in 1830, which brought into question the validity of an 1822 Rhode Island law laying a tax upon the Providence Bank. Citing *Dartmouth* and other contract clause decisions, counsel for the bank maintained that the institution's 1791 charter, like other corporate charters, was a contract protected by the Constitution. The state tax, so it was contended, impaired the obligation of this contract, for the taxing power could in effect be exercised to destroy the bank.

Marshall rejected this argument, finding no express or implied promise of exemption in the charter. Because the power of taxation was "of vital importance," he said, its relinquishment was "never to be assumed." Any special privileges attaching to corporations exempting them "from the burdens common to individuals" had to be expressed in the charter itself. "The power of legislation, and, consequently, of taxation, operates on all the persons and property belonging to the body politic," he observed. "This is an original principle, which has its foundation in society itself." The taxing power accordingly did not need to be reserved when the state granted property to individuals or corporate bodies. Although this power might be abused, the Constitution "was not intended to furnish the corrective for every abuse of power which may be committed by the state governments. The interest, wisdom, and justice of the representative body, and its relations with its constituents, furnish the only security, where there is no express contract."[96]

This decision is often cited as evidence of the Marshall Court's "retreat" from the vigorous nationalism that characterized the pronouncements issued during the preceding two decades. It is undoubtedly true that in response to political and economic pressures and as a result of changes in personnel, the Court during the last decade of Marshall's chief justiceship adopted a more accommodating posture toward the claims of state sovereignty.[97] Yet *Providence Bank* was not inconsistent with the principles laid down in earlier "nationalist" decisions, and there is no reason to assume the case would have been decided differently if, say, it had appeared on the docket in 1819.

The same is true of *Barron v. Baltimore* (1833), the last constitutional opinion Marshall wrote for the Supreme Court.[98] Although not a contract clause case, *Barron* fits in with the larger theme of those cases. The plaintiff, a Baltimore wharf owner, complained that the regrading and paving of city streets had caused the silting up of the waters surrounding his property, destroying its commercial value. In seeking damages for an uncompensated "taking" of private property, he cited the Fifth Amendment, which declares that "private property shall [not] be taken for public use without just compensation." This case thus raised the important question of whether the Bill of Rights amendments applied to the state governments. Counsel maintained that those amendments in which the language was general (not specifically directed to the federal Congress) should be construed to restrict the legislative power of both the general and state governments. If this proposition could be sustained, the Supreme Court would gain vastly enlarged scope for the exercise of judicial power against state interferences with private rights.

Marshall for the Court emphatically declined the offer extended by Barron's counsel. The question presented by the case was "of great importance," the chief justice admitted, "but not of much difficulty." In deciding it he relied on his usual method of interpretation, beginning with a general principle arising from the nature of the Constitution and then proceeding with a textual analysis. The Constitution, he premised, established a government for the people of the United States, not for the individual states. It conferred powers to be exercised by the general government, and the limits it imposed, "if expressed in general terms," seemed necessarily to restrain that government. Although the Constitution, as shown by the restrictions contained in the tenth section of Article 1, secured the people against state legislative powers as well, this section strongly supported the opinion that the Bill of Rights was to apply only to the general government. The preceding ninth section, Marshall observed, contained restrictions "obviously intended" to restrain only the general government, even though some were expressed in general language. In the tenth section, however, all the enumerated restrictions applied in express terms to the states. The original Constitution, as evidenced by these two sections, thus clearly discriminated "between the limitations it imposes on the powers of the general government and on those of the states." Since every restriction intended to operate on state power contained express words for that purpose, "some strong reason must be assigned for departing from this safe and judicious course in framing the amendments, before that departure can be assumed."[99]

The Court could find no such reason. If the people wanted further protections against the acts of their state governments, the more rational course would have been to revise the particular state constitutions rather than resort to the cumbersome process of amending the federal Constitution. Surely the framers of the Bill of Rights amendments, like the framers of the original Constitution, would have declared "in plain and intelligible language" an intention to apply those amendments to the states. The chief justice reinforced this construction by recalling the history of the adoption of the Bill of Rights, which furnished abundant evidence that these amendments were proposed as additional security against the exercise of power by the general government.[100]

Although it is correctly described as a concession to state sovereignty, *Barron* was in no sense a retreat from the nationalist principles Marshall had articulated during three decades as chief justice. The decision was perfectly consistent with those principles and with the rules of construction he employed in all his great cases. In truth, the Court had no choice but to deny Barron's bold and unprecedented claim of Fifth Amendment protection against the actions of the Baltimore municipal government. At no time in its history could the Marshall Court have seriously entertained the idea of applying the Bill of Rights to the states. Had the case arisen in 1819, rather than in 1833, the result would have been the same. To suppose that the Court in the latter year, for reasons of mere political expediency, chose to read the Constitution in a way that denied Bill of Rights protections against the actions of state governments is to indulge in historical fantasy.[101]

Until the Fourteenth Amendment, the contract clause served as the Court's principal weapon for protecting private rights against state legislation. Chief Justice Marshall made this clause an effective instrument of judicial review, having no doubt that its purpose was to impose a great barrier to state interferences with the vested rights of property and contract. Yet, as shown by *Providence Bank*, he never regarded the clause as a general prohibition on unwise or obnoxious laws. He recognized the potential of pushing arguments based on the contract clause to absurd extremes that would severely hamper the ability of governments to perform their functions. Throughout all his contract clause cases, Marshall strove to discern the constitutional line between prohibited and legitimate state sovereignty. In another important group of constitutional cases, he had to consider the limits of both federal and state sovereignty in relation to the competing claims of each.

5

NATIONAL SUPREMACY AND STATES' RIGHTS

Constitutional Nationalism

The great constitutional decisions of John Marshall, observed Edward S. Corwin, "transfixed State Sovereignty with a two-edged sword, one edge of which was inscribed 'National Supremacy,' and the other 'Private Rights.'"[1] The contract clause cases exemplify the "private rights" edge of his constitutional rapier. In another set of cases Chief Justice Marshall wielded with equal effect the "national supremacy" edge of his weapon. The leading decisions in this category—*McCulloch* v. *Maryland* (1819), *Cohens* v. *Virginia* (1821), *Osborn* v. *Bank of the United States* (1824), and *Gibbons* v. *Ogden* (1824)—are a virtual treatise on constitutional nationalism, a body of doctrines and principles that Marshall wove into the fabric of American constitutional law.[2] Although useful for analytical purposes to distinguish these opinions from those expounding the contract clause, the result in both kinds of cases was the same: an abridgment of state sovereignty imposed by the judicial department of the United States. In the contract cases the denial of state sovereignty was based on an express constitutional prohibition. In the cases now to be considered the basis for denial was the doctrine of national supremacy, the logic of which implied a prohibition on state power whenever it conflicted with legitimate federal power.

Marshall premised constitutional nationalism on a theory of the Constitution as the constituent act of the people of the United States, not a compact among sovereign states. From this starting point he read the

111

Constitution as having created a real government, one of enumerated powers yet supreme within the sphere of action allotted to it. The grant of enumerated powers was to be understood as conferring upon the general government ample discretion to choose the means for executing its express powers. The Constitution, in addition, conferred upon the federal judiciary broad jurisdiction to decide cases arising under the Constitution and laws of the United States and imposed the duty of preserving federal law as the "supreme law of the land." The Supreme Court was accordingly empowered not only to nullify state laws that were repugnant to federal law but also to overrule decisions of state courts that failed to uphold federal supremacy.

In antebellum America this nationalist reading of the Constitution provoked impassioned denunciations as tending to destroy the state governments and establish a single consolidated national government. Opposition to the nationalizing decisions of the Marshall Court was founded on the doctrine of states' rights, which drew upon the Antifederalist critique of the Constitution in 1787 and 1788 and upon Jeffersonian Republican resistance to Federalist policies in the 1790s. Nowhere was states' rights a more potent ideology than in Marshall's own state of Virginia, its strength and continuity evident from the ratifying convention of 1788 through the protest against federal assumption of state debts in 1790, the resolutions of 1798 and 1799 against the alien and sedition laws, and first defiance of the Supreme Court in 1815. After 1819 a resurgent antifederal spirit in the Old Dominion hardened into the political dogma of states' rights republicanism that became increasingly identified with the defense of property in slaves.

Like constitutional nationalism, states' rights doctrine derived from a theory of the Constitution. In contrast to the nationalist concept of the Constitution as the act of the American people, states' rights theorists posited the idea of the Constitution as a compact in which the states were the constituent parties. In entering this compact the states surrendered only that portion of their sovereignty necessary for the general government to carry out its expressly enumerated national purposes. Defenders of states' rights placed much emphasis on the words of the Tenth Amendment, which declared that "the powers not delegated to the United States by the Constitution, nor prohibited by it to the States, are reserved to the States respectively, or to the people." Both nationalists and states' righters agreed that the Constitution established a system of divided sovereignty but disagreed over the extent to which power had been allotted to the general government on the one hand and retained by the states on the other.

The disagreement arose from different modes of interpreting the Constitution, which in turn sprang from different conceptions of the nature of the union. Nationalists, who viewed the union as composing the collectivity of the American people, maintained that the powers conferred upon the general government should be construed broadly to enable that government to operate effectively in performing its great national objects. States' righters, who viewed the union as a confederation of states, contended that the general government must be strictly confined to its express powers and to those means that were indispensably necessary to execute them. Nationalists and states' righters also sharply disagreed on the proper procedure for settling disputes that involved the competing claims of federal and state sovereignty. The former asserted that the Constitution conferred this authority upon the Supreme Court. The latter denied that the Constitution made any such provision and insisted that the states, as parties to the compact, must be the ultimate judges of the extent of their own powers.

From a modern perspective it is difficult to appreciate the argument for states' rights, associated as it is with the defense of slavery, nullification, and secession in the nineteenth century and with the defense of racial segregation in the twentieth. Not only has it been indelibly tarnished as the parent of secession and support of racial oppression, but as a constitutional theory states' rights seems anachronistic in an age of instantaneous electronic communications, high-speed transportation, and integrated national economy. The United States has long since become a consolidated nation-state administered by a massive bureaucracy. Yet despite the worst fears of Antifederalists and states' righters, consolidation has not resulted in the overthrow of the republican regime constituted in 1787 and has stopped well short of establishing a unitary national government in place of the compound system of general and state governments. The governmental system of the United States is still indisputably federal notwithstanding the vast enlargement of federal sovereignty at the expense of state sovereignty.

If the verdict of history since 1865 has upheld the nationalist reading of the Constitution, during the antebellum period states' rights doctrine held sway in much of the country, particularly in the South. At a time when most Americans bestowed primary loyalty upon their state governments and regarded the federal government as a distant, abstract, nearly invisible entity having little impact upon their daily lives, devotion to states' rights accorded with the deepest sympathies of the people. To read the arguments put forward by states' rights proponents as simply masking selfish interests (of slaveowners, for example) does not do them full justice. Nor can the alarm raised by the specter of "consolidation" be dismissed as groundless, however absurdly exaggerated it appears in hindsight. This was essentially a revival of the argument advanced by Antifederalists in 1787 and 1788 that the government prescribed by the Constitution, though in form republican and federal, would in practice evolve into a consolidated government; that a consolidated government of such extensive jurisdiction could not long remain republican; and that it must inevitably degenerate into monarchy, despotism, and tyranny.

In brief, states' righters, like their Antifederalist predecessors, believed that the compound system of divided sovereignty was inherently unstable and that the preservation of freedom and republicanism required the least possible abridgment of state sovereignty consistent with maintaining the union. Unlike Antifederalists, who in seeking to defeat ratification portrayed the Constitution as a radical change from the Articles of Confederation, states' righters had to adapt their arguments to a situation in which the Constitution had in fact been approved and gone into effect. They accordingly premised their interpretation of that instrument on the assumption that the system adopted in 1788 was not essentially different from the former confederation of states. At the same time, because of the new government's consolidating potential, eternal vigilance was required to maintain constitutional purity. Any perceived augmentation of federal power became a fateful step toward destruction of the republic.

Where states' righters sought to minimize the significance of the change from Confederation to Constitution, Marshall and his fellow nationalists insisted that in ratifying the Constitution the American people made a deliberate and decisive rejection of confederalism, or league of sovereign states, in favor of a general government organized on national principles. Marshall also believed that the Constitution's compound system of general and state governments was at best precariously stable, but he considered it far more likely to revert to the former

confederation of states than to evolve into a single consolidated government. His nationalist perspective inclined not forward to the nation-
state that emerged after the Civil War but backward to the 1787 idea of a
government of the union whose objects were primarily conservative and
defensive: to preserve the union against external invasion and internal
turbulence.[3] The experience of the 1780s remained central to his
thinking when considering both the extent of federal powers granted by
the Constitution and the limitations imposed by it on state powers.

On this question of the nature of the union hinged the conflicting
views of nationalists and states' righters concerning the extent of federal powers, the limits on state sovereignty, and the principles of constitutional interpretation. The debate on these issues had begun with the
inception of the Constitution and remained unsettled at the outbreak
of the Civil War in 1860. This constitutional dialogue had taken place
in the executive cabinet and the halls of Congress as well as in the
courtroom of the Supreme Court. Beginning in 1819 and continuing
during the next several years, the Court occupied center stage in the
debate. By an extraordinary coalescence of circumstances the Court in
swift succession heard a series of cases in which the claims of national
power and state sovereignty came into direct collision. By an equally
remarkable coincidence these cases occurred at a time of peak intensity
in the great national debate. The announcement of *McCulloch*, for instance, came during the midst of angry protests and retaliatory actions
against the federally chartered Second Bank of the United States.
Around this time, too, Congress was deliberating on a proposed federal
program of internal improvements and, ominously, on a proposal to
prohibit the introduction of slavery into the territories.

Marshall's opinions in the great "sovereignty" cases heard between
1819 and 1824 are justly celebrated for their comprehensive investigation into the meaning of the Constitution concerning the scope of national powers and restrictions on state authority. In the decision of
"concrete controversies," observed a leading constitutional scholar, "the
very foundations of the constitutional system were exposed, as only
Marshall could expose them."[4] Commentators have characterized these
opinions as partaking more of the quality of pronouncements on politics and government than of mere judicial determinations of the law.
Thus *McCulloch* has been praised as an "epochal state paper," the
"greatest of Marshall's treatises on government," and criticized as a "po-

litical state paper."[5] The chief justice in these cases is typically portrayed as essentially a statesman or politician, using his tribunal as "a platform from which to promulgate sound constitutional principles, the very cathedra indeed of constitutional orthodoxy." In this capacity as judicial legislator, he boldly "rewrote the fundamental law of the Nation," transforming a "government of limited and enumerated powers" into a "government of expansive powers."[6]

Chief Justice Marshall would have been quick to deny this assessment, which despite its tone of praise was essentially the same as that made by the most vehement states' rights critics of his decisions. Although recognizing the opportunity presented by these cases to expound constitutional nationalism, he regarded himself as first and foremost a judge whose duty was to decide legal controversies, not promulgate constitutional dogma. And in truth he did not deviate from this role when making his utterances from the bench.[7] In none of his nationalizing opinions did he use the case as a pretext for advocating his brand of nationalism or for answering the theorists of the states' rights school. He did not indulge in constitutional exegesis for his own gratification but to fulfill his duty to consider and respond to arguments put forward by counsel. The passages devoted to expounding the Constitution were not superfluous, extrajudicial obiter dicta but integral to the formation of a reasoned judgment in the case before him. The chief justice, of course, did not act alone. In all the great cases affirming a nationalist interpretation of the Constitution, he had the unanimous or nearly unanimous concurrence of his brethren.

IMPLIED POWERS AND NATIONAL SUPREMACY:
MCCULLOCH V. MARYLAND

In *McCulloch* v. *Maryland,* decided at the 1819 term, the Supreme Court upheld the power of Congress to incorporate the Second Bank of the United States while denying the right of a state to tax the bank. *McCulloch* was an arranged case brought to challenge a Maryland act laying a stamp tax on all banks not chartered by the state legislature. The Second Bank, chartered by act of Congress in 1816, had opened for business in 1817, establishing branches at various locations throughout the country.[8] When James McCulloch, cashier of the Baltimore branch, circulated bank notes that had not been issued on special stamped paper as prescribed by the state law, the state sued him in the local county court. After the Maryland Court of Appeals upheld judgment against McCulloch, the case came up to the Supreme Court by writ of error.

As Marshall observed at the outset of his opinion, the constitutionality of a federally chartered national bank was scarcely an "open question" in 1819.[9] Congress had first issued such a charter in 1791, when the constitutionality of the measure was fully aired in both the legislature and in the cabinet. The question arose again in 1811 when Congress, then under Republican control, refused to renew the bank's charter. Within five years, however, financial disarray resulting from the War of 1812 produced a change of mind among many Republicans, enough of whom put aside their constitutional scruples to secure passage of the bill creating the Second Bank of the United States. The bill was signed by President James Madison, who as a congressman in 1791 had been the leading opponent of the bank.

McCulloch's case thus called upon the Supreme Court to determine the validity of a measure whose constitutionality had been debated and affirmed by the other departments of government. Under the circumstances a holding that Congress had no authority to charter a bank would have been extraordinary. Yet the decision in the bank case provoked harsh public censure in the months following its announcement. This response can be attributed in great part to the unpopularity of the Second Bank, particularly in the southern and western sections of the country, where its policy of contraction proved ruinous to many state banks. At the same time, investigation into the practices of several branch banks revealed mismanagement and corrupt speculation. In the ensuing financial panic and economic depression that gripped the country, the bank became the focus of blame and resentment as the cause of this misery. The tax levied by Maryland was but one example of hostile legislation against the bank enacted in various states in 1818 and 1819.[10]

The impassioned denunciations of *McCulloch* arose not merely from the ruling in the bank's favor but from the broad and emphatic terms in which the Court affirmed Congress's authority to charter the institution. The implications of the decision for the recently revived debate over the extent of federal powers alarmed the jealous guardians of state sovereignty, who regarded the national bank and its branches as tangible proof of the federal government's aggressive encroachment upon the rights of the states and liberties of the people. Not only had Congress forced upon the states an institution whose policies were considered inimical to the people's welfare but the federal judiciary was now declaring that the states could not exercise their sovereign power of taxation to regulate or control this federal instrumentality. The bank case thus aroused all the latent antifederal fears about consolidation that had been lurking near the surface since the Constitution had gone into effect in 1789.

After an argument extending over nine days, Chief Justice Marshall delivered the Supreme Court's judgment on March 6, 1819. His opening paragraph underscored the importance of the occasion: "The constitution of our country, in its most interesting and vital parts, is to be considered; the conflicting powers of the government of the Union and of its members, as marked in that constitution, are to be discussed; and an opinion given, which may essentially influence the great operations of the government."[11] The opinion sought to answer two questions: First, did Congress have power to incorporate a bank? Second, could the state of Maryland constitutionally tax the bank?

The chief justice devoted the greater part of his opinion to the first question. As a prelude to this inquiry, he discussed the nature of the Constitution, the sources of its authority, and the rules for expounding the instrument. These observations responded to arguments by Maryland's counsel founded on the compact theory of the Constitution and designed to prove that the powers of the general government were delegated by the states, which retained all powers not expressly relinquished. Marshall countered by articulating the theory that underlay his constitutional nationalism, namely, that the Constitution was the ordinance of the people of the United States. He derived this theory from the mode of ratification by conventions elected by the people and from the words of the preamble. Conceding that in adopting the Constitution the people acted in their separate states and not as a single mass, he insisted that ratification was no less a measure of the people themselves as distinct from a measure approved by the states as states. The government established by the Constitution was "emphatically, and truly, a government of the people. In form and in substance it emanates from them."[12]

From this theory Marshall formulated another of his celebrated nationalist tenets: the general government, "though limited in its powers, is supreme within its sphere of action." This proposition was evident not only from general reasoning but from that clause declaring the Constitution and laws of the United States to be the "supreme law of the land." Was the power of creating a corporation within the sphere of authority allotted to the general government? Clearly it was not among the enumerated powers, but neither the original Constitution nor the Tenth Amendment (in contrast to the Articles of Confederation) excluded "incidental or implied powers" by confining the government to "expressly" delegated powers. Whether this particular power was delegated to the general government thus depended "on a fair construction of the whole instrument." To make this "fair construction," however, one had to understand the nature of the Constitution. The framers, Marshall observed, deliberately eschewed writing a Constitution that partook "of the prolixity of a legal code." They intended to mark only the "great outlines," to designate the "important objects," leaving the multiplicity of subordinate governmental powers involved in those objects to "be deduced from the nature of the objects themselves." Therefore, said Marshall in a memorable phrase, in conducting an inquiry into the extent and scope of the delegated powers, "we must never forget, that it is *a constitution* we are expounding." By this remark he meant only that the Constitution should not be read as a detailed blueprint for governing; it did not signify approval of the idea of an evolving Constitution.[13]

The chief justice had now carefully prepared the ground for erecting another pillar of constitutional nationalism, the so-called doctrine of "implied powers." Briefly stated, this doctrine held that a general government entrusted with "ample powers" must be presumed to have been entrusted with "ample means" to execute those powers, though these means were not spelled out in the Constitution.[14] Reasoning from the nature of the Constitution, it followed that Congress should have broad discretion in selecting the means that would best accomplish the great purposes confided to it. This principle of construction was founded not only in reason but in the text of the Constitution itself, in that clause granting Congress power to pass all laws "necessary and proper" for executing its enumerated powers. Counsel for Maryland had argued that the word "necessary" was to be understood in the restrictive sense that would have confined Congress to those means only that were "absolutely" or "indispensably necessary."

Marshall expounded this clause at length, invoking common usage, common sense, and other parts of the Constitution to demonstrate that "necessary" must be read less restrictively as enabling Congress to select means that were "convenient" or "conducive" to the beneficial exercise of its express powers. "This provision," he said, "is made in a constitution intended to endure for ages to come, and, consequently, to be adapted to the various *crises* of human affairs. To have prescribed the means by which government should, in all future time, execute its powers, would have been to change, entirely, the character of the instrument, and give it the properties of a legal code." This passage has often been erroneously cited to show that Marshall endorsed the notion of *judicial* adaptation of the Constitution. The context clearly shows, however, that he meant the process of constitutional adaptation to be a *legislative* responsibility.[15]

A careful examination of the "necessary and proper" clause, said Marshall, manifested an intention that its words should not "be construed to restrain the powers of Congress, or to impair the right of the legislature to exercise its best judgment in the selection of measures to carry into execution the constitutional powers of the government." He then formulated a rule for determining the constitutionality of implied powers: "Let the end be legitimate, let it be within the scope of the constitution, and all means which are appropriate, which are plainly adapted to that end, which are not prohibited, but consist with the letter and spirit of the constitution, are constitutional."[16] Applying this criterion, the chief justice had little difficulty in showing that the act incorporating the bank was within the scope of Congress's constitutional powers.

In the briefer second part of his opinion, Marshall employed the principle of national supremacy to demonstrate the existence of implied restrictions on state powers. Counsel for Maryland had contended that the state tax on the bank was constitutional because the states retained their full sovereign powers of taxation except as expressly prohibited from laying import, export, and tonnage duties. The chief justice replied that the "paramount character" of the Constitution had the capacity to restrain the exercise of state sovereignty in cases where it was incompatible with a constitutional federal law. To determine whether Maryland's tax was repugnant to the law incorporating the national bank, he followed his usual method of examining the question first in terms of general principles and then by construing the Constitution. A government's power of taxation, he observed, was theoretically unlimited but was secured from abuse by the influence of constituents over their representatives. This security, however, did not protect the national bank, or any other means employed by the general government to carry out its designated objects, from taxes imposed by a state government. Such means were given by a different constituency—the people of the Union—"and upon theory, should be subjected to that government only which belongs to all."[17]

Marshall admitted that a state's taxing power was coextensive with its sovereignty but denied that this sovereignty extended to means adopted by Congress in execution of its enumerated powers. Those powers were conferred not by the people of a single state but by the people of the United States upon a government whose laws were declared to be supreme. If a state's taxing power was measured by the extent of its sovereignty, the Court would have an "intelligible standard" to apply, one that avoided "clashing sovereignty" and "the incompatibility of a right in one government to destroy what there is a right in another to preserve." Just as the rule formulated in the first part of the opinion avoided judicial investigation into the degree of necessity in determining the constitutionality of an act of Congress, so by this standard judges were "not driven to the perplexing inquiry, so unfit for the judicial department, what degree of taxation is the legitimate use, and what degree may amount to the abuse of power. The attempt to use it on the means employed by the government of the Union . . . is itself an abuse, because it is the usurpation of power which the people of a single State cannot give."[18] The denial of such a right of taxation on the part of the states was founded not only on "just theory" but also on "a fair construction" of the Constitution. To permit any degree of taxation would reverse the supremacy principle; it would enable a single state government to control and defeat the lawful measures of the general government, rendering the supremacy clause an "empty and unmeaning declamation."[19]

The rule in *McCulloch* effectively shielded instrumentalities of the federal government from state taxation. Marshall applied it to void not only the obviously discriminatory and punitive tax enacted by Maryland (and, five years later, the Ohio tax that gave rise to *Osborn* v. *Bank of the United States*) but also a seemingly benign municipal tax on United

States stock. In *Weston v. Charleston* (1829), the chief justice struck down this tax on stock on the ground that it directly interfered with the federal power to borrow money.[20] Acknowledging the "delicate and difficult" duty of applying a rule to limit a state's power of taxation, he reiterated his conviction that "as a necessary consequence" of national supremacy the general government should be able to exercise its powers "free and unembarrassed by any conflicting powers" held by the states.[21] Marshall expounded national supremacy in such comprehensive terms that they could be invoked in subsequent years to justify attempts to extend tax exemptions to corporations and agencies that were indirect instruments of federal power. Yet he never envisioned national supremacy as an offensive weapon to encumber or obstruct the operations of the state governments. He conceived it rather as a conservative and defensive constitutional principle to enable the general government to freely exercise its limited powers and to resist state encroachment on its jurisdiction.

In *McCulloch* Chief Justice Marshall restated principles that had enjoyed a long currency in American constitutional discourse. As early as 1791, for example, Alexander Hamilton had offered a classic defense of implied powers in advising President Washington to sign the bank bill. Marshall was thoroughly familiar with Hamilton's opinion, having published a lengthy extract of it (along with Jefferson's opinion) in a note to his *Life of Washington*. His construction of the "necessary and proper" clause also closely followed Hamilton's. Scarcely a passage in the first part of *McCulloch* could not be traced to Hamilton's advisory opinion or to some earlier writing, speech, or legal argument. Yet the enduring fame of *McCulloch* does not rest on the originality of its ideas but in the way its author gathered up various familiar strands of interpretation and wove them together into a masterly exposition of the Constitution.

McCulloch came down emphatically in favor of reading the Constitution as conferring on Congress wide latitude in determining the extent of its express powers. Such a reading also abridged state powers more stringently than did the express prohibitions. As a statement of the doctrine of implied powers and principle of national supremacy, and more generally as an inquiry into the nature and meaning of the Constitution, *McCulloch* ranks among the greatest of Marshall's opinions. Later generations of legislators and jurists frequently invoked its eloquent phrases to justify the great expansion of national power that occurred in the late nineteenth and twentieth centuries. As an expression of constitutional nationalism, however, *McCulloch* is not to be understood as a prescient anticipation of the modern liberal state, in which a federal government of vastly augmented powers has assumed primary responsibility for regulating the economy and promoting social welfare. Neither praise nor blame for this development is properly ascribed to Marshall or his Court.

Despite contemporary fulminations against the "consolidating" doctrines of *McCulloch*, the nationalism endorsed by that opinion is more accurately defined in negative or defensive terms—concerned primarily with preserving the union against powerful centrifugal tendencies that constantly threatened its dissolution. The opinion purported not to enhance the powers of the federal government but to enable that government to exercise its powers effectively and to prevent state encroachments upon its legitimate operations. By "implied powers" Marshall meant no more than that Congress should be able to choose the means for executing an enumerated power. He did not intend to suggest that Congress, in addition to its delegated powers, could tap a vast reservoir of other powers that were not expressly granted but could be implied because Congress was the legislative branch of the national government.[22] Nor did Marshall's argument so much affirm a "broad" (a term he did not use) construction of Congress's powers as reject the restrictive construction adopted by Maryland's counsel. The latter construction, Marshall contended, would emasculate the general government, preventing it from carrying out the important objects entrusted to it by the Constitution. A government so tightly tethered would scarcely be more effective than Congress under the former Confederation. His overriding concern was that strict construction would inexorably transform the union into a league of sovereign states—a belated triumph for antifederalism.

It is worth remarking that Marshall, in contrast to certain nationalist congressmen, never appealed to the "general welfare" clause as a source of national power, for example, as conferring on Congress a general power over internal improvements. Although the clause never came before him judicially, he privately remarked in 1828 that he had "never believed that the words 'to pay the debts and provide for the common defence and general welfare of the United States' were to be considered as a substantive grant of power, but as a declaration of objects for which taxes etc. might be levied." On the question of internal improvements, Marshall considered a general power as inexpedient whether or not it was constitutional. To make internal improvements for "military purposes or for the transportation of the mail," however, the power could "be exercised to great advantage, and, there is much reason for thinking, consistently with the constitution."[23]

JUDICIAL NATIONALISM: *COHENS* V. *VIRGINIA* AND *OSBORN* V. *BANK OF THE UNITED STATES*

McCulloch v. *Maryland* dealt with the scope and extent of the legislative powers of the general government and established a standard for determining when the exercise of a federal power operated as a limitation on the otherwise sovereign power of a state. It also implicitly reaffirmed the authority of the Supreme Court to void a state law and to reverse a decision of a state court. More broadly, it asserted the right and duty of the Supreme Court to decide questions involving the conflicting powers of the general and state governments. Marshall did not need to justify this assertion in his opinion, however, for the arguments of counsel did not challenge the Supreme Court's jurisdiction in the case. Just such a challenge was raised in two subsequent cases, *Cohens* v. *Virginia* and *Osborn* v. *Bank of the United States,* which elicited the chief justice's most elaborate inquiries into the constitutional foundations and extent of federal judicial power.

During the two years between *McCulloch* and the hearing of *Cohens* at the February 1821 term, attacks on the Supreme Court had continued virtually without cessation. The loudest and most sustained assault came from Virginia, led by the redoubtable Spencer Roane, eminent judge of the state supreme court. An opponent of the Constitution in 1788, Roane had distinguished himself as an outspoken champion of states' rights in resisting the Supreme Court's mandate in an 1813 case reversing a judgment of the Virginia Court of Appeals. At that time Roane and his fellow judges denied the Supreme Court's appellate jurisdiction over the judgments of state tribunals. This defiance in turn produced the Supreme Court's 1816 decision in *Martin* v. *Hunter's Lessee.* With Marshall not sitting because of a personal interest in the case, Joseph

Story delivered an opinion affirming the Supreme Court's authority under the Constitution to review decisions of state courts.[24] Three years later Roane, writing as "Hampden" in the pages of the Richmond *Enquirer*, delivered a stinging indictment of *McCulloch*. His essential charge was that the decision manifested a sinister design to overthrow the Constitution, to prostrate the rights of the states and of the people, and establish a consolidated government of unlimited powers. Roane's diatribe followed that of William Brockenbrough, another Virginia jurist, who called himself "Amphictyon." The swelling chorus of hostile newspaper criticism provoked Marshall to take up his pen in defense of the Court and its decision, carefully hiding his identity behind the pseudonyms "A Friend to the Union" and "A Friend of the Constitution." In all he produced eleven "Friend" pieces in the spring and summer of 1819, two in reply to Amphictyon and nine in reply to Hampden.[25]

The motive behind this extraordinary extrajudicial defense of *McCulloch* was the chief justice's growing apprehension that the antagonism directed against the Court was the entering wedge of a broader assault on the Constitution and the union itself aimed at its most vulnerable point, the federal judiciary. The Court's attackers,

> like skilful engineers, batter the weakest part of the citadel, knowing well, that if that can be beaten down, and a breach effected, it will be afterwards found very difficult, if not impracticable, to defend the place. The judicial department, being without power, without patronage, without the legitimate means of ingratiating itself with the people, forms this weakest part; and is, at the same time, necessary to the very existence of the government, and to the effectual execution of its laws.[26]

Marshall worried that Virginia's renewed "antifederal spirit" would produce measures that would effectively dismantle the national government. His suspicion that the real aim of the anti-Court agitation was to convert the Constitution "into the old Confederation" seemed to be confirmed by Roane (Hampden) himself, who claimed that the present general government was "as much a federal government, or a 'league,'" as was the former confederation."[27]

None of the charges Roane leveled against *McCulloch* cut more deeply than his contention that the Supreme Court had no jurisdiction to decide that case or any other involving a clash of powers between the general and state governments. Frankly likening the Constitution to a league of independent sovereign states or compact between the general government and state governments, Roane insisted that in such a system there was no superior authority that could bind the contracting parties, who alone were the proper judges to decide whether infractions of the compact had occurred. If the general government, as one party to the compact, could not be the exclusive or final judge of the meaning of the compact, then the judiciary, as a subordinate department of that government, was not an impartial and competent tribunal to decide on the extent of the powers delegated to the government of the union.[28]

Marshall retorted that the Constitution was neither a league nor a compact but was "itself a government, created for the nation by the whole American people." The people, not the general government or the state governments, were the sole "party" to this act. It followed from this understanding of the nature of the Constitution that the judicial department of the general government was "not a partial, local tribunal" but a "national" tribunal created for the purpose of deciding national questions. In deciding those questions that assumed a judicial form, the judiciary was the government itself, acting on behalf of the whole people, not as the agent of a particular government. The judges, moreover, being selected "from the great body of the people" and made "perfectly independent" by tenure for life, were as disinterested as "imperfect human institutions" could make them. To confide such questions to this tribunal, then, was not at all a case of allowing a party to sit in his own cause.[29]

If reasoning from the nature of the Constitution did not make plain the framers' intention of entrusting to the judiciary the duty of deciding controversies concerning the respective powers of the general and state governments, the question was settled beyond all doubt by the express declaration in Article 3: "The judicial Power shall extend to all Cases, in Law and Equity, arising under this Constitution, the laws of the United States, and Treaties made, or which shall be made, under their Authority."[30] Here in the concluding pages of his "Friend" essays Marshall announced the theme he would develop at length in *Cohens* and *Osborn*, namely, the "arising under" clause as the basis for an enlarged conception of the jurisdiction conferred upon the federal judiciary.

Cohens was nicely timed to give Marshall an opportunity to respond judicially to Roane and other states' rights champions who denied the federal judiciary's authority to adjudicate cases that hinged on the interpretation of the respective powers of the general and state governments. The case began in June 1820 with a criminal indictment against the brothers Philip and Mendes Cohen, Norfolk merchants, for selling lottery tickets authorized under the 1802 act of Congress incorporating the District of Columbia. This sale was alleged to be in violation of an act of the Virginia legislature prohibiting the sale of lottery tickets not authorized by the laws of the commonwealth. In September 1820 the Norfolk borough court found the Cohens guilty and assessed a fine of one hundred dollars. This judgment was not reviewable by any higher state court, so the brothers took their case directly to the Supreme Court on a writ of error under section 25 of the Judiciary Act.

A case could not have been better designed to alarm the zealous guardians of states' rights. That Virginia should be cited to appear at the bar of the Supreme Court to defend its right to enforce its own penal laws was regarded as a monstrous invasion of state sovereignty and independence. Before the case was argued, the state legislature issued a report and resolutions denying the Supreme Court's jurisdiction. Another resolution instructed the lawyers appearing for the commonwealth to argue only the question of jurisdiction, and if that should be sustained, they should "consider their duties at an end."[31] Virginia's counsel urged a number of arguments against the jurisdiction. They contended that the case did not arise under the Constitution or a law of the United States; that the Supreme Court's appellate jurisdiction did not extend to state judiciaries; and, most important, "that a sovereign and independent State is not liable to the suit of any individual, nor amenable to any judicial power, without its own consent."[32]

On March 3, 1821, Chief Justice Marshall on behalf of a unanimous Court upheld the Supreme Court's jurisdiction. He began his opinion by taking up the most important objection, that the jurisdiction was excluded by the circumstance that a state was a party. This objection brought forth a lengthy analysis and construction of Article 3, section 2, which divided federal jurisdiction into two classes of cases: first, those whose jurisdiction depended on the character of the cause, which included all cases arising under the Constitution and laws of the United States; and second, those whose jurisdiction depended on the character of the parties, which embraced controversies between two or more states, between a state and citizens of another state, and between a state and foreign states, citizens, or subjects. Once again relying on a literal reading of the Constitution's words as the safest guide to intent, Marshall observed that in the first class jurisdiction extended to "all cases" arising under the Constitution and laws. Any exception among cases of this character could only be sustained by appeal to "the spirit and true meaning" of the Constitution that was so obvious as to overrule its express words.[33]

Did the principle that a sovereign state could not be sued without its consent exclude jurisdiction in this case? Without denying the principle, Marshall maintained that "a just construction" of the Constitution showed that the state had given its consent, that is, had relinquished its "sovereign right of judging in every case" and "entrusted that power to a tribunal in whose impartiality it confides."[34] In support of this construction he restated the national supremacy principle first enunciated in *McCulloch:* "The general government, though limited as to its objects, is supreme with respect to those objects." The Constitution abridged state sovereignty by express prohibitions and by implied restrictions necessary to maintain the general government's supreme authority. State sovereignty was also surrendered, added the chief justice, where "no other power is conferred on Congress than a conservative power to maintain the principles established in the constitution." The judiciary was an institution for peacefully performing the important duty of maintaining "these principles in their purity." In short, the nature and spirit of the Constitution did not sanction any departure from its express words that would oust jurisdiction because a state was a party. The federal judiciary had cognizance of a case arising under the Constitution and laws "whoever may be the parties to that case."[35]

Marshall further supported an enlarged construction of the "arising under" clause by appealing to the "political axiom" that "the judicial power of every well-constituted government must be co-extensive with the legislative."[36] In framing a Constitution "for ages to come" and "designed to approach immortality as nearly as human institutions can approach it," the framers surely were not so unwise as to have failed to provide the general government "with the means of self-preservation from the perils it may be destined to encounter." Such an omission certainly could not be inferred from the historical circumstances attending the formation of the Constitution, notably the inability of the Confederation government to obtain compliance with its laws. One remedy for this radical defect was the Constitution's provision for a national judiciary. The Constitution, of course, could not provide against a determined and general resistance to the measures of the general government, but this was no reason for denying that the government possessed constitutional means to defend against partial and local opposition "to the general will."[37]

Assuming that federal jurisdiction did extend without exception to all cases arising under the Constitution and laws, Virginia's counsel objected that the Supreme Court could exercise only original jurisdiction where a state was a party. Article 3 declared that the Supreme Court was to have original jurisdiction in cases "affecting Ambassadors, other public Ministers and Consuls, and those in which a State shall be Party." In all other cases, including those arising under the Constitution and laws, it was to have appellate jurisdiction. But which rule was to apply to a case in which a state was a party and which also arose under the Constitution and laws? In this situation the Court's duty was "so to construe the constitution as to give effect to both provisions, as far as it is possible to reconcile them, and not permit their seeming repugnancy to destroy each other. We must endeavor so to construe them as to preserve the true intent and meaning of the instrument."[38]

The result of Marshall's intricate textual analysis of the "distributive" clause was that the "affirmative words" conferring original jurisdiction in cases where a state was a party should not be read "negatively" to deny appellate jurisdiction if the case also arose under the Constitution and laws. A negative reading, the chief justice pointed out, would in effect defeat the jurisdiction in cases arising under the Constitution and laws because such jurisdiction could only be exercised in appellate form. The true intent of the distributive clause was to enable the Supreme Court to exercise its appellate jurisdiction in every case cognizable by federal courts "in which original jurisdiction cannot be exercised." The Court could find no exception—such as the circumstance that a state was a party—to the grant of appellate jurisdiction in all cases arising under the Constitution and laws.[39]

This construction was unaffected by the Eleventh Amendment, which declared that federal jurisdiction should "not be construed to extend to any suit . . . commenced or prosecuted against" a state "by Citizens of

another State, or by Citizens or Subjects of any Foreign State." Both
the history and language of this amendment, argued Marshall, showed
that its purpose was merely to bar suits brought by individual creditors
against the states, not to restore the sovereign dignity of the states. No
intention could be read into it "to strip the government of the means of
protecting, by the instrumentality of its courts, the constitution and
laws from active violation."[40] After citing eminent legal authorities such
as Blackstone, Coke, and Bacon concerning the meaning of "suit" and
"writ of error," he concluded that the writ of error in the present case,
which was brought to reverse a judgment against the Cohens in the
state court on the ground that it violated the Constitution or laws of the
United States, was not a suit commenced or prosecuted against the
state in the sense meant by the Eleventh Amendment. In any event, the
case was not embraced by that amendment because the Cohens were
not citizens of another state.

The chief justice next considered a second major objection raised
by Virginia's counsel: that the Supreme Court's appellate power could
not be exercised to revise judgments of state courts. Despite the decision in *Martin* v. *Hunter's Lessee* and the long practice of bringing cases
from the state courts to the Supreme Court under section 25 of the
Judiciary Act, the state contended that the Constitution did not confer appellate jurisdiction over the state courts. The federal and state
judicial systems, counsel argued, were completely separate and independent of each other. The Supreme Court's appellate jurisdiction
was merely an authority to revise the decisions of inferior *federal*
courts.

In rejecting the "hypothesis" that the two systems were independent,
Marshall restated his own nationalist premises, which he claimed were
founded on both the spirit and express words of the Constitution.
"That the United States," he said, "form, for many, and for most important purposes, a single nation, has not yet been denied. In war, we are
one people. In making peace, we are one people. In all commercial
regulations, we are one and the same people." The government established by the American people for these and other national purposes
was "complete," "competent," and "supreme," and in carrying out its
purposes could "legitimately control all individuals or governments
within the American territory." It was not only reasonable in such a
government that the judicial power should extend to the state judicia-

ries but entirely compatible with the nature of a government declared to be supreme with respect to the objects entrusted to it.[41]

If federal jurisdiction embraced all cases arising under the Constitution and laws, Marshall reasoned, then federal courts should have either exclusive jurisdiction or power to revise state judgments in such cases. Concurrent jurisdiction without an appeal to the Supreme Court would subject the Constitution and federal laws to confusing and contradictory interpretations. Thus "the necessity of uniformity as well as correctness in expounding the constitution and laws of the United States, would itself suggest the propriety of vesting in some single tribunal the power of deciding, in the last resort, all cases in which they are involved." But again, the clinching argument was the constitutional text. The words conferring appellate jurisdiction were "broad enough to comprehend all cases" arising under the Constitution and laws no matter in what court they originated. Marshall added that both the historical circumstances of the Constitution and its "contemporary exposition" by the authors of *Federalist* and of the Judiciary Act reinforced the correctness of this construction.[42]

One last objection remained. Admitting the constitutional validity of section 25, counsel for Virginia denied that the act of Congress relied on by the Cohens was a law of the United States or such a law as could override Virginia's penal laws. In exercising its power of exclusive legislation over the District of Columbia, Congress was not the legislature of the union but a mere local legislature whose acts—such as that authorizing the lottery in this case—had no obligation outside the federal district. Marshall rejected this proposition, insisting that Congress's legislation for the district was no different in form, character, or obligation from that arising from its other powers. Congress, he said, "unites the power of local legislation with those which are to operate through the Union, and may use the last in aid of the first." It was "not a local legislature" but exercised its power of exclusive legislation for the district "in its high character, as the legislature of the Union."[43]

The entire thrust of Marshall's argument went to sustain the Supreme Court's jurisdiction, that is, its authority to adjudge the *merits* of the Cohens' claim. After hearing arguments on the merits, the Court rejected that claim a few days later and upheld the fine levied by the Norfolk borough court. It concluded that in establishing the corporate government of the District of Columbia, Congress did not intend for the corporation's acts to have any obligation beyond the geographical limits of the district—and certainly not so as to interfere with a state's police powers. This judgment did not, to be sure, mollify the outraged partisans of state sovereignty, who perceived correctly that the question of jurisdiction was everything in this case. Once again, the Supreme Court was subjected to wrathful harangues (with Roane leading the way), which in turn led to proposals for curbing the Court's powers.[44]

In view of the seemingly evident lack of merit to the Cohens' claim and of the risk of provoking further attacks on the federal judiciary, Marshall might well have declined hearing this case as the more prudent course. But the consequences of refusing jurisdiction overrode this consideration. The chief justice and his brethren had to look beyond the immediate case to the broader issue at stake—whether or not the Supreme Court was to be the ultimate expositor of the Constitution and federal laws and a tribunal of last resort for peacefully adjudicating disputes that involved a conflict between federal and state powers. Persuaded beyond all doubt that the Constitution itself ordained this role for the judiciary, Marshall concluded that the Court had no choice in this matter:

> It is most true that this court will not take jurisdiction if it should not, but it is equally true, that it must take jurisdiction if it should. The judiciary cannot, as the legislature may, avoid a measure because it approaches the confines of the constitution. We cannot pass it by because it is doubtful. . . . We have no more right to decline the exercise of jurisdiction which is given, than to usurp that which is not given. The one or the other is treason to the constitution.[45]

Three years after *Cohens* Marshall reaffirmed and extended the principles of judicial nationalism in *Osborn* v. *Bank of the United States*, which had been working its way to the Supreme Court since 1819. Like *McCulloch* this case arose from a state's attempt to tax the national bank. In February 1819 the Ohio legislature laid a prohibitive tax of $50,000 on each branch of the bank in the state. Despite the decision in *McCulloch*, state officials proceeded to collect the tax by entering the vault of the Chillicothe branch and taking away $120,000 in notes and specie. In response, the bank sought an injunction and instituted a suit for damages against the state officials in the United States Circuit Court. That court, in September 1821, issued a decree ordering the state officials to return the money and enjoining collection of the tax. The defendants appealed to the Supreme Court, where the case was argued in 1823 and again in 1824. In the midst of these legal proceedings the Ohio legislature adopted a report and resolutions denouncing federal jurisdiction in *Osborn* as a violation of the state's constitutional rights, rejecting the reasoning of *McCulloch,* and protesting the Supreme Court's jurisdiction to settle the "political rights" of sovereign states in suits "contrived between individuals."[46]

Osborn, like *Cohens,* raised the issue of a state's sovereign immunity to suits by individuals, though the state of Ohio was not a party of record. In argument counsel for Osborn (one of the Ohio officials involved in collecting the tax) urged a number of points for reversing the decree of the federal circuit court. First, however, the court had to consider the constitutionality and effect of the provision in the 1816 incorporating act that authorized the bank to sue in the federal circuit courts. Two questions presented themselves: Did Congress intend by this provision to give a right to sue in the federal courts? If so, could Congress constitutionally confer this jurisdiction?

Marshall answered both questions affirmatively in his opinion for the Court pronounced on March 19, 1824. The words of the incorporating act, he said, expressly conferred jurisdiction on the federal circuit courts to hear suits brought by and against the bank. He sustained Congress's constitutional power to confer this jurisdiction by the same broad reading of the judiciary article of the Constitution he had employed in *Cohens.* Again he invoked the "axiom" that the legislative, executive, and judicial powers "of every well constructed government, are co-extensive with each other." The framers embodied "this great political principle" in the clause extending federal judicial power to all cases arising under the Constitution and laws of the United States. This clause enabled the federal judiciary "to receive jurisdiction to the full extent" of federal law when questions arising under that law assumed a judicial form.[47]

Controversies in which the bank was a party typically involved questions depending on the law of contract, not on any act of Congress. How could such cases be considered as arising under a law of the United States? Marshall answered this objection by observing that there was "scarcely any case, every part of which depends on the constitution, laws, or treaties of the United States." If it were necessary that the whole case depend on questions arising under federal law for federal jurisdiction to attach, then this clause "would be reduced to almost nothing." The chief justice also dismissed the objection that federal jurisdiction in cases arising under federal law could only be exercised in appellate form. That the Constitution placed such cases within the Supreme Court's appellate jurisdiction did not preclude original jurisdiction by inferior federal courts. "Original jurisdiction, so far as the constitution gives a rule, is co-extensive with the judicial power," he said.[48]

Although a case might depend on several questions of law and fact, the chief justice held that Congress could confer jurisdiction on the federal circuit courts so long as a federal question formed "an ingredient" of the original action. This condition was fully met in cases where the bank was a party, he said, for all of that institution's rights and capacities were founded on the act incorporating the bank. A case arising on a contract, for example, might ultimately be decided on the common law, but still the foundation of the bank's right to sue or to contract was a federal law. These questions entered into every case in which the bank was plaintiff even if not relied on by the defense. The plaintiff's right to sue could not "depend on the defence which the defendant may choose to set up," for this right was "anterior to that defence." Thus the act incorporating the bank "is the first ingredient in the case, is its origin, is that from which every other part arises."[49] There was no difference in principle, observed Marshall, between the act giving the bank access to the federal circuit courts and those acts authorizing federal officers and holders of patents to sue in those courts. At the same time he denied any resemblance between the act incorporating the bank and an act of naturalization. The former prescribed in detail the rights and capacities of the bank, while an act of naturalization did nothing more than place naturalized citizens on the same footing as natives with respect to the right to sue.

Marshall's construction of the "arising under" clause to uphold the constitutionality of original federal jurisdiction in this case was of immense importance in giving the much maligned Bank of the United States frontline legal protection. Without this jurisdiction, the Second Bank of the United States would have been forced to seek redress in the first instance in the state courts, where the prospects for justice were at best uncertain. Although the bank would still have the remedy of appealing an adverse state court decision to the Supreme Court, many of the staunch defenders of state sovereignty who denied original federal jurisdiction also denied the Supreme Court's appellate power over the state courts. In providing the bank immediate access to the federal courts, Congress, Marshall emphasized, was not bestowing any jurisdiction that was not already fully conferred by the Constitution. Just as Congress under the "necessary and proper" clause had broad discretionary power to select means for executing its express powers, so under the "arising under" clause it could choose to extend or not to extend federal jurisdiction to the full limit allowed by the Constitution.

After disposing of this constitutional question, the court took up seven objections to the lower court's decree, most of which turned on technical legal points. The last two raised broader questions, one concerning a state's sovereign immunity to lawsuits by individuals, the other reopening the issue of the constitutionality of a state tax on the national bank. The former objection asserted that the federal court could not exercise jurisdiction because the actual defendant below was the state of Ohio. Osborn's counsel insisted that a suit against the state's agents could not evade the barrier to federal jurisdiction posed by the Eleventh Amendment. Acknowledging the "full pressure of this argument," Marshall admitted that the state had a "direct interest" in this case. The "very difficult question" was whether the federal court in this case could "act upon the agents employed by the State, and on the property in their hands." He prefaced his answer with a favorite rhetorical device—reciting the dire consequences of the argument against which he was contending. A denial of jurisdiction, he warned, would mean that each state was "capable, at its will, of attacking the nation, of arresting its progress at every step, of acting vigorously and effectually in the execution of its designs, while the nation stands naked, stripped of its defensive armour, and incapable of shielding its agent or executing its laws, otherwise than by proceedings which are to take place after the mischief is perpetrated."[50]

The issue, as the chief justice framed it, was whether the federal courts could protect federal officials from a state's attempts to resist execution of federal laws. Did the Constitution's provisions concerning cases in which a state was a party extend "on a fair construction" to cases in which the state had a substantial interest but was not a formal party of record? A close inquiry showed that the framers did not provide for cases where the state had an interest without being a party. If jurisdiction was to depend on the state's interest, the Constitution supplied no rule for measuring that interest. Marshall concluded his investigation by formulating a rule that "in all cases where jurisdiction depends on the party, it is the party named in the record."[51] The Eleventh Amendment therefore did not embrace this case because Ohio was not a party of record. As in *Cohens*, the court restricted the reach of that amendment, holding in this instance that a state's sovereign immunity could not protect its agents from individual liability for acts committed under authority of an unconstitutional law.

There remained the state's contention that it could constitutionally tax the bank notwithstanding the decision in *McCulloch*. Although not questioning either the constitutionality of the bank or the holding that a state could not tax the offices, institutions, and operations of the national government, counsel maintained that the bank was a corporation engaged in private trade for private profit. As an essentially private institution, the bank could not claim exemption from state taxation. This argument had received little attention in *McCulloch*, and the Court used this occasion to supply the omission. Marshall reaffirmed the earlier decision by insisting that the bank was "a public corporation, created for public and national purposes," a statement reminiscent of his opinion in *Dartmouth*. The two cases were dissimilar, however, for the question in *Osborn* was not whether a state could alter the charter of a *private* corporation created by the state's sovereign authority but whether a state could tax a *public* corporation created by the federal government. The bank retained its character as a public corporation, said the chief justice, even though it had the capacity to transact private business. Indeed, the bank's faculty for lending and dealing in money was indispensable to accomplishing its public purposes, enabling it to be "a machine for the fiscal operations of the government."[52] It was therefore necessary that the bank's commercial transactions be exempt from state control. As in *McCulloch*, the Court ruled that the Ohio act, which was "certainly much more objectionable than" the Maryland act, was void as repugnant to a federal law.

In this concluding section of *Osborn* Marshall uttered his most famous pronouncement about the nature of judicial power. Counsel had argued that if Congress intended the bank to be exempt from taxation, the act of incorporation would have expressly declared this exemption. Marshall replied that it was not unusual for an act "to imply, without expressing," such an exemption, citing the examples of revenue collectors, mail carriers, and other public agents who are protected in the line of duty without any act of Congress explicitly providing this protection. Their security was provided by the judicial department. "That department," said Marshall, "has no will, in any case. If the sound construction of the act be, that it exempts the trade of the Bank, as essential to the character of a machine necessary to the fiscal operations of the government, from the control of the States, Courts are as much bound to give it that construction, as if the exemption had been established in express terms." He continued:

> Judicial power, as contradistinguished from the power of the laws, has no existence. Courts are the mere instruments of the law, and can will nothing. When they are said to exercise a discretion, it is a mere legal discretion, a discretion to be exercised in discerning the course prescribed by law; and, when that is discerned, it is the duty of the Court to follow it. Judicial power is never exercised for the purpose of giving effect to the will of the Judge; always for the purpose of giving effect to the will of the Legislature; or, in other words, to the will of the law.[53]

As plainly shown by the context of this passage, the "judicial power" here distinguished was nothing more than the ordinary and uncontroversial practice by which courts construed the acts of legislatures. Yet the passage can be read broadly to embrace the practice of judicial review, which Marshall understood to be a special category of statutory construction. Hence a court's exercise of judicial review was no more an act of "will" than was statutory construction. Modern legal realists tend to dismiss Marshall's disclaimer of judicial will as empty rhetoric, belied by his own career as a shaper of American constitutional law. Marshall, wrote a distinguished twentieth-century jurist, "gave to the constitution of the United States the impress of his own mind; and the form of our constitutional law is what it is, because he moulded it while it was still plastic and malleable in the fire of his own intense convictions."[54] Much the same thing was said of the chief justice in his own time, though not to praise but to denounce him. In either case he would have indignantly rejected the notion that he exercised will in expounding the Constitution and laws.

In stating that courts were "the mere instruments of the law" and could "will nothing," Marshall by no means endorsed the "machine" model of judging. Judges were not simply automatons who mechanically fitted the appropriate precedent or statute to the case at hand. They exercised "judgment," what he modestly called "mere legal discretion." But discretion, even "mere legal discretion," implies choice. The chief justice recognized and admitted that the task of "discerning the course prescribed by law," of applying the law to questions of right arising from disputes between individuals, compelled judges to choose among a range of plausible interpretations. So long as in making this choice they were "guided by sound legal principles"—the well-known principles of the common law, including the commonly accepted rules for interpreting statutes—judges did not exercise will.[55]

Courts and judges, then, operated within the relatively confined realm of legal discretion, which still gave them opportunity to shape the law, even in a sense to "make" it. The possibilities for creative jurisprudence were greatest, of course, in the uncharted field of constitutional law. Quite apart from the chief justice's superior intellectual powers and genius for leadership, the Marshall Court, simply by being the first to consider a particular question, could not help but make path-breaking decisions. The point, though, is that even in cases where it issued important constitutional pronouncements the Court professed to be exercising judgment, not will. If judgment in constitutional cases consisted of giving the Constitution a "fair construction"; of trying to discover its meaning or "spirit" in its actual words and, where the words were not unambiguously clear, by reading them with reference to the subject, context, and purposes disclosed in the instrument itself; and of giving due consideration to alternative constructions and explaining why they were defective, then Marshall and his Court cannot be fairly charged with transcending the boundaries of legal discretion.

To maintain that the Marshall Court "willed" a particular result—for example, that *Cohens* and *Osborn* expanded federal jurisdiction beyond what Congress intended and what the Constitution prescribed—it is not enough to show that the Court could have adopted a less nationalistic stance. It would be necessary to show that the Court's methods and reasoning in reaching that result did not adhere to "sound legal principles." Yet the dominant impression one gets from reading Marshall's great opinions is their close resemblance to ordinary legal adjudications. He investigated momentous questions of constitutional law using the same methods of legal analysis and reasoning that he employed in his mundane cases. These investigations were undertaken, moreover, not simply to expound the Constitution but to decide the particular case before him. Chief Justice Marshall never forgot that his domain was a court of law and that this circumstance was at once a limitation on and source of strength for the exercise of judicial power.

THE COMMERCE POWER: *GIBBONS* V. *OGDEN*

In addition to *Osborn*, the docket of the 1824 term of the Supreme Court contained another case of immense national significance: *Gibbons* v. *Ogden*, popularly known as the "steamboat monopoly" case. *Gibbons* presented still another variation on the theme of nationalism and states' rights. Where *McCulloch* endorsed a broad reading of Congress's implied powers and *Cohens* and *Osborn* set forth an expansive view of the reach of federal judicial power, *Gibbons* dealt with the nature and extent of one of the general government's enumerated powers, the regulation of commerce with foreign nations and "among the several States." No part of the Constitution has proved a more fertile source of national power than the commerce clause. Upon this constitutional foundation Congress erected the federal regulatory state that emerged in the twentieth century. As the first Supreme Court case to construe the commerce clause, *Gibbons* has often been cited as a landmark judicial precedent for extensive national power. Like Marshall's other nationalizing opinions, however, the principal significance of *Gibbons* lay not so much in building up and centralizing federal power as in circumscribing state power.

The case originated in legal efforts to break a monopoly on steamboat navigation in New York waters, which the legislature of that state had granted to Robert Livingston and Robert Fulton in 1808, shortly after the successful demonstration of Fulton's *Clermont* on the Hudson River. Steamboats soon developed into an important means of transportation along the coasts and on the rivers penetrating the interior of the country. State jealousy threatened to disrupt the free development of interstate trade by this new technology, however, as several states passed laws forbidding steamboats licensed by the New York monopoly to navigate their waters and others began to grant their own steamboat monopoly rights. These measures called to mind the ruinous retaliatory commercial restrictions enacted by the states during the Confederation.[56]

In New York the Livingston-Fulton interests had repeatedly fought off legal challenges to the monopoly, most recently in 1820, when the state court of appeals upheld an injunction obtained by Aaron Ogden against Thomas Gibbons. Ogden held a license under the New York monopoly to operate a steamboat ferry from New York City to Elizabethtown, New Jersey. Gibbons, the operator of a rival steamboat line, held a federal coasting license under a law enacted by Congress in 1793. He appealed the New York decision under section 25 of the Judiciary Act, claiming his right under federal law to operate steamboats notwithstanding the New York laws that granted Ogden's exclusive right.

The case attracted widespread public interest because the Court's decision was likely to have momentous economic consequences. The immediate question was whether steamboat navigation on the coastal and inland waters of the United States would continue to be controlled by state-oriented monopolies or be opened to free competition. More broadly, the case promised to clarify the federal government's role in establishing a unified economic policy, either by restricting state legislation or by promoting its own programs. Unlike *McCulloch* and *Osborn*, where federal power was aligned with a monopolistic financial institution, in *Gibbons* state power was arrayed on the side of an unpopular monopoly. The Court thus had a rare opportunity to render a decision against states' rights that would also meet with broad public approval.

The hearing of the appeal was delayed until the 1824 term, when it was exhaustively argued over five days. Among the questions thoroughly aired were these: What was commerce? Did the term also embrace navigation? Did the power to regulate commerce reside exclusively or principally with Congress? Or did Congress and the states share this power "concurrently"? Chief Justice Marshall delivered the Court's answer to these questions on March 2, 1824. He began by asserting that strict construction did not properly apply to the government of the Constitution, however appropriate that rule might have been under the Articles of Confederation. The conversion of a league into a government changed the "whole character" of the relationship between the states and the general government, he said, "the extent of which must be determined by a fair consideration" of the Constitution. Nothing in the Constitution countenanced strict construction if by that term was meant a "narrow construction" that, ignoring the plain language of the instrument, "would cripple the government, and render it unequal to the objects for which it is declared to be instituted, and to which the powers given, as fairly understood, render it competent." The meaning of the Constitution, as he had so often urged before, must be extracted from its words understood "in their natural sense." And where the meaning was doubtful "from the imperfection of human language," the "well settled rule" was to look to the "objects" for which a power was given. "We know of no rule for construing the extent of such powers," said the chief justice, "other than is given by the language of the instrument which confers them, taken in connexion with the purposes for which they were conferred."[57]

Marshall then examined the language of the commerce clause. The word "commerce," he contended, embraced not merely "traffic"—the buying and selling of goods—but "intercourse"—commercial relations in all its branches including "navigation." If navigation was not a constituent element of commerce, then Congress had no power over the subject and Gibbons's appeal must fail, for the transporting of passengers by ferry clearly belonged to navigation. In fact, however, there could be no doubt that the general government from its commencement had exercised the power to regulate navigation and that the word commerce had been "uniformly understood" to include navigation. This enlarged meaning was not only consistent with other parts of the Constitution but was implicitly confirmed by Congress's "universally acknowledged power" of laying embargoes.[58]

The next inquiry concerned the extent of the commerce power, particularly as it related to commerce "among the several States." Marshall interpreted this phrase to mean that Congress's power of regulation was limited to commerce concerning more than one state and did not reach "the exclusively internal commerce" of a particular state.[59] Thus limited, however, the power to regulate did not stop at the boundary lines of a state but was to be exercised wherever foreign or interstate commerce existed—which could be in a particular district, county, or town within a state. The power to regulate, moreover, was "complete in itself, may be exercised to its utmost extent, and acknowledges no limitations, other than are prescribed in the constitution." This power was "vested in Congress as absolutely as it would be in a single government" having the same restrictions found in the Constitution. Congress's "wisdom and discretion" and the vigilance and influence of the people were the "sole restraints" on the abuse of this power.[60]

Given that Congress's power to regulate commerce was plenary, was this power exclusive or did the states retain a right to exercise the same power within their jurisdictions? Ogden's counsel strenuously contended for the doctrine of "concurrent power," conceding only that state regulations must yield when there was direct collision with federal law—and that the present case did not involve such a collision. With equal vigor Gibbons's counsel maintained that this power was exclusive in nature. From these arguments Marshall fashioned a unique synthesis that leaned toward exclusive power while recognizing as a practical matter the states' concurrent power in this area.

The chief justice devoted most of his attention to the concurrent power argument. Counsel had cited the Constitution, acts of Congress, and state laws to demonstrate that the states could concurrently exercise the power to regulate commerce. Marshall denied that this was the correct inference to be drawn from examining those sources. The prohibitions on the states from laying import and export duties, for example, were not restrictions on an existing power to regulate trade but on the states' taxing power. Similarly, state inspection laws did not derive from a power to regulate commerce even though such laws might affect commerce. These laws, along with quarantine and health laws, laws regulating internal commerce, and laws concerning turnpikes, roads, and ferries, formed "a portion of that immense mass of legislation, which embraces every thing within the territory of a State, not surrendered to the general government: all which can be most advantageously exercised by the States themselves."[61] The chief justice here recognized the existence of a broad area of reserved state powers known as the "police power." At the same time he took great pains to maintain a conceptual distinction between the police power and the power to regulate commerce.

Congress in exercising its power over commerce and the states in exercising their acknowledged police powers might adopt similar laws, Marshall explained, but this similarity did not "prove that the powers themselves are identical." Likewise, the conflicts concerning power that must inevitably arise between the general and state governments in this "complex system" did not prove that the one government had "a right to exercise, the powers of the other."[62] In short, none of the examples cited in argument implied any recognition of a concurrent power over commerce but merely reflected an understanding that the states in virtue of their internal trade and police powers could enact legislation that affected interstate commerce. Marshall thus never explicitly denied that the states retained a concurrent power to regulate commerce. He merely said that a case had not been made at the bar for this proposition. Every law that had been adduced and acknowledged as a legitimate exercise of state sovereignty could be shown to derive from some other source than the commerce power.

The chief justice then briefly considered the hypothesis advanced by Gibbons's counsel that the commerce power resided exclusively with Congress. The phrase "'to regulate,'" he said by way of summarizing this argument, "implies in its nature, full power over the thing to be regulated" and "excludes, necessarily, the action of all others that would perform the same operation on the same thing." The commercial regulations enacted by Congress constituted "a uniform whole, which is as much disturbed and deranged by changing what the regulating power designs to leave untouched, as that on which it has operated." If Congress chose not to legislate on the subject of trade and navigation monopolies, this very silence evinced an intention to leave this branch of commerce unfettered by state monopolies. Marshall admitted the "great force" of the exclusive power argument, and Justice Johnson in a separate concurring opinion accepted it as sufficient to void the New York monopoly. The chief justice, however, just as he did not absolutely reject the concurrent power theory, stopped short of committing himself to the exclusive power doctrine. He was content to say only that the Court was "not satisfied that it has been refuted."[63]

Marshall and the Court ultimately avoided having to make a choice by deciding the case on the narrower ground of a collision between the state laws and a federal statute. Gibbons had asserted his right to operate his steamboats by virtue of a license issued under the federal coasting act of 1793, which granted certain privileges and exemptions to vessels enrolled in the coasting trade. Ogden's counsel denied the law's applicability to this case, contending that it did not confer a right to trade or navigate; that Gibbons's ferryboats were not engaged in the coasting trade but merely employed in transporting passengers for hire; and that, if the federal law did give a right to navigate, the New York law did not take away this right but only prevented navigation by means of steam.

Marshall rejected this construction, insisting that the coasting act implied "unequivocally, an authority to licensed vessels to carry on the coasting trade." The privileges it conferred, he said, could not "be enjoyed, unless the trade may be prosecuted." Although the words of the coasting license did not specifically authorize a voyage from New Jersey to New York, such a voyage was certainly comprehended within the coasting trade, "a term well understood."[64] The chief justice also maintained that transporting persons was part of the coasting trade, at the same time dismissing this point as irrelevant to the case. The complaint against Gibbons was not that he operated a ferry service but that his boats were propelled by steam. "The real and sole question," he said, "seems to be, whether a steam machine, in actual use, deprives a vessel of the privileges conferred by a [federal coasting] license."[65] On this point a review of the "vast and complex system" of legislation concerning commerce showed that Congress never contemplated any distinction based on the means of propulsion. Steamboats could be licensed for the coasting trade "in common with vessels using sails" and were "entitled to the same privileges." They could "no more be restrained from navigating waters, and entering ports which are free to such vessels, than if they were wafted on their voyage by the winds, instead of being propelled by the agency of fire." Thus the New York laws were "in direct collision" with the federal law.[66]

In comparison to the emphatic language defining commerce in comprehensive terms and endorsing an expansive interpretation of Congress's power to regulate foreign and interstate commerce, the actual holding in *Gibbons* has an air of anticlimax. The Court did not pronounce the New York monopoly laws "unconstitutional," that is, repugnant to the commerce clause, but merely held them to be in conflict with the federal coasting act. The opinion, to be sure, established a clear precedent for Congress's power to superintend and promote the commercial development of the country. It "vitalized enumerated powers" and set in motion the career of the commerce clause as a virtually inexhaustible fount of national regulatory power.[67] Indeed, *Gibbons* is chiefly remembered and praised today for its dynamic nationalism, its prescient anticipation of the consolidating potential of the commerce clause.

Marshall surely recognized the opportunity to give a broad scope to the positive powers of Congress. Yet this objective was subordinate to his judicial task of reaching a satisfactory resolution of the particular case. As a legal controversy *Gibbons* was less about defining the extent of federal power than about setting limits on state sovereignty. More precisely, it was an inquiry into how far an affirmative federal power operated as a negative upon state legislation. The case compelled the Court to confront the perplexing problem of American federalism: where to draw the line of demarcation between federal and state sovereignty. In this respect *Gibbons* has a studied ambiguity that made it an uncertain guide for subsequent cases arising under the commerce clause.[68]

The opinion reflects a determined effort to avoid drawing a precise boundary between the federal commerce power and the permissible field of state legislation. Marshall implicitly acknowledged that this question must perpetually arise and could only be settled, more or less, over the course of many adjudications. In a single case there was no need to pursue this "delicate inquiry" any further than was necessary to decide the particular question before the Court.[69] Whether intentionally or not, *Gibbons* opened the door to greater exercise of federal judicial power and enhanced the Supreme Court's role as "final arbiter in federal-state relations." The chief justice, of course, never doubted that the Constitution had "devolved this important duty" on the Supreme Court.[70]

As an attempt to arbitrate between the competing claims of federal and state sovereignty, *Gibbons* by no means reflects an uncompromising nationalism. The opinion permitted an ample field for state legislative activity in the area of commerce and the economy. The scope given to Congress's authority to regulate commerce, broad as it was, did not encompass intrastate commerce. Nor did it touch the mass of state powers grouped under the rubric of the "police power." Moreover, the decision did not endorse the exclusive power theory, the notion that the commerce clause by itself operated as a general prohibition on the states. Marshall had previously discussed exclusive power in *Sturges* v. *Crowninshield*, which concerned the effect of the federal bankruptcy clause on state bankruptcy laws. In that case he admitted that if the nature of a delegated power required "that it should be exercised exclusively by

Congress, the subject is as completely taken from the State Legislatures, as if they had been expressly forbidden to act on it." However, he then went on to deny that Congress's power to establish uniform laws on the subject of bankruptcies was exclusive and to declare that it was "not the mere existence of the power, but its exercise, which is incompatible with the exercise of the same power by the States."[71] This passage, which Ogden's counsel repeatedly cited, no doubt influenced the Court's determination to decide *Gibbons* on the ground of the state law's incompatibility with an actual exercise of the federal commerce power.

Marshall's often stated preference for a literal construction of the constitutional text also inhibited him from reading the word "exclusive" into the commerce clause and from interpolating into the list of prohibitions on the states a ban on measures concerning foreign and interstate commerce. If the exclusive power doctrine had prevailed, cases would still have arisen in which the state law was asserted to be a regulation of internal trade or police. The Court would then have to undertake the onerous and probably futile task of precisely delineating between laws regulating foreign and interstate commerce and laws regulating intrastate trade and police. But this line, like that between bankruptcy and insolvency laws, "must be in a great degree arbitrary," said Marshall. The two were so closely connected "as to render it difficult to say how far they may be blended together."[72] On the other hand, if a collision could be shown to exist between a federal and state law, it was "immaterial" whether the latter emanated from a concurrent power to regulate commerce or from a power to regulate internal trade and police.[73] According to the principle of national supremacy, the law would have to yield to the law of Congress in either case. In short, even if a state law was an otherwise legitimate exercise of sovereignty, it must give way if inconsistent with a federal law.

Gibbons, then, stopped short of converting an affirmative grant of power to Congress into a general prohibition on the states. Marshall did not read the commerce clause as acting on state legislation in the same way as the contract clause. State laws invalidated under the contract clause were unconstitutional, contrary to an express prohibition on laws impairing the obligation of contracts. The supreme law in these cases was the Constitution itself. In *Gibbons* and in subsequent commerce clause cases, the state law was not declared unconstitutional but merely incompatible with a specific federal regulation of commerce. Here the supreme law was a law enacted by Congress in pursuance of the Constitution. In this more limited sense the affirmative powers of Congress, particularly those exercised under the commerce clause, could still serve as a formidable instrument abridging state sovereignty. *Gibbons*, indeed, demonstrated how effectively the principle of national supremacy could operate through a federal law. The Court construed an act for licensing vessels in the coasting trade as a regulation of interstate commerce sufficient to bring it into collision with New York's steamboat monopoly laws.

Still, the Court was not disposed to find such a collision in every case. In *Willson* v. *Blackbird Marsh Co.*, decided in 1829, a Delaware company sued the owner of a sloop for damaging a dam it had erected over a small tidal creek. The sloop's owner, whose vessel was licensed under the same federal act asserted by Gibbons, claimed the dam was an unlawful hindrance to navigation. The company contended that the state law authorizing construction of the dam was a legitimate exercise of the police power, undertaken for the public good (improvement of health, for example); that the commerce clause was not intended to prevent such measures; and that the state law did not interfere with any act of Congress. In a brief opinion for the Court, Marshall accepted this argument on behalf of the state law.

Congress, he said, had passed no law that bore on the subject of navigation of tidal creeks. The state law was neither repugnant to the commerce power "in its dormant state" nor in conflict with any law regulating commerce.[74] The Court accordingly reinforced its conditional view of the reach of the commerce clause over state legislation. For the state law to be declared void two conditions had to be met: first, Congress had to exercise its power through legislative enactment, and second, there had to be an actual "collision"—an inconsistency, incompatibility, or repugnancy—between the federal and state law. At the same time, however, Marshall reaffirmed the principles of national supremacy enunciated and applied in *Gibbons* and in *McCulloch*. He never admitted that the states' "concurrent power of legislation extended to every possible case in which its exercise . . . has not been expressly prohibited."[75] Using the supremacy clause, he enforced the Constitution's implied restrictions on state authority as vigorously as he enforced its express prohibitions.[76]

In the line of cases from *McCulloch* through *Gibbons*, Chief Justice Marshall presented a masterly statement of constitutional nationalism, advancing a series of propositions that ultimately became settled principles of American constitutional law. Broadly speaking, constitutional nationalism enhanced federal powers, restricted state sovereignty, and asserted the Supreme Court's role as arbiter of conflicts arising from the clash of federal and state sovereignties. It also propounded a view of the Constitution as emanating from the whole American people for the purpose of establishing an effective national government—one of limited powers, to be sure, yet supreme within its allotted jurisdiction. As merely a general outline, designating only the important objects, such an instrument was to be construed in an enlarged or liberal sense, not in a restrictive sense appropriate to a detailed legal code. Relying on arguments derived from the nature and text of the Constitution and expounding certain key passages—the "supreme law," "necessary and proper," "arising under," and commerce clauses—Marshall made a compelling case for nationalism. He articulated a constitutional vision that inspired and facilitated the creation of the mighty nation-state that the United States was eventually to become.

Yet the consolidation of national power was more of an unintended consequence than a conscious design of constitutional nationalism. Marshall aimed not to constructively enlarge federal powers but to counteract the noxious doctrine of states' rights. In the conclusion to *Gibbons* he once again animadverted upon strict construction and its baneful consequences:

> Powerful and ingenious minds, taking, as postulates, that the powers expressly granted to the government of the Union, are to be contracted by construction, into the narrowest possible compass, and that the original powers of the States are retained, if any possible construction will retain them, may, by a course of well digested, but refined and metaphysical reasoning, founded on these premises, explain away the constitution of our country, and leave it, a magnificent structure, indeed, to look at, but totally unfit for use.[77]

This passage nicely expresses the tenor of his nationalist jurisprudence, which was to interpret the Constitution to enable the general government to operate effectively—that is, with supreme authority within its assigned sphere. Constitutional nationalism, in sum, was largely defensive in character, not looking to build a powerful federal state but to protect and defend the general government against persistent antifederal forces that imperiled the "more perfect Union" formed by the Constitution of 1787.

6

THE LIMITS OF
JUDICIAL POWER

Law and Politics

A pervasive theme of Marshall's opinions is his attempt to mark out the boundaries of judicial power, principally as exercised by the Supreme Court of the United States. In this endeavor the chief justice repeatedly affirmed the distinction between law and politics first announced from the bench in *Marbury*. According to this distinction, the judicial branch disclaimed "all pretensions" to decide questions "in their nature, political."[1]

Three years before *Marbury*, while serving in Congress, Marshall had pointed out that the Constitution extended the judicial power not to *"all questions"* but to *"all cases in law and equity"* arising under the federal Constitution, laws, and treaties. It did not confer on the judiciary "any political power whatever." To come within the judicial power a question had to "assume a legal form, for forensic litigation, and judicial decision. There must be parties to come into court, who can be reached by its process, and bound by its power; whose rights admit of ultimate decision by a tribunal to which they are bound to submit."[2] That the Supreme Court could act only within the confines of deciding legal cases was and is the most important limitation on its power. Marshall's great achievement was to make this limitation serve as the foundation of the Supreme Court's claim to expound the Constitution and to void legislative acts deemed to be contrary to the fundamental law.

Restricted to deciding "cases," the Supreme Court nevertheless could

not avoid confronting questions—notably, though not exclusively, in
the constitutional cases—that fell within the shadowy borderland between law and politics. The vast majority of cases, to be sure, belonged
squarely to the conventional domain of law. Contracts and commercial
transactions, land titles, civil procedure, marine insurance and admiralty causes formed the bulk of the Court's business.[3] Collectively, these
cases underscored the Supreme Court's role as a court of law, as primarily an appellate tribunal for adjudicating disputes between private
individuals. In its profusion of ordinary business the Court established
itself as an authoritative expounder of common law and equity, admiralty law, and the law of nations. Marshall well understood that public
confidence in the Court's ability to reach impartial judgments in the
great constitutional law cases depended on its undisputed mastery of
the traditional fields of legal science.

Throughout his chief justiceship Marshall exhibited a shrewd and
discriminating sense of the limits of judicial power. Although *Marbury*
established at the outset the judiciary's claim to review acts of the executive and legislative, the central thrust of his decisions was to allow the
political departments broad scope to accomplish the objects confided
to them by the Constitution and laws. The province of courts, the chief
justice was fond of reiterating, was ordinarily "to decide upon individual rights, according to those principles which the political departments of the nation have established."[4] Courts possessed no "will"
independent of the laws. Their duty was merely to declare what the law
is, not what it *should be*. To prescribe what the law should be was precisely the definition of legislative power, a sphere that was off-limits to
the judiciary.

On a number of occasions Marshall made a point of differentiating
between courts, which were concerned with "objects unconnected with
government," and the executive and legislative, which were concerned
with exercising "sovereignty without affecting the rights of individuals."[5]
This differentiation found expression in a variety of cases but most commonly where the assertion of individual rights was intermingled with
questions bearing on the conduct of foreign relations and war.

Judicial deference to the political departments in matters of foreign
policy was an established doctrine of American constitutional law before Marshall came to the bench. As a lawyer arguing *Ware* v. *Hylton* in
1793, he heard a classic formulation by Justices John Jay and James

Iredell, both of whom denied the competence of courts to decide the policy questions involved in pronouncing a treaty void.[6] Marshall himself expressed similar views in defending President Adams's action in turning Jonathan Robbins over to British authorities under the extradition article of the treaty of 1794. This case, he said, was "for executive not judicial decision." Although points of law were involved in the decision to extradite, these were "questions of political law, proper to be decided by the executive and not by the courts." Robbins's extradition case was essentially one between two sovereign nations, whose respective claims upon each other could not be litigated in a court of law. As "the sole organ of the nation in its external relations," the president was the proper person to whom national demands could be made and by whom national acts were to be performed.[7]

Marshall here spoke as a Federalist congressman defending the conduct of a Federalist president, but as chief justice he consistently acknowledged the foreign policy prerogatives of successive Republican administrations. In one of his first cases the Supreme Court decreed restoration of a French vessel that had been condemned as lawful prize in the federal circuit court. Marshall held that the governing law in the appeal was the Convention of 1800 between the United States and France, which provided for the mutual restoration of captured property "not yet *definitively* condemned." This treaty was not in force at the time of the original decree, President Jefferson having promulgated its final ratification the same day the chief justice announced the Supreme Court's decision—a coincidence strongly suggesting cooperation between the executive and judiciary in disposing of this case. The Court had no choice but to regard the convention as obligatory law, said Marshall, even though it operated retrospectively in this case. If on considerations of policy a nation contracted to sacrifice "individual rights, acquired by war," it was "not for the court, but for the government, to consider whether it be a case proper for compensation."[8]

In an 1812 case Marshall denied a claim by two American citizens for recovery of a vessel that had been captured by a French privateer, condemned as prize, and refitted as a warship of the French navy. In this latter capacity the ship had been forced by bad weather to take refuge in Philadelphia, where the original owners filed their libel. The case presented "the very delicate and important inquiry," observed the chief justice, "whether an American citizen can assert in an American court a title to an armed national vessel, found within the waters of the United States." An affirmative answer to this question might have upset relations between two nations then at peace with each other, for the French government would have regarded such a judicial decision as an affront to the nation's sovereignty and dignity.

Reasoning from authorities on the law of nations, Marshall derived "a principle of public law, that national ships of war, entering the port of a friendly power open for their reception, are to be considered as exempted by the consent of that power from its jurisdiction." Of course, this consent could be withdrawn at any time, but this was a decision to be made by the political branches, not the judiciary. Only "the sovereign power of the nation" was "competent to avenge wrongs committed by a sovereign," and "the questions to which such wrongs give birth are rather questions of policy than of law." Since the United States government had not revoked its consent to waive jurisdiction, the federal tribunals could not inquire into the title of the French warship, though under ordinary circumstances courts were open to individuals claiming property.[9]

Marshall again resorted to the distinction between legal and policy questions in a case concerning the seizure of British property during the War of 1812. He refused to sanction a lower court decree upholding the seizure and sale of such property on the ground that Congress had passed no act explicitly confiscating enemy property. For the Court to sustain the legality of the seizure would have been to make a policy judgment about the prosecution of the war. "When war breaks out," he wrote, "the question, what shall be done with enemy property in our country, is a question rather of policy than of law." Congress was perfectly free to adopt confiscation of enemy property as an appropriate war measure, but until the legislature declared its will in express terms the Court had no discretion to enforce confiscation by implication.[10]

The piracy cases occurring in the wake of the Latin American revolts following the War of 1812 also blended legal and political questions. Indictments were brought in the federal courts against crewmen serving on privateers fitted out in United States ports and commissioned for service on behalf of newly proclaimed governments in revolt against Spain and Portugal. The courts in these cases had to decide whether such privateering amounted to unlawful piracy or to legitimate acts of war. In the leading case Marshall laid down the general proposition that courts must follow the policy adopted by the legislative and executive departments with respect to the conflict between a former colony and the mother country. If that policy was neutrality and recognition of civil war, then the courts could not "consider as criminal those acts of hostility which war authorizes, and which the new government may direct against its enemy." A contrary decision would in effect adopt a different policy and "transcend the limits prescribed to the judicial department."[11]

Marshall presented perhaps his fullest statement on the theme of judicial deference to the legislative and executive in matters pertaining to foreign relations in *Foster and Elam* v. *Neilson* (1829). The case was a land title dispute, the plaintiff claiming under an 1804 Spanish grant and the defendant denying the validity of this grant on the ground that the land lay within the Louisiana Purchase of 1803. The land in question lay just east of the Mississippi River and thus fell within West Florida, a territory the United States claimed, and Spain denied, was included within the 1803 purchase. After reviewing at length the history of negotiations regarding Louisiana and West Florida and various acts of Congress, the chief justice denied the plaintiff's claim under the Spanish grant. He concluded that the "American construction" of the meaning of the Louisiana Purchase, "if not entirely free from question," rested on strong arguments that could not "be easily confuted." In any event, the courts could not adopt a contrary construction, for that would infringe upon the prerogatives of the political departments of the government to assert the national interests. Such power was not confided to the judiciary, a department whose ordinary duty was simply "to decide upon individual rights, according to those principles which the political departments of the nation have established." A question concerning national boundaries was "more a political than a legal question; and in its discussion, the court of every country must respect the pronounced will of the legislature."[12]

The case also involved construction of the 1819 treaty between the United States and Spain by which the latter yielded all claims to its Florida possessions. An article of that treaty provided for Spanish land grants made before 1818 to be ratified and confirmed to those in possession of the lands. Marshall held that the Court could not apply this article to the case even assuming its provisions were favorable to the plaintiff's title. American courts, he conceded, were to regard a treaty as the law of the land, as equivalent to a legislative act. Yet when its terms amounted to a contract, one party engaging to perform a specific act, "the treaty addresses itself to the political, not the judicial department." Prior execution of the treaty by Congress was necessary before it could "become a rule for the Court."[13]

The line between law and politics was hardest to draw in the great constitutional cases, for here the Court undertook not merely to interpret a law but to adjudge the very legality of the legislature's exercise of political power. These cases have monopolized scholarly attention because of their importance to the emerging field of constitutional law and to the developing institutional role of the Supreme Court. Yet constitutional adjudication figured in a mere handful of the total judgments handed down by the Court during Marshall's tenure.[14] Exclusive focus on this aspect of its work may yield a misleading picture of an "activist" Marshall Court, constantly poised to exercise its power to construe the Constitution and curb legislative powers. What stands out as the more revealing characteristic of Marshall's chief justiceship is the degree to which the Court refrained from bold assertions of power and deferred to the political branches of the government. Caution, prudence, and moderation were the hallmarks of his leadership. The chief justice, to be sure, did not hesitate to claim and to exercise judicial power where he believed the Constitution had conferred jurisdiction. The Court, he often remarked, was under the equal obligation not to "usurp power" and not to "shrink from its duty." The usurping and the refusing to act were equally "treason to the constitution."[15]

EXECUTIVE DISCRETION

In recognizing a vast area of political discretion that was not amenable to judicial inquiry, Marshall differentiated between executive and legislative discretion. The executive department had considerably narrower scope for action than did the legislative department. The executive was bound by the laws as well as by the Constitution; its discretion to execute the laws was limited by the terms prescribed by Congress. Where individual rights clashed with executive action, the judiciary could intervene to determine whether such conduct exceeded the authority assigned by law. *Marbury* was the first and most notorious in a series of cases in which Marshall had to balance the claims of executive discretion against an assertion of private rights. It established the principle that where the law commanded an executive officer to perform a certain act and failure to perform this act injured the rights of an individual, a court of law was the appropriate forum for the aggrieved person to seek redress. The Court concluded that the secretary of state, though acting under the president's orders, had no authority to withhold Marbury's commission. The refusal to deliver the commission was a denial of legal right that the Supreme Court could properly inquire into (though it ultimately decided on other grounds that it had no jurisdiction to remedy this wrong by mandamus).

In only one other case besides *Marbury* did Marshall presume to make the highest government officers answerable to judicial process. On circuit in 1807, he issued a subpoena *duces tecum* to President Jefferson commanding him to produce certain documents said to be material to the defense of the accused traitor, Aaron Burr. The chief justice justified this action in terms of his legal duty to uphold the rights of the accused in criminal prosecutions (spelled out in the Sixth Amendment), among which was the right to compulsory process for obtaining witnesses. He could find no exception that would exempt the president from the general obligation to be a witness. Marshall conceded that the demands of the office might excuse the president from attending in person, but this rather constituted "a reason for not obeying the process of the court, than a reason against its being issued." The issuing of "a subpoena to a person filling the exalted station of the chief magistrate" was "a duty which would be dispensed with much more cheerfully than it would be performed; but if it be a duty the court can have no choice in the case."[16]

As for the delicate question of whether the president had a right to withhold all or part of the requested document, Marshall accorded due recognition to the executive's need to preserve confidentiality and his duty to maintain national security. If a document contained information that "would be imprudent to disclose" and that the president did not wish to disclose, "such matter, if it be not immediately and essentially applicable to the point, will, of course, be suppressed." The chief justice clearly implied that the ultimate determination of materiality was a matter for judicial decision, not executive discretion. He denied that granting the motion for a subpoena showed disrespect for the

president, insisting that the court "feels many, perhaps peculiar motives, for manifesting as guarded a respect for the chief magistrate of
the union as is compatible with its official duties." In this instance legal
duty compelled him to issue the subpoena, to take an expansive view of
the rights of a defendant accused of a capital crime. On the real possi-
bility that Burr might eventually be convicted, Marshall, in a rare inter-
jection of personal feelings in a legal opinion, stated that he would
"deplore most earnestly, the occasion which should compel me to look
back on any part of my official conduct with so much self-reproach as I
should feel" in denying the defendant's request.[17]

Marshall, as suggested, was inclined to adopt a strict view of executive
discretion when its exercise impinged on individual rights. If in such
cases executive action was not explicitly authorized by statute, he was
disposed to uphold the party's asserted rights. In a North Carolina circuit case heard in 1812, the chief justice dismissed a libel that alleged a
violation of the nonintercourse laws.[18] His decision involved interpreting the effect of two presidential proclamations, the first suspending
those laws and resuming trade with Great Britain, the second renewing
the operation of nonintercourse laws and interdicting trade with the
British. Although the law clearly authorized the president to issue the
first proclamation, the chief justice expressed an opinion—one in
which "he owned he had not full confidence"—that the law did not vest
the president with power to issue the second. The court therefore
could not sustain a libel based on that proclamation.[19]

Even in wartime Marshall held to a strict view of presidential discretion, disagreeing in this respect with Justice Story. On circuit in 1813
the Massachusetts jurist maintained that Congress's declaration of war
against Great Britain vested full sovereign authority in the president to
adopt all appropriate measures to prosecute the war, including confiscating enemy property. In overruling Story on appeal in 1814, the chief
justice insisted that confiscation was a policy question "proper for the
consideration" of Congress alone, "not of the executive or judiciary."
Until Congress expressly declared its will to confiscate enemy property
in a statute for that purpose, the president could not assume such authority as deriving from his prerogative to prosecute the war.[20]

Other decisions touching on the exercise of executive power concerned the conduct of subordinate military and civilian officers. Several
early cases originated in actions taken by American naval commanders

to enforce the acts of Congress suspending American trade with France. In one such case the naval officer was held to be liable for damages for seizing a neutral vessel even though he was faithfully obeying instructions from the secretary of the navy. Those instructions, however, were founded on a misconstruction of the law. Although executive instructions "could not give a right," Marshall initially believed "they might yet excuse from damages." He reluctantly yielded this opinion to that of the Court majority, which held that instructions could not "change the nature of the transaction, or legalize an act which without those instructions would have been a plain trespass."[21]

The conduct of civil officers came under scrutiny in a series of cases arising from the Jefferson administration's embargo on American foreign commerce. Marshall interpreted the embargo laws strictly to protect individual rights against abuse by overzealous customs officers. Such an official, he ruled in an 1811 circuit case, had no discretion to take an embargo bond that varied materially from that prescribed by statute: "It is a point on which the judgement of the officer is not to be exercised. . . . He is a ministerial officer whose business it is to pursue the statute, & if he fails to do so the statute will not sanction his act."[22] In another circuit case decided late in his career, Marshall employed similar reasoning to invalidate the act of a Treasury Department agent in imprisoning a defaulting navy purser. The agent, he said, "exceeded the authority given by law" and therefore the imprisonment was "illegal."[23]

LEGISLATIVE DISCRETION

Despite serving early notice that the judiciary would invalidate legislative acts deemed repugnant to the Constitution, the Marshall Court over the course of three decades displayed marked deference to Congress. Adhering to a restricted conception of judicial review, the Court after 1803 never again declared an act of Congress unconstitutional. Judicial review, it turned out, was much less important in checking Congress than it was in restricting the state legislatures. Unlike Congress, the state legislatures, in addition to being bounded by specific constitutional prohibitions, were restrained by the principle of national supremacy. The federal judiciary, as Marshall understood its proper function to be, consequently had a correspondingly greater obligation to invoke judicial review to nullify state laws—not only those that transgressed the Constitution but also those that were inconsistent with a federal statute or treaty.

The only federal statute the Marshall Court refused to sanction was a section of the Judiciary Act that purported to confer original jurisdiction to the Supreme Court beyond that specified in the Constitution. Congress, said Marshall in *Marbury*, had no discretion to add to or to subtract from the original jurisdiction assigned by the Constitution. Implicit in the same decision, however, was that Congress did have considerable power to control the Court's appellate jurisdiction. Indeed, discerning readers of *Marbury* might have foreseen that judicial review, as an instrument for checking Congress and the state legislatures, would be less formidable than Congress's ability to check the judiciary by making "exceptions" to and by otherwise regulating the Court's appellate jurisdiction.[24] In exercising judicial review, the Supreme Court has always been ultimately answerable to the people through their elected representatives.

Marshall, to be sure, well understood the Court's vulnerability to political forces, and this understanding powerfully reinforced his inclination to concede to Congress ample discretion to conduct its legislative business without judicial intervention. As early as 1805, for example, he adumbrated the construction of the "necessary and proper" clause that he fully developed in *McCulloch* fourteen years later. It was erroneous, he said, to suppose this clause meant that Congress could pass no law that "was not indispensably necessary to give effect to a specified power." On the contrary, "Congress must possess the choice of means, and must be empowered to use any means which are in fact conducive to the exercise of a power granted by the constitution."[25]

No better illustration of Marshall's acceptance—long before *McCulloch*—of Congress's immense discretion to determine the extent of its own powers can be found than in his conduct in the embargo cases. While privately denouncing the embargo policy as obnoxious, the chief justice never questioned the duty of the federal courts to enforce these stringent laws, which arguably stretched federal powers beyond their constitutional limits.[26] Had the question been presented to him, Marshall undoubtedly would have sustained the constitutionality of the embargo in much the same terms as he later upheld the law incorporating the national bank in *McCulloch*. As it was, he tacitly recognized Congress's authority to enact embargo laws by virtue of its power to regulate foreign commerce. To an argument that an embargo bond was void at common law "because made in restraint of trade, in restraint of common right," he replied that such a bond could not be considered invalid if "at the time the policy of the law restrained trade." In other words, Congress had discretion under its regulatory power to restrain trade, even to prohibit it entirely.[27]

McCulloch gave Marshall an opportunity to make explicit the rule of judicial restraint he had implicitly followed from the beginning in determining whether a given act of Congress was a legitimate exercise of powers conferred by the Constitution. According to this rule, all appropriate means that were "plainly adapted" to carrying out a delegated power, that were "not prohibited" but consisted "with the letter and spirit of the constitution," were "constitutional." In applying this standard to an act of Congress, the Court could not "inquire into the degree of its necessity." Such an inquiry would transcend the bounds of legal discretion and become an exercise in political discretion. In Marshall's words, it would "pass the line which circumscribes the judicial department, and . . . tread on legislative ground. This court disclaims all pretensions to such a power."[28]

To make this concession was simply to recognize that judicial power was incompetent to decide whether an act passed in virtue of an affirmative power of Congress transcended the limits of that power. The chief justice assuredly did not mean to suggest that this admission was equivalent to giving Congress a blank check to do whatever it deemed expedient. His point, rather, was that the limits on the powers of the federal legislature were to be principally defined and enforced through the political process. To forswear judicial interference with this process was not merely a prudent act of self-denial but, more fundamentally, an acquiescence to the will of the majority as expressed through the people's elected representatives. In short, *McCulloch* placed on Congress— and, ultimately, on the American people—much of the burden and responsibility for settling the meaning of the Constitution, for adapting that instrument "to the various *crises* of human affairs."[29]

By this standard the Supreme Court would rarely invoke its power to nullify an act of Congress, yet even this restricted scope of judicial review was no insignificant check upon the federal legislature. The mere acknowledgment that the judicial power could inquire into the constitutional validity of legislation no doubt had its inhibiting effect. As if to ensure that judicial review would exert a continuing silent influence over the legislature's deliberations, the chief justice issued timely reminders of the Court's duty to uphold the fundamental law over legislative enactments. Not coincidentally, in the very decision that sustained the constitutionality of the Bank of the United States, Marshall politely but firmly advised Congress that its discretion was not boundless, that it could not "under the pretext of executing its powers, pass laws for the accomplishment of objects not entrusted to the government." In such a case the Court would have "the painful duty . . . to say that such an act was not the law of the land."[30]

If judicial review was the judiciary's ultimate weapon to curb legislative discretion, the Court's ordinary power to construe the laws could restrain Congress's exercise of legislative power. The duty of a court, Marshall frequently remarked, was to apply the law according to the intention of the legislature. A judge could not inquire into the "policy" of legislation, could not consider "the wisdom or folly of any particular system"—this was solely for legislative consideration. Marshall understood the term "policy of the law" to refer only "to the object of the legislature, and to the means by which that object is to be effected, as disclosed in the words they have employed."[31]   In striving to effect the legislature's intention, a court could look only to the words of the statute for evidence of that intention. Once the legislature had enacted policy into law, had declared what the law shall be, it then became the judiciary's sole prerogative to determine the meaning of that law in cases coming before it. The law's meaning as discerned by judicial construction was not necessarily identical to the subjective intentions of the legislators at the time of adopting the act.

In cases that required him to interpret acts of Congress, Marshall employed standard canons of construction that could limit the reach and operation of the law, particularly where it affected individual rights. One such maxim was that laws imposing a penalty were to be construed strictly. This rule was "perhaps not much less old than construction itself," the chief justice remarked. It was "founded on the tenderness of the law for the rights of individuals; and on the plain principle that the power of punishment is vested in the legislative, not in the judicial department."[32] He applied this rule not only to federal criminal statutes but also to noncriminal penal statutes such as the embargo and nonintercourse laws. In each instance he attempted to balance the rights of the individual with his duty to carry out Congress's will in punishing crimes and enforcing its commercial and foreign policies.[33] This rule was not to be carried so far, Marshall cautioned, as to disregard "the sense of the legislature" or "to imply, that the intention of the legislature, as manifested in their words, is to be overruled." Construction could not "defeat the obvious intention of the legislature," but where the words might reasonably admit of two constructions, "the more restricted construction ought to prevail," especially where the punishable act was "rendered culpable only by positive law."[34]

The rule that penal statutes should be construed strictly was of a piece with the more general rule that legislative enactments were never to be construed as violating natural law or the law of nations, which was "a law founded on the great and immutable principles of equity and natural justice."[35] Chief Justice Marshall applied this rule on a number of occasions, notably in cases of international law dealing with neutral rights and confiscation of enemy property. In interpreting acts for prosecuting a war, for example, he remarked that they could "never be construed to violate neutral rights, or to affect neutral commerce, further than is warranted by the law of nations as understood in this country."[36] He further assumed that the United States adopted the more civilized and humane understanding of that law that prevailed in the advanced commercial nations of Europe. Thus Congress in declaring war could not be presumed to have authorized confiscation, since the modern rule, "introduced by commerce in favor of moderation and humanity," was opposed to the idea that war automatically vested enemy property in the belligerent government. Because Congress had not by express legislation confiscated enemy property, Marshall applied the law of nations to restore seized property to its owner. In another case he refused to condemn property as prize of war because no statute for that purpose had been adopted. "Till such an act be passed," he said, "the Court is bound by the law of nations which is a part of the law of the land."[37]

As with the case of penal statutes, Marshall was mindful not to exceed the limits of discretion in bringing the positive statutes enacted by Congress into line with the principles of justice and reason. Construction should "avoid gross injustice," even mischief and inconvenience, but should not "be carried so far as to thwart the scheme of policy which the legislature has the power to adopt."[38] The extent to which a judge should consider the consequences in expounding laws depended on the nature of the case. If "rights are infringed" or "fundamental principles are overthrown," that intention had to "be expressed with irresistible clearness to induce a court of justice to suppose a design to effect such objects." If, however, a "political regulation" produced inconvenience, so long as that intention was "expressed in terms which are sufficiently intelligible to leave no doubt in the mind," a court could not adopt a "constrained interpretation" to prevent the inconvenience. In the latter case a court must presume that the legislature had weighed the costs and benefits at the time of enacting the legislation. In any event, it was inappropriate for a court to make such a calculation. Thus Marshall broadly interpreted a statute giving the government priority of payment out of the effects of insolvent debtors to the United States as embracing the case of a private merchant whose bill of exchange had been purchased by the government.[39] Similarly, he construed the patent laws to sustain the right of an inventor to sue for damages against a person who had built and used his machine before the patent had been issued. Although "some injustice" might result from this construction, Marshall concluded that "the great fundamental principles of right & of property do not appear to be so vitally wounded as to induce the court to resist & struggle against the obvious meaning of words."[40]

Marshall conscientiously attempted to keep construction from wandering "from the beaten track prescribed" for courts into "the devious and intricate path of politics."[41] Even where construction might serve the immediate interests of policy, he refused to take judicial shortcuts to spare Congress responsibility for legislating. If the words of the law imperfectly conveyed the legislature's intentions or did not authorize objects the legislature may have had in mind, Congress itself would have to amend the statute to suit its will. However convenient it might be to cure defects or supply omissions by creative construction, a court, said Marshall, must resist the temptation to encroach on the legislative field.

SLAVERY AND THE SLAVE TRADE

The limits of judicial power as exercised by the Marshall Court are well illustrated in cases dealing with slaves and Indians. In no other cases were the claims of justice, humanity, and morality placed in such seeming stark opposition to the commands of positive law. Since the Constitution and state laws sanctioned slavery, judicial discretion was virtually powerless to affect that institution directly, though it might occasionally intervene to release persons unlawfully held in bondage. As for the dispossession of Native American tribes, the Supreme Court could declare that the Constitution and federal laws protected Indian rights but could not by itself enforce this protection.

An owner himself of a modest number of slaves, Marshall recognized the evil of slavery and resignedly accepted it as part of the civil order. Slavery was contrary to natural law, for "every man has a natural right to the fruits of his own labour" and "no other person can rightfully deprive him of those fruits, and appropriate them against his will."[42] Apart from being troubled by the moral evil of slavery, Marshall expressed even greater apprehension about its pernicious economic and potentially calamitous political and social consequences. In Virginia, he remarked, slavery made honest labor seem "disreputable," causing many of the young and industrious who were "not rich enough to remain at home in idleness" to leave the state. Like many enlightened southerners of his generation, he hoped for the eventual demise of slavery, but abolitionist and southern proslavery fanaticism made him despair that this goal could be achieved by peaceful means. In his mind preservation of the Constitution and union took precedence over the immediate eradication of slavery.[43]

An early member of the American Colonization Society and officer of the local society, Marshall publicly supported efforts to colonize emancipated slaves on the African continent. Restoring the descendants of Africans to their ancestral homeland was not only a "great cause of humanity" but also a prudent step toward avoiding political and social convulsion. He shared the belief common among moderate opponents of slavery that the two races would not be able to live peacefully together. Nothing portended "more calamity & mischief to the southern states," he feared, "than their slave population." Removal should be "a common object, by no means confined to the slave states. . . . The whole union would be strengthened by it and relieved from a danger whose extent can scarcely be estimated."[44]

As a lawyer Marshall occasionally argued cases that exposed the contradiction between slaves as human beings entitled to freedom and as property protected by law. None of these cases called into question the legality of slavery but raised only the narrow issue of whether particular persons were wrongfully held in bondage. For example, he represented both slaves and masters in suits for freedom founded on descent from a free woman. Freedom suits were akin to common law tort actions and were resolved according to the standard rules of evidence and of statutory construction that applied to ordinary cases.

In one notable case Marshall represented the interest of the slaves of John Pleasants, a Quaker whose will provided for freeing his slaves if Virginia passed a law allowing private manumission. Such a law was enacted, but the legatees raised legal objections to the manumission clauses of the will. In a case where more than four hundred slaves stood to gain their freedom, Marshall's reported argument on their behalf was strikingly devoid of the rhetoric of liberty. Instead, he presented a dry, technical argument dealing with the doctrines of trusts, executory devises, and the rule against perpetuities. The slaves' right to freedom was contingent on proving that the testator's bequest of liberty was "good, upon the soundest principles of law." In a legal system that protected property in slaves like any other vested property right, an argument for freedom could not succeed merely by appealing to the principles of natural justice. It was necessary to show that a person's status as a slave was "illegal" according to the same system of laws that protected slavery generally. The slaves of John Pleasants benefited from the venerable legal principle that courts in cases of wills should strive to effect the testator's intention.[45]

As chief justice, Marshall took a similarly narrow, legalistic approach in cases involving slaves or the slave trade. Since the law of slavery was almost exclusively local, relatively few such cases came into the federal courts. These included a handful of freedom suits originating in the federal circuit court for the District of Columbia, where the local laws of Maryland and Virginia were in force. In three such suits Marshall and the Court reversed circuit court judgments in favor of the petition and in two others upheld a judgment denying the petition. All were decided as routine cases of statutory construction and application of the rules of evidence.[46]

In *Mima Queen* v. *Hepburn* (1813), for example, the chief justice adhered strictly to the rule that hearsay evidence to establish a specific fact was inadmissible, refusing to allow an exception that would aid the petitioner in proving descent from a free woman. Sympathy for the claimant could not justify departing from the strict path of law, he said: "However the feelings of the individual may be interested on the part of a person claiming freedom, the Court cannot perceive any legal distinction between the assertion of this and of any other right, which will justify the application of a rule of evidence to cases of this description which would be inapplicable to the general cases in which a right to property may be asserted." To make an exception in this case would set a dangerous precedent that would undermine the security of property rights.[47]

Marshall also heard several cases arising from federal laws dealing with the slave trade. One concerned a ship libeled for violating federal laws forbidding the construction and fitting out of vessels engaged in the slave trade. As before, the chief justice warned against allowing personal feelings to influence legal judgment: "The peculiar odium attached to the traffic, in which this vessel is alleged to have engaged, ought not to affect the legal questions which belong to this case."[48]

Marshall's one significant case concerning slavery and the slave trade was *The Antelope*, decided by the Supreme Court in 1825. In 1819 a privateer with mostly American officers and crew sailed out of Baltimore under a commission from a Latin American revolutionary state. Off the coast of Africa the privateer captured an American and several Portuguese slave ships, each carrying a cargo of Africans, and then a Spanish vessel, *The Antelope*, carrying a large number of Africans. By a complicated chain of events *The Antelope* and the Africans, numbering nearly three hundred, were brought into Savannah, Georgia, by a United States revenue cutter for adjudication in the federal court. Claims for the vessel and cargo were filed by the Spanish and Portuguese consuls and also by the United States. Justice William Johnson's circuit court decree dismissed the United States' claim, except as to those Africans taken from the American vessel, and divided the remaining number between the Spanish and Portuguese claimants. The federal attorney appealed this decree to the Supreme Court, where it was placed on the docket in 1822 but not argued until 1825.[49]

The purpose of the appeal was to assert the United States' claim to all the Africans brought into the country on *The Antelope*. If this claim was upheld the Africans would be set free and returned to Africa, as provided by various federal statutes prohibiting the importation of

slaves and outlawing the slave trade.[50] As Chief Justice Marshall remarked, this case brought into dramatic conflict "the sacred rights of
liberty and of property"—the Africans claiming their freedom and the
Spanish and Portuguese subjects claiming these same Africans as their
legitimately acquired property. At the outset he reiterated his familiar
admonition that the "Court must not yield to feelings which might se-
duce it from the path of duty, and must obey the mandate of the law."[51]

The case was essentially one of international law, and the central
question was whether that law prohibited the international trading in
slaves. In answering this question, Marshall looked more to the actual
practices of nations than to the principles of natural law as the source
of that law of nations whose "mandate" the Court "must obey."[52] He
noted that "Christian and civilized nations" had all engaged in this "abhorrent" traffic "as a common commercial business." A trade that had
long been sanctioned by the laws of all commercial countries "could
not be considered as contrary to the law of nations." True, in recent
times the United States and Great Britain had been "assiduously employed" in suppressing "this unnatural traffic," and public opinion in
both countries was extensively in favor of interdicting this trade. In
these circumstances, where the slave trade's "illegality" was "asserted by
some governments, but not admitted by all," it was not surprising that
"public feeling should march somewhat in advance of strict law, and
that opposite opinions should be entertained on the precise cases in
which our own laws may control and limit the practice of others."[53]

In looking to British decisions for guidance, the chief justice relied
heavily on an 1817 opinion by Sir William Scott, eminent judge of the
High Court of Admiralty. Scott maintained that the right of searching a
vessel was strictly a belligerent right that could not be exercised by a nation at peace, except against pirates, "who are the enemies of the
human race." But "trading in slaves, however detestable," was not
piracy. Nor was it contrary to the law of nations, "as fixed and evidenced
by general, and ancient, and admitted practice, by treaties, and by the
general tenor of the laws and ordinances, and the formal transactions
of civilized states." Scott concluded that the right of search could not
"be exercised on the vessels of a foreign power, unless permitted by
treaty." On the strength of this opinion, Marshall reasoned that British
courts would restore slaving vessels even of nations that had prohibited
the slave trade but had not by treaty conceded the right of search.[54]

Now "for the first time" the Supreme Court had to consider the proposition that the slave trade was prohibited by international law. Having previously indicated his answer to this question, Marshall further prepared the ground by contrasting natural law and morality with "legality" conferred by actual practice. That the slave trade was "contrary to the law of nature will scarcely be denied," he said, and that "every man has natural right to the fruits of his own labour" was "generally admitted." It seemed naturally to follow "that no other person can rightfully deprive him of those fruits, and appropriate them against his will." From the "earliest times," however, "war has existed" and conferred "rights in which all have acquiesced"—including the right of the victor to "enslave the vanquished." Although Christian nations had long since renounced the notion that war gave a right to enslave captives, it was still the law of nations on the benighted continent of Africa. "Can those who have themselves renounced this law," Marshall asked, "be permitted to participate in its effects by purchasing the beings who are its victims?"[55]

Unlike a "moralist," a jurist could provide only a "legal" answer to this question by searching for the law "in those principles of action which are sanctioned by the usages, the national acts, and the general assent, of that portion of the world of which he considers himself a part, and to whose law the appeal is made." According to this standard, international law sanctioned the slave trade, and a jurist could not declare it illegal. Individual states could outlaw the slave trade but only for their own people. By the "universally acknowledged" principle of the equality of nations, no state could "rightfully impose a rule on another," that is, no one country could "make a law of nations." The slave trade remained legal in those countries that had not prohibited it. A court of the United States must accordingly restore a foreign slave vessel captured by an American ship on the high seas in peacetime.[56]

If Marshall's answer to the general question seemed favorable to the Spanish and Portuguese claims, his actual disposition of the particular case substantially increased the number of Africans awarded to the United States and thus designated for eventual release and transportation back to Africa. The chief justice ruled that the Spanish consul had the burden of proving the number of Africans taken from *The Antelope*, which resulted in a much lower number than had been awarded on circuit. In addition, he dismissed the Portuguese claim entirely. Since no

Portuguese subject had during the preceding five years appeared to assert his title and since it was a notorious fact that Americans and others carried on "this criminal and inhuman traffic under the flags of other countries," there was "irresistible testimony, that no such claimant exists, and that the real owner belongs to some other nation, and feels the necessity of concealment."[57] This dismissal further increased by more than a hundred the number of Africans turned over to the United States.

If legal discretion could not free all the unfortunate Africans brought in on *The Antelope*, Chief Justice Marshall perhaps took grim satisfaction that his appellate decree made a significant gain for human liberty over the original decree. In the circumstances a jurist would have to settle for less than what a moralist would have decreed. Constrained by judicial precedent and restricted to searching for the applicable rule in "positive" international law—the extant practices, laws, treaties, and formal transactions of "civilized" nations—he concluded that *The Antelope* was not a ripe moment for declaring the illegality of the slave trade. To have carried judicial discretion further would have been to stray into the forbidden territory of politics, of judicial lawmaking. Although many nations, including the United States, had individually outlawed the slave trade, there was as yet insufficient evidence of collective action to suppress it. Given that public opinion in the civilized world was decidedly hostile to the continuation of the slave trade, an international Congress might soon be expected to convene for the purpose of outlawing it. In the meantime, it was not for the court of a single nation to anticipate that event, to preempt the field of legislative activity.

In the handful of slave cases that came before the Marshall Court, no important public issue—certainly not the legitimacy of slavery—was implicated in their decision. Their interest lies principally in showing the chief justice's characteristic determination to stick to the well-trod path of the law, untempted by the seductive call of the emotions. In each of these cases Marshall frankly acknowledged the limits of judicial power, conceded that courts could not always reconcile morality and law, "feelings" and "duty," inclination and judgment. He did not mean to say that considerations of morality and natural justice had no place in legal adjudication but only that courts could not disregard the plain intention of positive law. If positive law declared with "irresistible clearness" a design to violate natural law, a court could not "thwart" this policy, could not inquire into its wisdom or folly. Paradoxical as it seemed, if the law explicitly embraced an immoral object and was not otherwise unconstitutional, the legal duty of the court to enforce that law was the "morally" correct thing to do. However abhorrent or disagreeable this duty might be, in Marshall's mind the greater and unpardonable judicial sin was to usurp the legislature's prerogative to declare what the law shall be.

THE CHEROKEE CASES

The contradiction between natural law and positive law also figured prominently in cases concerning the rights of the Cherokee Indians, which came before the Supreme Court in 1831 and 1832. Unlike slaves, Native Americans, though not citizens, enjoyed the status of free persons. They claimed not personal freedom but the right to remain in possession of their lands; and, in contrast to slaves who had only a natural right to freedom, their assertion of natural right also had a foundation in the Constitution and federal laws. Although the slave cases were uncontroversial and attracted little notice outside the courtroom, the Cherokee cases thrust the Supreme Court into the center of a partisan controversy that called into question once again the judiciary's role in the American polity. By merely agreeing to hear the cause of the Cherokees, the Court became a player in a political contest in which it was aligned with the opponents of the administration of President Andrew Jackson. In this awkward and uncomfortable position the Court faced the challenge of preserving its reputation as an impartial legal tribunal. Where legal rights were asserted and the Court had jurisdiction, however, Chief Justice Marshall was not one to shrink from controversy, insisting on the Court's duty to act no matter what the consequences. His efforts to separate law from politics never entailed sacrificing legal rights in order to avoid political conflict.

The Cherokee cases originated in the hesitant and ambivalent Indian policy of the federal government, the constant push of white settlers upon Indian lands, and the aggressiveness of state governments impatient to assert their jurisdiction over remaining Indian lands lying within state boundaries.[58] Empowered by the Constitution to regulate commerce with the Indian tribes and to make treaties for the purchase

of Indian lands, the general government tried to follow an orderly policy of removing Indians beyond the pale of white settlement while guar-
anteeing title to their unceded lands. The assumption was that Indians
were nomadic hunting peoples who could never be incorporated in
"civilized" white society and that the tribes would accordingly continue
to sell their lands as white settlement advanced.

In 1802 Georgia ceded its western lands to the United States in return for a promise that the federal government on behalf of the state
would purchase all Indian lands within the state boundary as soon as
possible and on reasonable terms. By the 1820s little progress had been
made in extinguishing Indian titles. The Cherokees had taken up agri-
culture and refused to sell any more of their lands. In 1827 they
adopted a constitution and declared themselves an independent state.
In response Georgia enacted a series of laws seizing Cherokee territory,
extending state law over this territory, and annulling all Indian customs
and laws. These extreme actions encountered no opposition from the
Jackson administration, which lent a sympathetic ear to assertions of
state sovereignty, particularly in regard to Indian affairs. In 1830 the administration secured passage of the Indian Removal Act, by which the
Indians could choose to remove west of the Mississippi River or submit
to state law. In these circumstances the Cherokees, supported by well
placed politicians and statesmen motivated both by genuine sympathy
for the plight of the Indians and by desire to embarrass the administration, brought their cause to the Supreme Court. *Cherokee Nation* v. *Georgia* (1831) was an original action brought to restrain the state of
Georgia from executing its laws in the Cherokee territory.[59]

Until this case Marshall's most important statement about Indian
rights occurred in *Johnson* v. *McIntosh* (1823), a land title dispute between white litigants, one of whom claimed under direct grants from Indians.[60] The chief justice here elaborated a theory of an Indian "title of
occupancy," a fully protected legal right that he distinguished from the
discovering nation's "absolute ultimate title." Under this theory the government of the United States (which succeeded to rights of the British
crown) had the exclusive right to extinguish (by purchase) the Indian
title of occupancy and to convey absolute title in the soil to individuals.
Such a title could not be acquired by direct purchase from Indians.[61]
Johnson defined an Indian right of property that attempted to bring traditional English property law in line with the actual circumstances gov-

erning relations between whites and Indians. As he was to do in *The Antelope* two years later, Marshall paid due homage to the principles of natural justice while grounding his decision largely in actual practice and
positive law. Because of society's unquestioned right "to prescribe those
rules by which property may be acquired and preserved," land titles necessarily depended "on the law of the nation" where the land lies. In resolving the case the Court therefore had to examine "not singly those
principles of abstract justice, which the Creator of all things has impressed on the mind of his creature man, and which are admitted to
regulate, in a great degree, the rights of civilized nations," but also the
principles adopted by the American government for settling land disputes.[62] In the resulting inquiry he left no doubt that Indian property
rights were based not merely on "abstract justice" but firmly embedded
in American law.

The British Crown's claim to absolute title in the soil of the North
American continent, Marshall explained, was never asserted to deny
the right of the original inhabitants to occupy the soil. This title was asserted, rather, against other European nations, who in order to avoid
conflicts among themselves, adopted the principle of discovery. According to this principle, the discovering nation gained title "against all
other European governments, which title might be consummated by
possession." It gave to the discovering nation "the sole right of acquiring soil from the natives, and establishing settlements on it." The principle said nothing about relations between the discoverer and the
native inhabitants, which "were to be regulated by themselves." As
those relations developed, native rights "were, in no instance, entirely
disregarded; but were necessarily, to a considerable extent, impaired."
Their legal and just claim to occupy and retain possession of the soil
was recognized, "but their rights to complete sovereignty, as independent nations, were necessarily diminished." In asserting their right of
"ultimate dominion," European nations exercised the right to grant the
soil even while it remained in possession of the natives. "These grants,"
said Marshall, "have been understood by all to convey a title to the
grantees, subject only to the Indian right of occupancy," and he found
abundant recognition of these principles in the historical record from
discovery to the present.[63]

The Crown's absolute title in the soil and exclusive right to extinguish the Indian right of occupancy was "incompatible with an absolute

and complete title in the Indians." Admitting this state of affairs to have arisen largely through the superior force and arts of European civilization, Marshall sounded the theme he would repeat in *The Antelope*. Whether or not advanced civilizations had "a right, on abstract principles," to expel primitive hunting societies from their territory, conquest gave "a title which the courts of the conqueror cannot deny, whatever the private and speculative opinions of individuals may be, respecting the original justice of the claim which has been successfully asserted."[64]

As a pragmatic jurist, not a moralist, the chief justice was concerned only with finding the "legal" answer. Marshall was not entirely successful, however, in suppressing a tone of apology, even embarrassment, in discussing the fate of Native Americans. He spoke of the "pompous claims" of European nations to North America and the "extravagant . . . pretension of converting the discovery of an inhabited country into conquest." Since in fact the Europeans were able to sustain these fantastic assertions, he remarked somewhat abashedly, the principle that discovery conferred absolute title to the soil became "the law of the land." The same was true of the "concomitant principle" that Indians were "to be considered merely as occupants, to be protected, indeed, while in peace, in possession of their lands, but to be deemed incapable of transferring the absolute title to others." Such a restriction was contrary "to natural right, and to the usages of civilized nations," he ruefully admitted, but was nevertheless "indispensable" to the American system of settlement and "adapted to the actual condition of the two people." It could therefore, "perhaps, be supported by reason, and certainly cannot be rejected by courts of justice."[65] Clearly, the chief justice experienced no little discomfort in announcing these principles as the law he had to apply to this case.

Still, the Indian right of occupancy was a recognized legal right of possession that was to be respected by American courts. Its subordinate status in the hierarchy of English common law property rights, moreover, was of little consequence to the Indian tribes. It did not matter to them that they could not convey absolute title. They were not restricted to selling their lands only to the federal government. They were perfectly free to sell land to individuals, including white persons, though the title conveyed was only the Indian title, the right of occupancy. This title would be held under the law of tribe, which retained power to annul the grant if it chose. If the tribe annulled the grant, said Mar-

shall, "we know of no tribunal which can revise and set aside the proceeding."[66] In the case at hand, the party's claim under an Indian grant
was presumably defeated by the Indians themselves when they subsequently ceded their territory to the United States without reserving the
particular tract.[67]

In taking up the Cherokee cases, Chief Justice Marshall was thus on
record in *Johnson* v. *McIntosh* as stating that Indian tribes had a legally
protected right to their lands. They possessed not only property rights
but also, he implied, rights of sovereignty as separate and distinct societies. Although not one to let his legal judgment be led astray by "feelings," Marshall expressed genuine sympathy for the cause of the
Indians and indignation at the "disreputable" conduct of government
towards them. The time had come, he wrote privately in 1828, "to give
full indulgence to those principles of humanity and justice which ought
always to govern our conduct towards the aborigines when this course
can be pursued without exposing ourselves to the most afflicting
calamities." Continued "oppression" of "a helpless people depending
on our magnanimity and justice for the preservation of their existence,
impresses a deep stain on the American character."[68] The chief justice,
we may be sure, was not displeased at having the opportunity to do as
much as a jurist could do to remove this stain, especially when the denial of Indian rights occurred in consequence of an assertion of the
noxious doctrine of state sovereignty.

The circumstances of *Cherokee Nation* v. *Georgia* counseled caution,
however. The state of Georgia refused to appear in court and made
clear its intention to ignore any decree the Supreme Court might issue
directing the state to rescind its Cherokee laws. An equally important
consideration was whether the executive department would enforce
such a decree. Jackson's political opponents eagerly spread rumors that
the president would ignore the Court's mandate. While no direct evidence could be cited to substantiate this charge, the president and his
party did denounce these judicial proceedings as being part of a
broader political campaign designed to unseat them in the election of
1832. Shortly before the case was argued, Congress debated a resolution to repeal section 25 of the Judiciary Act, which would have abolished the Supreme Court's appellate review of state court decisions. In
deciding on the legal rights of the Cherokees, the Marshall Court faced
a direct challenge to its authority.[69]

As it turned out, *Cherokee Nation* v. *Georgia* was not the case to consider the merits of the tribe's cause, for the Supreme Court ruled that it had no jurisdiction. As if to appease his conscience in having to deny the Indians a hearing, Marshall prefaced his opinion with a compassionate statement of their plea for justice that served as an implied censure of past government policy:

If courts were permitted to indulge their sympathies, a case better calculated to excite them can scarcely be imagined. A people once numerous, powerful, and truly independent, found by our ancestors in the quiet and uncontrolled possession of an ample domain, gradually sinking beneath our superior policy, our arts, and our arms, have yielded their lands by successive treaties, each of which contains a solemn guarantee of the residue, until they retain no more of their formerly extensive territory than is deemed necessary to their comfortable subsistence. To preserve this remnant the present application is made.[70]

To sustain jurisdiction it was necessary to show that the Cherokee tribe was a "foreign state" as that term was used in the jurisdiction clause of Article 3 of the Constitution. The chief justice was wholly persuaded that the Cherokees constituted a state, "a distinct political society, separated from others, capable of managing its own affairs and governing itself."[71] At the same time, however, their territory lay within the jurisdictional limits of the United States, and in certain respects they were subject to its laws and acknowledged themselves to be under its protection. As he was wont to do when confronted with unsatisfactory alternatives, Marshall claimed the middle ground and fashioned his own unique solution. Indian tribes were neither independent foreign nations nor subject communities incorporated into the United States. They were "domestic dependent nations," whose relationship to the United States resembled that of a "ward to his guardian."[72] In any event, it seemed clear that the framers did not mean to include Indians in conferring jurisdiction in disputes between a state and foreign states. This conclusion was supported as well by the language of the commerce clause, which explicitly distinguished Indian tribes from foreign nations.

Marshall also regarded as a serious objection to the jurisdiction that the bill of injunction sought relief beyond the Court's authority to act. It required the Court "to control the legislature of Georgia, and to restrain the exertion of its physical force." Such interposition was inappropriate, savoring "too much of the exercise of political power to be within the proper province of the judicial department." As far as remedying the wrongs committed against the Cherokee nation and securing the tribe against further injustice, the Supreme Court was "not the tribunal which can redress the past or prevent the future." Even on the matter of the Cherokees' claim to be protected in the possession of their lands, the Court could do nothing more perhaps than decide "the mere question of right . . . in a proper case with proper parties."[73]

As in *Marbury* v. *Madison*, another case in which the assertion of legal right drew the judiciary department into conflict with the administration, the chief justice escaped an awkward dilemma by denying jurisdiction. In both instances the denial was the legally correct as well as a politically prudent decision. Although he averted a crisis that threatened the Court's authority, Marshall was not entirely satisfied with his resolution of the Cherokee case. In an extraordinary departure from his policy of preserving unity on the Court, he encouraged publication of a separate dissenting opinion. He also approved the court reporter's plan to publish the entire Cherokee case, including arguments of counsel, the dissenting opinion, and other materials that supported the tribe's claims. "As an individual I should be glad to see the whole case," wrote Marshall. "It is one in which a very narrow view has been taken in the opinion which is pronounced by the Court. The judge who pronounced that opinion [i.e., Marshall himself] had not time to consider the case in its various bearings; and had his time been so abundant, did not think it truly proper to pass the narrow limits that circumscribed the matter on which the decision of the court turned."[74]

This publication, along with Marshall's hint about a "proper case with proper parties," encouraged the Cherokees and their friends to bring another case to the Supreme Court in 1832. The complaining party this time was not the tribe itself but one Samuel Worcester of Vermont, a missionary who had resided in the Cherokee territory. Worcester had been imprisoned under a Georgia act of 1830 prohibiting white men from living with the Cherokees without a license. His case, originally tried in the state court, came by writ of error under section 25 of the Judiciary Act. Freed of the constraints imposed upon him in the 1831 case,

Chief Justice Marshall in *Worcester* v. *Georgia* took the broadest possible approach in deciding on the legality of the missionary's imprisonment. The case involved not merely one man's personal liberty but also the "legislative power of a state, the controlling power of the constitution and laws of the United States, [and] the rights, if they have any, the political existence of a once numerous and powerful people."[75] He could have framed the case on the narrow ground of whether the Georgia law under which Worcester had been imprisoned violated the Constitution and laws of the United States. Instead, since that law asserted jurisdiction over the Cherokee nation, he devoted most of his opinion to examining the "rightfulness" of the Georgia legislature's claim to exercise "extra-territorial power."[76] By stating the issue this way, the chief justice ensured that the Cherokees would get a full hearing of their case.

Restating and elaborating themes presented in *Johnson*, Marshall examined in detail the history of relations between Europeans and native peoples since discovery of the North American continent. He scornfully dismissed the proposition that discovery gave European nations rights that "annulled the pre-existing rights of its ancient possessors." He was equally contemptuous of the notion that "nature" or the "great Creator of all things" conferred rights of property and dominion over "hunters and fishermen" upon "agriculturists and manufacturers." Conceding that such practical authority could be acquired by "power, war, [and] conquest," he proceeded to consider the "actual state of things." It was important to keep the origins in view, however, for this "recollection" could "shed some light on existing pretensions."[77]

Having indicated his predisposition in favor of the Cherokees, Marshall in clear and forceful language set about to show that the Indian tribes within the United States remained distinct political communities, occupying and rightfully possessing their own territories and exercising substantial powers of sovereignty within their boundaries. Their rights of dominion and property were recognized from the beginning and had never been lost throughout the long and often violent course of European colonization and settlement. They had not lost their rights by war and conquest, for they had never been conquered. The principle that discovery gave title to the government of the discoverer, said Marshall (reiterating the point established in *Johnson*), was only an accommodation among European nations to settle their competing claims. It merely determined which government had the exclusive right to purchase but "could not affect the rights of those already in possession." This principle ran through all the various charters establishing colonies. Despite language in the charters granting the soil from the Atlantic to the Pacific, no one at the time entertained the "extravagant and absurd idea that the feeble settlements made on the sea-coast . . . acquired legitimate power by them to govern the people, or occupy the lands from sea to sea." The charters asserted title only against Europeans. Moreover, they authorized the colonies to conduct war only for defensive purposes, "not for conquest."[78]

Marshall's examination of the "actual state of things" from the granting of the charters through the entire colonial period showed that Great Britain considered the Indian tribes "as nations capable of maintaining the relations of peace and war, of governing themselves, under her protection." This policy continued after the United States succeeded to the rights of the British Crown, as shown by a detailed analysis of the treaties entered into between the government and the Indians and of various acts of Congress. Although in these treaties the Indians acknowledged themselves to be under the protection of the United States, they "perceived in this protection only what was beneficial to themselves—an engagement to punish aggressions on them. It involved, practically, no claim to their lands, no dominion over their persons."[79] Marshall concluded that Indian tribes "had always been considered as distinct, independent political communities, retaining their original natural rights, as the undisputed possessors of the soil from time immemorial." The only limitation on their rights, one "imposed by irresistible power," was that they were excluded from trading or treating with any foreign state.[80]

Consequently, within the Cherokee territory, the laws of Georgia could "have no force" and Georgia citizens could not enter that territory without permission from the Cherokees themselves. After devoting nearly all of his opinion to showing that Georgia's laws were invalid for assuming extraterritorial operation, the chief justice blithely remarked that the Supreme Court had no jurisdiction to decide the case on this point alone. In brief concluding paragraphs he accordingly declared those laws to be repugnant to the federal Constitution, laws, and treaties. The Court then ordered the state court to reverse its original decision and release Worcester.[81]

Of this case President Jackson was alleged to have said, "John Marshall has made his decision, now let him enforce it."[82] There is no proof that Jackson ever uttered this statement; indeed, there is no evidence that he ignored his constitutional duty to enforce the Court's judgment even though from the beginning he bitterly resented the judiciary's interference in the Cherokee business. The president was not legally required to do anything until the state of Georgia first refused to carry out the Court's mandate. The state, as expected, ignored the order, but a second mandate that might have obliged the executive to act was never issued. In response to the impending crisis posed by South Carolina's attempt to nullify federal tariff laws, the Jackson administration persuaded the Georgia governor to pardon Worcester, who in turn dropped further proceedings on behalf of the Cherokees. The upshot was that the Jackson administration had a stronger hand to deal with nullification, the state of Georgia did not yield its sovereign pretensions, the Supreme Court preserved its authority, and the Cherokees gave up further legal efforts to prevent their removal from ancient tribal lands.[83]

Chief Justice Marshall stretched the limits of judicial power as far as he could in *Worcester* to give the Cherokee tribe's legal claims a full hearing at the bar of the Supreme Court. In this decision, perhaps more than in any other, the jurist went beyond strict legal necessity to make a pronouncement that trenched upon the political sphere. Although recognizing that the vindication of Cherokee legal rights would invite censure as trespassing upon the political realm, Marshall was genuinely moved by the Indians' plight and outraged by what he regarded as Georgia's unlawful conduct toward the tribe. Here law and morality were so clearly on the same side that a jurist might indulge his feelings to a greater extent than was possible in other cases, such as those involving slaves. In *Cherokee Nation* he had to subordinate morality to law, for to have allowed jurisdiction in that case would have forced the Court into an inappropriate exercise of political power. When, partly as a result of his own active encouragement, "a proper case with proper parties" came before the Court the next year, the chief justice was not content merely to decide the issue of Samuel Worcester's liberty but instead contrived to make that matter the entering wedge for considering the broader question of Cherokee rights. Because the Supreme Court had clear jurisdiction to decide Worcester's case, Marshall believed he had discretion to take up the Cherokee claims at large even if strict law did not oblige him to do so.

In handing down the *Worcester* decision, the Supreme Court, said Justice Story, could "wash their hands clean of the iniquity of oppressing the Indians, and disregarding their rights."[84] Implicit in this remark was an admission that more was at stake than just the matter of Indian rights. Sympathetic as he was to the dire predicament of the Cherokees, Marshall had other reasons for seizing the opportunity to pronounce the law in their case. To have remained silent in the face of a state's manifest violation of the Constitution and laws of the United States would have seriously compromised the Supreme Court's claim to be the guardian and expositor of the nation's fundamental law, if not the keeper of the nation's moral conscience. To risk this consequence, the chief justice must have reckoned, was a less acceptable alternative than to incur the wrath of a defiant state or to provoke a confrontation with the federal executive. Even though a favorable decision was not likely to be of any practical benefit to the Indians, still it mattered greatly that the Court should be perceived as faithfully discharging its duty.

7

PRINCIPLE, PRECEDENT, AND INTERPRETATION

As chief justice of the United States for thirty-four years, John Marshall established a model for judging that continues to inspire emulation in our day. He was the original and is still the leading exemplar of a judge in a federal constitutional republic charged with the duty not only of enforcing ordinary law but also of applying the Constitution to particular cases. The ways in which Marshall pursued the craft of judging have been touched upon in the course of discussing his opinions. The subject bears recapitulating in more systematic fashion for the light it casts on Marshall's larger design to "legalize" the Constitution, to make it amenable to the familiar and routine methods of resolving legal disputes.[1] How did he approach the task of interpretation? In searching for the principle or rule that governed a case, to what extent did he rely on the authority of precedents? In cases that required him to expound a legislative act, what rules of construction did he employ and how did he apply them? These questions address the larger issue of Marshall's understanding of judicial discretion and of the place and role of the judiciary in the American constitutional system.

PRINCIPLE AND PRECEDENT

One of the more persistent myths about Marshall is that he was indifferent, even disdainful of, precedent. He "saw issues with a vision unencumbered by reverence for precedent and not confined within the

181

calfskin covers of the English reporters," writes the author of a recent textbook on the Supreme Court. This remark misconstrues the role of precedent in Marshall's jurisprudence and grossly exaggerates the degree to which the chief justice "wrote on a clean slate."[2] Although it is true that the constitutional opinions contain relatively few citations to authorities and provide some basis for the myth, a bare perusal of the reports of Cranch, Wheaton, Peters, and Brockenbrough yields numerous opinions in which the chief justice engaged in a full, sometimes exhaustive, discussion of precedents. Like any judge, Marshall depended on past adjudications for guidance in determining the case before him. The degree of this dependence varied with the nature of the dispute, some cases amenable to decision only by reference to a long chain of authorities, others capable of being disposed of with little or no aid from precedent.

A great many cases were resolved not by applying principles derived from precedents but by employing the established rules for construing written instruments. Marshall's opinions interpreting statutes, for example, typically consisted of close analysis of the text itself, with no references to previous cases unless the same statute had been judicially expounded. The same was true of his constitutional opinions. Their relative dearth of citations bespoke not an inattention to precedent but rather his belief that an appeal to authority was largely irrelevant or inappropriate in deciding this particular kind of case. In *Dartmouth College* v. *Woodward*, for example, the chief justice deliberately refrained from relying on the English law of charitable corporations. Likewise, in *Osborn* v. *Bank of the United States*, the Court declined to review certain English decisions that had been brought to bear on the question of federal jurisdiction. As Marshall explained, "a question growing out of the constitution of the United States, requires rather an attentive consideration of the words of that instrument, than of the decisions of analogous questions by the Courts of any other country."[3]

In those cases where he was compelled to deal with precedent, Marshall adopted a moderate, circumspect attitude—always respectful of the opinions of other judges while never according them unquestioned deference. His discussion of authorities often had the character of a running dialogue with his fellow judges, past and present, "as if the very minds of the judges themselves stood disembodied before him."[4] Although never arrogantly presuming his own superiority of legal knowledge and powers of reasoning, Marshall was fully confident in his mastery of the methods of common law adjudication. Like Lord Mansfield, he founded his jurisprudence upon the ancient distinction between principle and authority, which was rooted in the assumption that law consisted of a body of principles existing independently of particular cases. Marshall reiterated this distinction time and again in his opinions. Typically, he would reach a tentative conclusion "upon principle" or "in reason" and then review the relevant authorities to determine how they bore upon the point at issue.[5]

In cases arising upon common law or equity, English precedents were most frequently cited in Marshall's court. The books of English reports constituted an immense repository of case law, providing illumination and guidance in resolving the myriad and often intricate disputes between private litigants that arose over property and grew out of commercial transactions. Modern English decisions, to be sure, did not have the binding authority of those made before the Revolution. They could "only be considered as the opinions of men distinguished for their talents & learning expounding a rule by which this country [Virginia] as well as theirs professes to be governed," said Marshall, adding: "When however they are reasonable, are conformable to general principles, and do not change a rule previously established such decisions cannot be entirely disregarded."[6]

Over time the chief justice heard an increasing number of citations of state court decisions and of decisions by the federal Supreme Court. On general law questions these precedents supplemented those contained in the English books. In seeking guidance on such questions, Marshall did not distinguish between English and American decisions, nor did he assume the latter to be the more competent authority simply because they had been made by American judges. The authoritative quality of a precedent did not depend on the particular jurisdiction of the court making the decision. All that mattered was whether the adjudged case correctly expressed the true legal principle and whether that principle applied to the case at bar. On circuit in Virginia, for example, he once had to choose between a decision of the Virginia Court of Appeals and a modern English decision in a case concerning principal and agent. In this instance he followed the English precedent because it laid down the general rule and appeared "to be directly in point."[7]

Adhering to precedents was unproblematic when they laid "down the positive rule in strict conformity with principle."[8] Adjudication, however, was more often an arduous intellectual exercise in reconciling principle and precedent. In this exercise Marshall assumed the validity of past judicial decisions, while regarding them merely as evidence of what the law is—evidence that could be challenged or discredited. If a legal point had been clearly settled by adjudged cases, the chief justice acknowledged his duty to submit to their authority even if they seemed not to conform strictly to the principles of reason and justice. Ever sensitive to the dangers of passing the line between judgment and will, he did not consider himself free to break the chain of authority simply because his own opinion inclined another way. "If this was a case to be decided by principle alone," he remarked during the Burr trial, "the court would certainly not receive this paper. But if the point is settled by decisions, they must be conformed to."[9] Likewise, in a circuit case heard in 1824 Marshall abandoned his original opinion that simple contract creditors in a court of law would also have the same rank in a court of equity. Examination showed that "the decisions are otherwise, and I must acquiesce in those decisions."[10]

A notable instance in which inclination drew Marshall one way and a string of precedents the other occurred on circuit in 1811, when Edward Livingston sued Thomas Jefferson for evicting him from the "batture" at New Orleans during the latter's presidency. Taking advantage of the venerable distinction between local and transitory actions, Jefferson pleaded to the jurisdiction, contending that the federal court in Virginia could not hear the case because the alleged trespass took place outside the district of Virginia. Marshall upheld this plea, not having the "hardihood" to challenge a distinction so encrusted in the common law that not even the great Mansfield had been able to dislodge it. Even though this rule produced "the inconvenience of a clear right without a remedy," the chief justice reluctantly concluded he "must submit to it."[11]

Marshall also recognized the duty of federal courts to abide by state court decisions on questions of local statutory law. This rule was "founded on the principle . . . that the judicial department of every government . . . is the appropriate organ for construing the legislative acts of that government." Accordingly, no court that "professed to be governed by principle" could presume that the courts of another jurisdiction "had misunderstood their own statutes, and therefore erect itself into a tribunal which should correct such misunderstanding." The courts of the United States were "no more at liberty to depart" from the construction of the law of another nation or of a state given by the courts of that nation or state "than to depart from the words of the statute."[12] In affirming this rule on circuit in 1821, the chief justice declared that if the Virginia Court of Appeals had decided a particular point under the state's statute of frauds, he would "have followed the precedent, however erroneous" he believed it to be.[13]

While recognizing the dominant and often binding authority of adjudged cases, Marshall (like Mansfield) was adept at dealing with precedents that posed a challenge to principle. Only rarely did he directly impugn the reasoning or correctness of a previous decision. Instead of denying the validity of a precedent, he preferred to parry or deflate its significance for the case at hand. For example, the poor quality of the reports, particularly the old English reports, afforded opportunities to declare a case to be an unsatisfactory authority because it was too "imperfectly," "vaguely," "obscurely," "loosely," or "carelessly" reported.[14] Assuming the reasonable accuracy of the report, the chief justice, when he deemed it necessary, employed a variety of tactics to prevent his case from being drawn into the magnetic field of precedential authority. For instance, he might cite the different practices or circumstances in the United States or in Virginia to deny the applicability of English cases. Thus, Lord Mansfield's reasons for adhering to a rule concerning pleading did "not apply in the United States, where costs are not affected by the length of the declaration." Similarly, after noting the "different practice" prevailing in Virginia concerning sales under a decree of a court of equity, Marshall stated "after mature consideration" that he could not be influenced by the course of English decisions on this subject. On another occasion, he replied to counsel's citation of English authorities by observing "that the law which governs the practice [of pleading] in England, is different from that which governs the practice in Virginia."[15]

In numerous opinions Marshall succeeded in weakening if not exploding precedents by distinguishing them from the present case. Close scrutiny of cited cases often revealed "points of dissimilitude" so "striking" or "material" as to impair their authority for the point under consideration.[16] It frequently happened, too, that alleged precedents were not precisely in point or had not clearly decided a particular question. "In recurring to precedent," said Marshall in a case arising on a marine insurance policy, "no direct decision by a court on the point, no direct affirmance of the principle has been adduced." In regard to two decisions cited as authority on a question concerning the claims of creditors upon a decedent's estate, he remarked: "Those cases, in my opinion, go a great way. I shall respect them in a case precisely similar, but shall not extend their application."

On another occasion Marshall pointed out that the précis of a case had misleadingly stated that case to have "expressly determined" a legal point, "but on examining the case itself" he found the chancellor's decision not "so express as it is stated to be in the index and marginal note." In a case where a vendor claimed his lien was retained against a vendee's creditors who held under a bona fide conveyance from the vendee, the chief justice observed: "To establish this principle on the authority of adjudged cases, the Court would require cases in which the very point is decided. We have seen no such cases." Marshall once refused to accept as authority a decision of the Supreme Judicial Court of Massachusetts, even though it was "expressly in point," because he thought it was opposed "to the whole course of decisions in England, as well as in this Court, and not supported by decisions in other States, or by a long course of decisions even in the State of Massachusetts."[17]

Another technique Marshall commonly employed to blunt the force of precedent was to confine a judge's decision to the particular circumstances of the case decided. "Every opinion, to be correctly understood, ought to be considered with a view to the case in which it was delivered," he observed, referring to the Supreme Court's opinion in *Ex parte Bollman and Swartwout*, a precedent of his own creation that proved troublesome during the Burr treason trial in 1807.[18] He resorted to this "maxim" whenever counsel seized upon general expressions or "dicta" (statements not essential to the decision of a case) in a judicial opinion to advance principles he believed lacked legal foundation. Statements going "beyond the case . . . may be respected, but ought not to control the judgment in a subsequent suit when the very point is presented for decision," he wrote in *Cohens*, when again he had to finesse his way around his own precedent—in this instance, *Marbury*. "The reason of this maxim is obvious," he explained. "The question actually before the Court is investigated with care, and considered in its full extent. Other principles which may serve to illustrate it, are considered in their relation to the case decided, but their possible bearing on all other cases is seldom completely investigated."[19]

The maxim proved particularly useful when the dicta of eminent jurists were cited to support a dubious legal proposition. It allowed Marshall to repel such authority without implying that his illustrious fellow judge had committed error or reasoned falsely. The errors and flawed reasoning, on the contrary, were committed by others in drawing unwarranted inferences from those opinions. "It is extremely dangerous," he cautioned, "to take general *dicta* upon supposed cases not considered in all their bearings, and, at best, inexplicitly stated, as establishing important law principles."[20] Marshall issued this warning while limiting the application of certain dicta uttered by Lord Mansfield.

In similar fashion he dealt with some unguarded statements of his mentor, Judge Pendleton of the Virginia Court of Appeals: "To consider the judge, in such a case, as laying down a new and important principle, contrary to uniform decisions, on vague and general expressions, would be doing injustice both to the judge and to the subject." He went on to show that Pendleton "did not mean to lay down the rule which is ascribed to him."[21] Marshall likewise evaded the snare of authority adduced from general propositions set forth by Judge Parsons of Massachusetts and Chancellor Kent of New York, jurists "whose opinions deserve to be greatly respected, and whose decisions must always have great influence with any court in which they are quoted." Close examination of the cases in which they expressed these statements showed that the principle laid down did "not necessarily extend to the case at bar" or that it had "been pressed much farther in argument than the eminent Judge who made it would be willing to carry it."[22]

In relying on the maxim that a judge's opinions must be understood by reference to the particular case decided, Marshall was quick to exploit any special circumstances that could aid his project of bringing precedent, properly understood, in line with principle. In the Burr treason trial, for example, counsel for the prosecution cited Sir Matthew Hale's treatise on English criminal law in support of the proposition that one who procured a treasonable assemblage, though not present, might be indicted as being part of that assemblage. This notion contradicted "every idea I had ever entertained on the subject of indictments," said Marshall, while acknowledging that it was "countenanced by the authorities adduced in its support." The repugnancy between Hale's dicta, taken in the expansive sense urged by the prosecution, and just principle led Marshall into a close investigation of these dicta to determine if Hale truly meant them to be so understood. At the outset he raised doubts by noting that Hale's treatise was based on a flawed manuscript. Had the revised manuscript served as the text, Hale's dicta, Marshall surmised, "would, if not expunged, have been restrained in their application to cases of a particular description." In these circumstances, it was "only doing justice to Hale" to ascertain whether his dicta would "admit of being understood in a limited sense." In the ensuing inquiry the chief justice found abundant evidence to show that the restricted meaning of Hale's dicta was the only sense in which the treatise writer was "to be reconciled with himself, and with the general principles of law."[23]

Another instance in which unimpeachable authority seemed to be at odds with correct principle occurred in a notable prize case arising out of the War of 1812. Marshall dissented from the majority opinion, contending for a less rigid application of the principle that residence or domicile determines the national character of a merchant. This was the conclusion to which he had been led, he said, "guided by the lights of reason and the principles of natural justice." Standing in the way, however, was a series of adjudications by Sir William Scott, judge of the British High Court of Admiralty, that were said to have settled the law in favor of strict adherence to the rule. Although respecting Scott as a "truly great man" whose decisions he would not depart from "on light grounds," Marshall delicately suggested that the British judge's mind leaned "strongly in favor of the captors": "In a great maritime country, depending on its navy for its glory and its safety, the national bias is perhaps so entirely in this direction, that the judge, without being conscious of the fact, must feel its influence." For this reason, the chief justice felt justified in investigating "rigidly the principles on which his decisions have been made" and in not extending them "where such extension may produce injustice." He followed with a detailed analysis of Scott's opinions and of other cases, finding none that decided in express terms that a merchant's property depended "conclusively" on his residence at the time of capture or upon his taking steps to leave the belligerent country before the capture. "Thus understanding the English authorities," he concluded, "I do not consider them as opposing the principle I have laid down."[24]

Time and again Marshall undertook a critical examination of precedents to determine the precise extent and applicability of the rule said to be established by them. With his probing and discerning mind, he was able to detect fine points of difference that allowed him to qualify the meaning of a previous judgment and thereby limit its reach. Typically, he would find that the rule had never been pressed to the extent urged in the case at bar. He exploited to full advantage the distinction between a general principle and one "universal in its application." The chief justice invoked this distinction, for example, in a case arising on the statute of frauds. The numerous decisions expounding that statute, both in England and the United States, were "admitted to bind this Court," he said. They had established the sound general principle "that a voluntary gift is void as to creditors, whose debts existed at the time the gift was made." But had these decisions converted a general rule into one so universal and rigid as to make the statute "equivalent to an act annulling all gifts or voluntary conveyances, made by a person indebted at that time, however large his fortune, and however inconsiderable his debts or his gift"? Marshall's review showed that in all the cases in which the principle was reiterated the gift in question was "property to a considerable amount" conveyed by formal deed. In no case had a court expressly declared that "every gift, however trivial," was void as to creditors.[25]

Marshall adverted to this distinction again in cautioning against undue reliance on the authority of treatises—in this instance a work by Joseph Chitty on the law concerning bills of exchange: "Elementary writers sometimes state general rules as if they were universal; and do not always make those discriminations which a comparison of the cases themselves shows ought to be made; nor trace results to the true principle which produces them."[26] Here Marshall succinctly expressed his own method of treating precedent and underscored his commitment to principles as standing apart from particular cases. The duty of a judge was not to give unquestioning deference to adjudged cases but to scrutinize them with a critical eye to nice discriminations found on a comparative review and to discover the "true principle" that governed them. From the confusing and contradictory adjudications of centuries of common law and equity jurisprudence, the judge was to extract the essence of law—the general principles running through and beyond particular cases.

In giving his primary allegiance to principle rather than precedent, Marshall was acting on the assumptions of eighteenth-century jurisprudence. Every technique he employed in dealing with precedent fell within the accepted canons of common law adjudication as passed down through generations of judges and codified in the pages of Blackstone. Having learned these methods and rules in the courtrooms of Pendleton and Wythe, Marshall, aided by extraordinary intellectual powers, developed a facility for using them that allowed him to carry judicial discretion further than less gifted judges. His skill in manipulating precedents, in exposing the inadequacy or irrelevance of cases as authority for the point to be decided, enlarged the range of choice open to him in selecting and applying the principles on which he based his decision. How he was able to maneuver freely through seemingly the tightest web of argumentation founded on precedents was perhaps best explained by Story: "But what seemed peculiarly his own was the power with which he seized upon a principle or argument . . . and showed it to be a mere corollary of some more general truth which lay at immeasurable distances beyond it."[27] The chief justice could penetrate farther into the maze of precedent, strip away error from truth, and reach a result that came closer to satisfying the competing claims of authority and principle.

The moderation and caution that characterized Marshall's jurisprudence were evident in the way he treated precedent. He did not carry the pursuit of principle to such an extreme that it risked becoming a pretext for imposing his own will on a legal judgment. The chief justice remained acutely sensitive to the dangers of overstepping the bounds of judicial discretion. Even as he felt the pull of principle, he acknowledged the constraints of authority. His project was to strengthen the foundation of authority, to bring it in accord with reason and principle so far as was within his power to do. When the two could not be harmonized, Marshall dutifully submitted to the claims of authority. Even in this situation, he might have an opportunity to invoke public policy as a rationale for preserving intact a chain of accumulated precedents whose basis in reason and principle had disappeared in the mists of time. Where expectations had been formed and titles established on a series of adjudications, for example, no other justification was needed to acquiesce in them. In law, as Marshall clearly understood, certainty was no less desirable than rationality and must often be the preferred choice of judicial wisdom. The sacrifice of reason was a small price to pay to avoid the mischievous consequences of overturning precedent.

STATUTORY CONSTRUCTION

Unlike precedents, which were not law but only the evidence of law, statutes were the law itself, the express will of the sovereign. In cases that depended on the construction of statutes, Marshall engaged in a somewhat different interpretive task from that of inquiring into the meaning and authority of adjudged cases. Instead of examining books of reports in quest of the applicable principle, he dealt with a single, discrete text that in itself was the sole authority for deciding the point at issue. One overriding principle governed such cases: a statute was to be so applied as to carry into effect the intention of the legislature. Legal investigation was accordingly confined to the single question of determining legislative intent by examining the words of the statute.

Broadly understood, nevertheless, statutory construction and expounding unwritten law by examining adjudged cases were analogous enterprises. If precedents could be regarded as collectively constituting a "text" of unwritten law, then the analogy becomes more apt. Whether explicating previous judicial decisions or construing a legislative statute, a judge confronted essentially the same question. Did the case at bar come within the principle established by a line of precedents or within the intention manifested by the words of a statute? Similar rules of interpretation were also to be applied. Words, whether uttered by a judge or embodied in a statute, were to be taken in their ordinary signification unless there was a clear intention to use them in a different sense. They were to be understood, too, in reference to the particular case decided or in relation to the particular purposes to be accomplished by the statute.

Both forms of legal inquiry involved the exercise of judicial discretion. Although it might seem that a judge would have much greater freedom to navigate in and around precedents than within the written text of a law, the constraints of authority operated in a manner similar to the words of a statute in restricting the range of choice. At the same time, the "imperfection of all human language," its inability to express accurately for all times and circumstances the precise meaning intended to be conveyed, created space for a judge to decide which interpretation of the words of a statute best carried into effect the will of the legislature.[28] Judicial power as exercised in expounding written law was largely founded on the imprecision, obscurity, and ambiguity of language that inevitably characterized even the most carefully drawn statute or other legal instrument.

Over the course of numerous decisions, Marshall adopted a pragmatic, common-sense approach to interpreting statutes that he invariably denominated "fair construction."[29] "Fair construction" strove to harmonize the parts with the whole, the letter with the spirit. It was "a medium between that restricted sense which confines the meaning of words to narrower limits than the common understanding of the world affixes to them, and that extended sense which would stretch them beyond their obvious import." It "gives to language the sense in which it is used, and interprets an instrument according to its true intention."[30] As much as possible, Marshall tried to make fair construction into minimal construction, departing in the smallest degree from the literal meaning of words. "[My] general rule of construction, and I think it a good one, is to adhere to the letter of the statute, taking the whole together," he wrote. In an earlier time, he noted, courts exercised greater freedom of construction, often going "far beyond the words." The modern practice, however, had "been a good deal restrained." Although courts still construed "words liberally, to reach that intention which the words themselves import," they rarely supplied omissions, such as including an omitted class of persons merely because they believed there was the same reason for bringing this class within the statute "as for comprehending those who are actually enumerated."[31]

As a modern judge, Marshall was reluctant to take words beyond their natural import, to discard the literal meaning in favor of one supposedly more faithful to the spirit of the law. He believed that the letter of the law was the most reliable guide to its spirit and that in most instances the two could be shown to be in accord, not in opposition. The burden of proof was always on the party seeking to vary the usual understanding of words or to infer an implication where there was no explicit provision.[32] For the "spirit of the law" was simply "the intention of the legislature, to be collected from the general language of the act, the scope of its provisions, and the object to be attained."[33] In preferring literal construction, Marshall understood that term in a broader sense than a strict grammatical or lexical reading of words unconnected to context or intention.

Construction was the art of discovering intention, and intention was to be found only in the words of the act, "taking the whole together."[34] The particular provisions of a law were to be construed in relation to each other and to the whole. A law, said Marshall, "was the best expositor of itself," every part of which was "to be taken into view, for the purpose of discovering the mind of the legislature." Words could not be understood in isolation, detached from their context, or without reference to the subject, nature, and purpose of the legislation. In keeping the whole law in view, one part might be "expounded by any other, which may indicate the meaning annexed by the legislature itself to ambiguous phrases." It was also appropriate in certain circumstances to consider several acts on the same subject in reference to each other, using the clear provisions of one to explicate obscure provisions in another.[35]

In statutory construction cases, Marshall encountered numerous instances in which the words of a law, taken by themselves, were of doubtful or ambiguous meaning. The typical case required him to determine the sense in which general words or expressions were used. Here the rule was "that general phrases may be explained, and restrained or enlarged by other words which demonstrate the sense in which those general phrases were used." A related rule was "that general expressions may be restrained by subsequent particular words" that showed the legislature's intention to use those general expressions "in a particular sense."[36] As general words might have a more or less restrictive meaning, so words having "a direct and common meaning" might "also be used in a less common sense." But they were not to be so understood, Marshall cautioned, unless the context showed a "clear design" or "manifest intent" to give them "a less obvious meaning."[37]

If the construction to be given words did not emerge clearly from the context, a jurist might properly call in aid the general subject of the legislation, the object and motives for its enactment, and the effects and consequences of a particular interpretation. Reliance on these aids was a "deductive" method of reaching intent, while attention to words in context was an "inductive" method. It was not unusual for Marshall to employ both methods in the same case, as nicely illustrated by his construction of a revenue law in *Pennington v. Coxe* (1804). The issue was whether a duty on sugar refined before the expiration of the law (which had been repealed) but not yet sent out was due and payable to the United States.

After a close analysis of the language of different sections of the act, the chief justice acknowledged that "great difficulty" remained in discerning the true construction. He then invoked the "object" of the law, which was to raise revenue, "and not to discourage manufactures." From this object he inferred the absence of certain motives on Congress's part in imposing a duty on refined sugars, which in turn led him to conclude there was "no reason" for adopting a certain construction "unless the words" required it. Referring to the particular language again, he could find no such requirement. Marshall by this point had concluded that Congress intended to lay the duty not on refined sugar per se but on the sending out of the refined sugar. He then devoted the remainder of his opinion to answering objections to this construction. Here again he referred broadly to the subject of revenue, noting that the apparent object of the laws was "to tax expense and not industry" and that this intent was "manifested with peculiar plainness" in the particular case of the duty on sugar.[38]

In *Pennington v. Coxe* and in other notable cases of statutory construction, Marshall combined intensive analysis of words with extensive analysis of subject, purpose, and consequence. He read a statute, so to speak, inside out and outside in to gather evidence of the mind of the legislature. Where appropriate, he assumed the character of grammarian and lexicographer in aid of his principal role of jurist. Depending on the nature and circumstances of the case, the results of his analysis confirmed or departed from a literal reading of words; gave a restrictive or an enlarged sense to words, or endorsed a "strict" or a "liberal" construction. The one result or the other was the product of that "fair construction" by which the chief justice tried to discern the true intent of the legislature.

A case where Marshall upheld a reading of words "in their natural and usual sense" was *United States v. Fisher* (1805). He construed an act for settling the accounts of receivers of public money to give the United States priority of payment out of the estates not only of public officers and of other receivers of public money but of any insolvent debtor to the government. Even though the title of the act and most of its provisions dealt with public officers, the section in question referred broadly to "any revenue officer, or other person," who became indebted to the United States. As this section appeared to embrace anyone who endorsed and failed to pay a bill of exchange purchased by the government, the chief justice said it was "incumbent" on those opposing this construction to prove "an intent varying from that which the words import." After carefully reviewing the law's various provisions and taking into account the "inconvenience" of a literal construction, he could find no justification for reading "other person" in a restricted sense.[39]

On the other hand, in *United States* v. *Palmer* (1818), the chief justice read the general phrase "any person or persons," employed in a statute defining crimes against the United States, restrictively to exclude persons who were not citizens and who served on a ship belonging exclusively to subjects of a foreign state from being tried as pirates under that act. Here he found ample reason from the words and the general subject to conclude that Congress intended the phrase to be "necessarily confined to any person or persons owing permanent or temporary allegiance to the United States."[40]

In *United States* v. *Wiltberger* (1820) Marshall interpreted the same law in refusing federal jurisdiction in a case of manslaughter committed by an American seaman on board an American vessel in a foreign river. One section of the statute provided for the punishment of manslaughter committed "on the high seas," but another section prescribed punishment for murder committed not only on the "high seas" but "in any river, haven, basin, or bay, out of the jurisdiction of any particular State." The question was whether Congress intended to punish manslaughter in these additional places as well. The chief justice refused to enlarge the construction of "on the high seas" beyond the phrase's "plain meaning" as used in the section dealing with manslaughter. It was reasonable to suppose, he admitted, that Congress might want to make manslaughter cognizable in the federal courts in the same places it prescribed for murder. But no such intention was to be implied from this probability. "It would be dangerous, indeed," he warned, "to carry the principle, that a case which is within the reason or mischief of a statute, is within its provisions, so far as to punish a crime not enumerated in the statute, because it is of equal atrocity, or of kindred character, with those which are enumerated." While invoking the rule that penal statutes were to be construed strictly,

Marshall relied principally on intention as manifested by the words of the statute. A minute investigation of the language satisfied him that Congress had not prescribed punishment for manslaughter in any place other than on the "high seas" and that the Court could not "enlarge the statute."[41]

The most difficult test of judicial discretion came when a court was asked to modify statutory language, supply omissions, draw implications—in short, to give a liberal construction to the legislature's words. Marshall justified liberal construction only to the extent necessary to reach an intention manifested positively by the language, subject, and purposes of the law and negatively by the absurd, repugnant, and meaningless consequences of a literal or strict construction. A "law requiring two repugnant and incompatible things," he said, "is incapable of receiving a literal construction, and must sustain some change of language to be rendered intelligible. This change, however, ought to be as small as possible, and with a view to the sense of the legislature, as manifested by themselves." Thus a simple change of a participle into the future tense of a verb could "destroy the repugnancy" contained in a particular passage of a law and "reconcile" it with another that "absolutely demonstrates" the legislature's intention.[42] In certain situations, as when "the whole context of the law" showed a "particular intent . . . to effect a certain object," a court could call in "some degree of implication . . . to aid that intent." From Congress's affirmative declaration in the Judiciary Act that the Supreme Court's appellate power extended to circuit court judgments of a value exceeding two thousand dollars, for example, the Court implied an intent to except from its jurisdiction judgments of less value.[43]

Along with a general rule of construction that penal statutes were to be construed strictly was another that statutes against frauds were "to be liberally and beneficially expounded."[44] Marshall applied this rule, without expressly referring to it, in interpreting a Virginia statute regulating conveyances. The act voided as to creditors and subsequent purchasers all deeds of trust and mortgages unless acknowledged, proved, and recorded according to the directions of the act. This legislation appeared to give directions only for conveyances of land, however, omitting mortgages of personal property. Acknowledging in *Hodgson* v. *Butts* (1805) that the statute was "very obscurely penned in this particular respect," the chief justice nevertheless concluded that it was sufficient to embrace deeds conveying personal property. "In a country where mortgages, of a particular kind of personal property [i.e., slaves], are frequent," he observed, "it can scarcely be supposed that no provision would be made for so important and interesting a subject." Since the legislature clearly intended to provide for mortgages of personal property and the "inconvenience resulting from the total want of such a provision would certainly be great," the Court was justified in liberally construing the law to effect that intention.[45]

In *Bond* v. *Ross* (1815), heard on circuit, Marshall again referred to "the obvious intention" of Virginia's conveyance law "to preserve the validity of a mortgage of a personal thing" and to the court's duty to construe it according to that intention "with the least possible violation to the words of the legislature." Although a discriminating review of the act's language produced satisfactory evidence indicating what court the legislature had in mind for the recording of such deeds, the chief justice was unable to effect this intention "without aiding the words" and construing the law as if certain phrases had been inserted. "There are certainly few cases in which this freedom of construction can be justified," he admitted. "If any act will justify it, it is the act for regulating conveyances." Even so, he was "not sure" that he would have given this opinion had it not been supported by a case decided in the state court of appeals.[46]

Marshall also resorted to liberal construction in a circuit case of 1820 that hinged on the meaning of an act providing for the remission of fines and forfeitures imposed for violations of the nonintercourse laws. The chief justice extended the law to embrace an American citizen's share of property jointly owned with British subjects. "In construing the act," he explained, "no reason can be perceived, for distinguishing between the interest of an American citizen, when joint and when sole; and it is an act intended for the protection of the citizen, which ought to be construed liberally, so as to effect that intention."[47]

A Supreme Court case of 1827 produced yet another variation on the theme of liberal construction. Marshall expounded the post office laws as authorizing the postmaster general to take bonds from a deputy postmaster, although no express words conferred this power. Such an interpretation, the chief justice admitted, might "be too free for a judicial tribunal, yet if the legislature has made it, if Congress has explained its own meaning too unequivocally to be mistaken, their Courts may be justified in adopting that meaning." The ensuing recital of various provisions showed that such bonds were fully within Congress's contemplation.[48]

In every case of statutory construction, Chief Justice Marshall conducted a critical, at times exhaustive, inquiry into legislative intention. If intention could be discerned, then the Court would have an objective, external standard for rendering a judgment. Drawing primarily upon the meaning of words in their ordinary sense and as modified by the context, he gave due attention as well to the broader subject of the legislation, to the objects it was intended to accomplish, and to the consequences of interpretation. Sometimes a delicate balancing of these various elements was required to reach a satisfactory determination of the legislative mind. There was always the danger, of course, that construction might imperceptibly cross the line from *interpreting* law to *making* law. Innocently or not, a judge might assume an identity between legislative intention and his personal view of a law's meaning and spirit.

Marshall was alert to this danger, sometimes taking unusual precautions to keep discretion in check. He consistently refused, for instance, to fill in gaps in the federal criminal code, even though an assumption of jurisdiction in these cases would probably not only have been approved but expected by the executive and legislative departments. Indeed, judicial self-denial as exhibited in *United States* v. *Palmer* provoked Secretary of State John Quincy Adams to denounce the decision as "founded upon captious subtleties."[49] In his irritation with a decision that appeared to hamper the administration's efforts to combat piracy, the secretary of state failed to grasp the larger significance of the Court's self-restraint. The judiciary's duty to enforce the will of Congress, the chief justice might have explained, did not extend to implementing policy goals based on supposition or probability. The Court could not allow short-term inconvenience to influence its judgment in such cases; rather, it had to consider the consequences of setting a precedent that led down the slippery slope to making law. Marshall repeatedly called attention to the necessity of preserving the distinction between legislative and judicial functions, particularly in expounding criminal and other penal laws. The legislature's province was to declare a rule "in explicit terms"; the court's province was "to apply the rule to the case thus explicitly described—not to some other case which judges may conjecture to be equally dangerous."[50]

FAIR CONSTRUCTION AND CONSTITUTIONAL INTERPRETATION

To the novel task of expounding the Constitution of the United States, Chief Justice Marshall applied the familiar tools and methods of statutory construction. "The object of language is to communicate the intention of him who speaks," he wrote, "and the great duty of a judge who construes an instrument is to find the intention of its makers."[51] When he referred to the "intention of the framers" in his constitutional opinions, the chief justice meant the same thing as he did when speaking of legislative intention in ordinary cases of statutory construction. He had in mind the intention of the instrument itself as disclosed by its words, not the subjective, historical intent of those who framed it. He explicitly endorsed this meaning of intent in reference to a proposed constitution for Virginia in 1830. That constitution, he declared, "ought to be construed *in its words*, and not in the opinion any member might have expressed upon it. They entertained different opinions: those opinions were not to regulate the construction of the Constitution. . . . Let the Constitution speak its own language, and be construed by those whose office it was to construe it."[52]

The distinction in Marshall's constitutional jurisprudence between the intention of the instrument and the so-called "original intent" of the framers emerged most clearly in *Dartmouth*, when he frankly acknowledged that the framers in 1787 and 1788 probably did not have in view the protection of corporate charters. Debtor relief legislation, he conceded, was the historic mischief that induced the framers to adopt the contract clause. At the same time, the comprehensive language of that provision revealed an intention to provide not only against the prevailing abuses of the day but also against future unforeseen mischief that legislative ingenuity might devise. It was this intention, Marshall insisted, an intention embodied in the express words of the Constitution, that must guide a judge in expounding the contract clause.[53]

The search for the intention of the Constitution was conducted by the same rules of fair construction that applied to statutes. "In performing the delicate and important duty of construing clauses in the constitution of our country, which involve conflicting powers of the government of the Union, and of the respective States," the chief justice wrote, "it is proper to take a view of the literal meaning of the words to be expounded, of their connexion with other words, and of the general objects to be accomplished by the prohibitory clause, or by the grant of power." The spirit of the Constitution was "to be respected not less than its letter," but the spirit was "to be chiefly collected from its words."[54] A judge should try to reach intention through the words, not read words according to some preconceived intent derived from the supposed spirit of the instrument.

Fair interpretation of the Constitution also meant keeping construction to a minimum. "Where words conflict with each other, where the different clauses of an instrument bear upon each other, and would be inconsistent unless the natural and common import of words be varied, construction becomes necessary, and a departure from the obvious meaning of words is justifiable," said Marshall. In all other cases, however, a judge was not authorized to disregard the "plain meaning of a provision" unless "the absurdity and injustice of applying the provision to the case, would be so monstrous, that all mankind would without hesitation, unite in rejecting the application."[55]

Marshall directed much of his constitutional interpretation against "strict construction," against what he considered to be an unauthorized restrictive reading of general words. He placed virtually the whole burden of proof upon those who wished to qualify general language and to introduce exceptions said to accord with the true intent and spirit of the Constitution. In expounding the contract clause, for example, he tried to show that confining its meaning to narrower limits than its words imported failed one or more tests of proof laid down by the rules of fair construction. By those same rules, he could sustain the literal, nonrestrictive sense of the words merely by showing that this sense was not so unreasonable or unjust as to authorize the Court to except particular kinds of contracts from the contract clause's protection or to exempt certain state laws from its operation. Applying the rules of fair construction, he concluded that the Constitution protected "executed" as well as "executory" contracts, public contracts (land grants and corporate charters) as well as private contracts, and that bankruptcy laws discharging a debtor's full liability were unconstitutional. He refused to yield to the Court majority in sanctioning prospective bankruptcy laws, discerning no more intent to distinguish between retrospective and prospective interferences with contracts than to distinguish between "executory" and "executed" contracts or between private and public contracts.

If fair construction was employed in the contract cases principally against a restrictive sense of the word and against a restrictive reach of the prohibition, Marshall readily conceded that the general prohibition did not extend to all contracts. Grants of political power and marriage contracts, for example, were legitimate objects of state regulation and control. The prohibition was to be understood as embracing only contracts that "respect property, or some object of value, and confer rights which may be asserted in a court of justice."[56] Since this restriction was not controverted, Marshall did not need to justify excepting certain contracts from the prohibition. Fair construction supplied the rule, if needed. The Constitution's provisions were "neither to be restricted into insignificance, nor extended to objects not comprehended in them nor contemplated by its framers." To have construed "contract" in its most latitudinous sense would have had the mischievous consequence of proscribing virtually all state legislative power, clearly not an object "comprehended" within any provision of the Constitution.[57]

The chief justice expounded other prohibitory clauses of the Constitution in the same way, taking into view the literal meaning of words and the objects of the provision. He held that the clause prohibiting the states from emitting bills of credit embraced loan office certificates issued in small denominations. These certificates, he maintained, were bills of credit in everything but name. That they were not legal tender made no difference, for the prohibition was "general," extending "to all bills of credit, not to bills of a particular description." To make an exception "without the aid of other explanatory words" would venture on judicial arrogance. Moreover, since the same clause also prohibited tender laws, to read the ban on bills of credit thus restrictively would violate the accepted rules of construction. Here the context clearly showed intention and aided proper construction of the clause. To the argument that the great mischief of paper money was its status as tender and that the prohibition must therefore be understood in this particular sense, he replied: "Was it even true that the evils of paper money resulted solely from the quality of its being made a tender, this court would not feel itself authorized to disregard the plain meaning of words, in search of a conjectural intent to which we are not conducted by the language of any part of the instrument."[58]

Marshall also held that a licensing fee imposed on importers was repugnant to the clause that prohibited a state from laying import or export duties except as "absolutely necessary" for enforcing its inspection laws. A duty on imports was literally "a duty on the thing imported" and might be levied after as well as during the act of importation. Literal construction was confirmed by the context, particularly the exception in favor of inspection laws, which showed "the extent" in which the term was understood. So, too, in looking "to the objects of the prohibition," he could "find no reason" to exempt the licensing act from its operation. If the states could enact such laws, it would defeat the purpose of the prohibition, which was to preserve Congress's control over the subject of foreign commerce. He acknowledged that the prohibition should not be carried too far, observing "that in our complex system, the object of the powers conferred" on the general government "and the nature of the often conflicting powers" remaining in the states should be kept in view "in expounding the words of any particular clause." In this case, however, the "sound principles of construction" did not permit the Court to say that the prohibition ceased, and the power of the state to tax commenced, at the instant of importation.[59]

If strict construction was inappropriate for the clauses prohibiting the exercise of state powers, it was no less so for those clauses granting powers to the federal government. *McCulloch* emphasized the nature of the Constitution as conferring powers in general terms, marking only the "great outlines," designating only the "important objects"—all of which evinced an intention to include within the grant ample means to execute the enumerated power. The ensuing construction of the "necessary and proper" clause concluded that the provision was not "restrictive of the general right . . . of selecting means for executing the enumerated powers."[60] *Gibbons* expounded one of the enumerated powers, the commerce power, in comprehensive terms as encompassing the power to regulate navigation and as extending Congress's regulatory control to the interior of a state. Where *McCulloch* and *Gibbons* liberally interpreted Congress's legislative powers, *Cohens* broadly construed the judiciary article's grant of federal judicial power in the "arising under" clause to extend to cases in which a state was a party.

In each of these opinions, Marshall conducted his inquiry into intention by means of reciprocal, overlapping arguments focusing on words, context, nature and objects, and consequences. He blended minute linguistic analysis with consideration of the broader structure, purposes, and nature of the Constitution. As intention could be discerned only in the actual language adopted by the framers, so the sense in which they used words was illuminated by reference to intention as manifested in other parts or in the whole text and structure of the Constitution. Without adhering to a set formula or strict order of argumentation, the chief justice's constitutional expositions exhibited a similar pattern of dialogue between text and intention, letter and spirit.

Construing the grants of power to Congress was not precisely the same thing as construing the prohibitions on state powers. Although Marshall rejected strict construction in both kinds of cases, the general language of the prohibitory clauses provided more definite clues to intention than did the general language of the granting clauses. Perhaps for this reason he deemed it more appropriate in expounding Congress's powers to discuss the nature and general purposes of the Constitution before taking up the particular clause in question. Taken by themselves, for example, the words of the "necessary and proper" clause did not offer much guidance to the interpreter. The first part of *McCulloch* accordingly deduced from the nature and framework of the instrument a general intention to recognize implied powers and to allow Congress discretion to choose the means to execute its enumerated powers. With this point of reference Marshall could proceed to a fair construction of the words of the "necessary and proper" clause.

A lexical analysis of "necessary" showed that it commonly imported something less than "an absolute physical necessity" and was used in a variety of senses. To determine the particular sense meant in this clause, the chief justice sought constructive aid from the subject, context, and intention. Under the heading of subject, "the execution of the great powers on which the welfare of a nation essentially depends," he argued essentially in negative terms that applying a narrow construction to the powers of government was totally impracticable and that the rule had in fact never been adopted. The context, particularly the association of "necessary" with "proper," further indicated an intention to qualify the "strict and rigorous meaning" and suggest "the idea of some choice of means of legislation." Context blended into intention as Marshall went on to show that the clause was "placed among the powers of Congress, not among the limitations on those powers," and that its language conveyed the idea of "an additional power, not a restriction on those already granted." He stated the result of this investigation not positively that the clause enlarged the powers of Congress but negatively that it did not restrain those powers or deny Congress's right to exercise discretion in choosing the means to execute its constitutional powers. He had now confirmed by "induction" the intention he had previously arrived at by "deduction."[61]

The importance of *McCulloch* lies no less in its exemplary illustration of the principles of fair construction than in its espousal of constitutional nationalism. Throughout his career as a legal interpreter, Chief Justice Marshall continually relied on these principles to discover intention, to discern the meaning of the law as embodied in precedents, statutes, or the Constitution. No matter what the case, whether a mundane suit for debt or a great controversy involving the clashing sovereignties of the state and general governments, he aspired to apply these principles so as to declare the law without transcending the limits of judicial discretion. All of his inquiries into intent were so many checks upon discretion, designed to show that he was not making law but carrying into effect a law made elsewhere.

Marshall most certainly would have preferred his reputation as a judge to be measured by his fidelity to the principles of fair construction than by the particular results of his interpretations. Indeed, he devoted the greater part of his defense of *McCulloch* to vindicating the reasoning of his exposition of the Constitution. Critics complained that the chief justice virtually rewrote the Constitution, constructively enlarging federal powers while abridging state powers. He indignantly denied the charge as a gross misrepresentation of his efforts to expound the meaning of the Constitution according to accepted canons of legal interpretation. The opinion, he repeatedly protested, did not contend that the "necessary and proper" clause enlarged the powers of Congress, only that it did "not restrain" those that were granted.[62] He neither sought to augment Congress's powers nor to diminish state powers but merely to demonstrate the errors of reading the Constitution's words restrictively. The issue, as he defined it, was whether a fair construction or a strict construction of the Constitution should prevail and which of the two came closer to discerning its true intention.

Marshall's quarrel with strict construction was not that it was an improper mode of legal interpretation but that it was incorrectly applied to certain clauses of the Constitution. He denied that there was a "technical rule applicable to every case" that enjoined a judge to interpret legal instruments "in a more restricted sense than their words import." As he so often pointed out, "the nature of the instrument, the words that are employed, the object to be effected, are all to be taken into consideration, and to have their due weight." If strict construction meant only to deny "that enlarged construction, which would extend words beyond their natural and obvious import," he fully agreed with the principle.[63] The problem with strict construction as urged by the advocates of states' rights was that it went to the opposite extreme, confining the meaning of words to narrower limits than their plain sense imported even when no restrictive intent could be shown.

This rigid strict construction was bad law, said Marshall. Its labored attempts to prove an intent to depart from the "plain meaning" of words by some theory or evidence not grounded in the Constitution's text violated the received maxims of legal construction. In *Cohens*, for example, the argument for a restrictive view of federal jurisdiction relied on an abstract theory of state sovereignty. Although not denying the existence of this principle in the Constitution, Marshall showed how the instrument itself had so far modified and abridged state powers that no exception to federal jurisdiction could be implied from the principle. So, too, the critics of *McCulloch* looked outside the Constitution, to the law of nations and to the common law, for evidence that grants of power to the federal government should be construed strictly. Marshall countered that the law of nations and the common law endorsed no particular rule of construction for legal instruments other than that they should be "construed liberally, or restrictively, as may best promote the object for which they were made." The critics, he pointed out, had selectively chosen examples—a treaty between hostile nations and a contract between two individuals—that might appear to justify strict construction in those particular cases but were wholly inapposite for cases of expounding a constitution.[64]

A recurring theme of Marshall's answer to the attacks on the Supreme Court was that the error of excessive constructionism, of ignoring the text of the Constitution while attempting to explain its meaning by reference to external sources, was more properly ascribed to the Court's critics than to the chief justice and his brethren. In this regard, his most effective reply to the critics was that their rule of construction utterly failed the test of consequences. If this rule were adopted, the result would leave the Constitution "a magnificent structure, indeed, to look at, but totally unfit for use." It "would essentially change the constitution, render the government of the Union incompetent to the objects for which it was instituted, and place all its powers under the control of the state legislatures. It would, in a great measure, reinstate the old confederation."[65]

Marshall rested his argument for a nonrestrictive interpretation on the manifestly pernicious consequences of strict construction. A jurist had no choice but to reject a construction that was so patently contrary to the letter and spirit of the Constitution, that would in fact cast aside the fundamental law created by the American people in 1787 and 1788. Marshall's defense of *McCulloch* thus boiled down to a single point: the Supreme Court had no discretion to choose between fair construction and strict construction. The American people had previously made that choice by discarding the Articles of Confederation and adopting the Constitution. Strict construction could not be and had never been the rule for interpreting the Constitution. Not the least of the unacceptable consequences was that a court in adopting such a rule would overstep the boundaries of judicial discretion.

Marshall attributed the emergence of strict constructionism to a persistent antifederal spirit that had never been reconciled to the decision of 1788. "The zealous and persevering hostility with which the constitution was originally opposed, cannot be forgotten," he wrote. "The deep rooted and vindictive hate, which grew out of unfounded jealousies, and was aggravated by defeat, though suspended for a time, seems never to have been appeased." What antifederalism failed to accomplish in 1788, the strict constructionists of the states' rights school were now undertaking with renewed vigor— "to strip the government of those effective powers, which enable it to accomplish the objects for which it was created; and, by construction, essentially to reinstate that miserable confederation" of the 1780s.[66]

As these remarks make clear, Marshall did not pretend to take a neutral, disinterested view of this debate over construction. Both his constitutional jurisprudence and his political views were decidedly hostile to the doctrine of states' rights. A perennial question raised about his judicial career concerns the extent to which his political beliefs shaped his interpretation of the Constitution. The proposition that these beliefs had no influence on his jurisprudence cannot be seriously maintained; indeed, Marshall himself made no such claim. Having participated in the events of the founding period, he had formed a certain understanding of the meaning of those events. The essence of this understanding was that the adoption of the Constitution was a transforming moment, a rare, almost miraculous occasion when the American people exercised their sovereignty to create a new constitutional framework. In particular, the Constitution represented the people's conscious, deliberate repudiation of a confederal "league" of sovereign states in favor of a general government of national jurisdiction.

That the Constitution provoked bitter opposition and was approved only after a closely contested campaign for ratification merely confirmed its nature as a radical break with the immediate past. The key to understanding the meaning of the Constitution, according to Marshall, lay in learning the "lessons" of the critical 1780s.

> I have always thought the interval between the conclusion of our revolutionary war and the adoption of our present constitution the most interesting and the most instructive portion of our history. . . . It has been always matter of wonder to me that with the lessons of that very instructive period before our eyes, any intelligent man should be found who would carry us back to a system so totally incompetent to the objects for which men congregate in society, and yet such is the direct tendency of some of the favorite dogmas of the day.[67]

This perception of the meaning of the political settlement of 1788 was the underlying premise of Marshall's constitutional jurisprudence, the point of departure from which he construed the grants of power to the general government and the prohibitions on the powers of the states. In this sense his constitutional pronouncements reflected the judge's "bias" in favor of the nationalizing and centralizing features of the instrument. Yet this "bias" was not at all the same thing as willful or arbitrary opinion or prejudice. The political principles and ideals upon which he fashioned his constitutional expositions were not narrow, partisan views but represented a broad consensus, one that embraced both the majority that brought the Constitution into being in 1788 and the minority who in good faith accepted the decision. Marshall never doubted that this consensus, which continued to operate by tacit consent in subsequent generations, truly reflected the best and deliberate sense of the American people. It constituted a sufficient external standard by which a judge could expound the law of the Constitution.

No text explains itself, and in its passage through the medium of the interpreter it receives the indelible stamp of that medium. Legal interpretation is a complex interaction between legal text and jurist to which the latter brings a set of assumptions, principles, and beliefs accumulated over a lifetime. The common law system of adjudication to which Marshall was bred had always recognized the difficulty, if not the impossibility, of realizing the ideal of objectivity in the act of interpretation. It took for granted the fallibility of the judge and the corresponding imperative to check judicial "will." Precisely for these reasons it had devised a set of methods and rules whose purpose was to filter out as much as possible the purely subjective elements—the personal prejudices and whims of the individual judge—that got in the way of principled, unbiased judgment. So long as he carried out the interpretive enterprise by conscientiously applying the rules sanctioned by centuries of common law adjudication, Marshall cannot be justly charged with allowing personal or partisan predilections to distort his legal judgment.

MARSHALL AND MADISON REVISITED

As a jurist and expounder of the Constitution, Marshall remained essentially true to the constitutional principles of James Madison, his fellow Virginian and founder. Despite the different political paths they took during the 1790s, these two statesmen always regarded each other with respect. The one's inveterate dislike of Jefferson and the other's close friendship with him did not interfere with their maintaining cordial relations with one another. They both believed that an essential purpose of the Constitution was to abridge the state sovereignties, to prevent the flagrant abuses committed by factious majorities in the state legislatures that were so prevalent during the 1780s. As chief justice, Marshall and his Court exercised judicial review almost exclusively against state laws, principally by means of a broad reading of the contract clause. In Marshall's hands the contract clause proved to be an effective means of accomplishing the same purposes Madison had in mind for his proposed legislative "negative," or veto, over state legislation. Madison, to be sure, may have thought the Marshall Court went too far in restraining the states, but his complaints on this account were not directed at the contract clause decisions.

Indeed, Madison never publicly criticized the Court, and in private only one of Marshall's opinions, *McCulloch* v. *Maryland*, incurred his strong censure. Even here he did not react directly to the decision itself but to a letter from Spencer Roane enclosing his "Hampden" essays.[68] Although he did not object to the Court's sustaining the constitutionality of the Second Bank or to its voiding of Maryland's tax, Madison was seriously disturbed by what he regarded as "the high sanction given to a latitude in expounding the Constitution." Marshall's rule of construction seemed "to break down the landmarks intended by a specification of the Powers of Congress, and to substitute for a definite connection between means and ends, a Legislative discretion as to the former to which no practical limit can be assigned." According to the Court's "doctrine," Congress might exercise any power "not expressly prohibited" so long as that body deemed it an expedient means of executing an enumerated power.

Madison dismissed the Court's declaration that it would uphold the Constitution "against legislative encroachments," for the decision of such a case would inevitably involve the Court in questions of policy or expediency, of which the judiciary properly refused to take cognizance. The Court in effect relinquished "all controul on the Legislative exercise of unconstitutional powers." Madison traced the Court's "error in expounding the Constitution" to its assumption that the sovereign powers vested in the general government necessarily implied "an unlimited discretion" in Congress to choose the means of executing them. "It may surely be remarked," he observed, "that a limited Government may be limited in its sovereignty as well with respect to the means as to the objects of its powers; and that to give an extent to the former, superseding the limits to the latter, is in effect to convert a limited into an unlimited Government."[69]

Pointed as it was, Madison's critique was totally devoid of the strident and doctrinaire tone adopted by states' rights ideologues who denounced *McCulloch* and attacked the Court as an institution. Indeed, the elder statesman took pains to distance himself not only from Roane but from Jefferson as well. Unlike them, he did not express alarm at a usurping federal judiciary bent upon prostrating the state governments and erecting a consolidated government over the union. That the Court's rule of construction tended to break down the barrier between the general and state governments was less troubling than that the Court had gratuitously conferred tremendous power on the legislative branch of the federal government. As a republican theorist, Madison had always believed that legislatures, as the direct representatives of the popular will, posed the most dangerous threat to free and stable government. Congress was scarcely less immune to the pressures of majority factionalism than were the state legislatures. His great fear was that Congress, armed with immense discretionary power and supplied with a rule that seemed to equate utility with constitutionality, would effectively amend the Constitution—completely bypassing the amendment process outlined in the instrument itself.[70]

Had he been privy to it, Marshall no doubt would have regarded Madison's indictment of *McCulloch* as much more formidable than that delivered by Roane. In reply he assuredly would have denied that his rule of construction tended to alter the nature of the government as one of specified and limited powers. He might have attempted to reassure Madison that the judiciary department would be more vigilant and disposed to arrest the career of an aggrandizing Congress than the latter believed was possible. Certainly, too, he would have expressed agreement with Madison's call for "a reasonable medium between expounding the Constitution with the strictness of a penal law, or other ordinary statute, and expounding it with a laxity which may vary its essential character, and encroach on the local sovereignties with which it was meant to be reconcilable."[71] Madison did not spell out what he meant by "reasonable medium," but he clearly implied that strict construction (at least as advocated by Roane and other states' rights theorists) was erroneous. What other rule, Marshall might have asked, could a jurist have formulated than the one advanced by the Court or one similar to it?

Madison's disagreement with Marshall on the proper rule for construing the powers of the general government reflected his somewhat different perception of the constitutional equilibrium established in 1787. Marshall continued to believe that the delicate balance was far more likely to be upset by centrifugal forces emanating from the states than from centripetal forces issuing from the general government. His overriding concern was that strict construction would ultimately convert the Constitution into the old Confederation. Madison was no less committed than Marshall to preventing the constructive revival of the Confederation, but he was much more attuned than was the chief justice to the dangers arising from the consolidating potential of a constructive enlargement of federal powers. In 1819 Madison was far less sanguine than he had been in 1788 that the national legislature could avoid the factionalism that plagued the state legislatures. Marshall remained confident that the force of public opinion and the structure of Congress, with an assist from the national judiciary, would keep that body more or less within its constitutional limits. In the end, both Madison and Marshall might have agreed that the former had identified a problem that admitted of no wholly satisfactory solution.

Whatever their differences on the appropriate construction of national powers, Marshall and Madison in other respects were in basic agreement about the nature of the American federal system. Both were dedicated to preserving the constitutional settlement of 1787, and for both the events of that decade were central to forming their understanding of the meaning of that settlement. Both firmly believed that the federal judiciary was the constitutionally authorized tribunal to resolve disputes about the proper boundary between federal and state jurisdictions. Even at the height of the protest against the "consolidating" doctrines of the Marshall Court, Madison was admonishing his zealous friends of their error in denying that this trust was conferred on the judicial department. That department's jurisdiction in cases arising under the Constitution, he reminded Roane, "must be admitted to be a vital part of the System." He emphatically rejected Jefferson's scheme for referring such questions to conventions of the people in the individual states, reiterating at the same time his belief that the framers intended the federal judiciary to "be the Constitutional resort for determining the line between the federal and state jurisdictions."[72]

In their last years Marshall and Madison were united in combating the noxious doctrine of nullification, a constitutional heresy that the latter readily perceived to be a far graver threat to dismantle the founders' great achievement of the 1780s than had ever been posed by the specter of consolidation. In repudiating nullification, Madison became an increasingly staunch defender of the federal judiciary as the arbiter of the federal system and as the institution best suited to giving an authoritative exposition of the Constitution.[73] "A political system that does not provide for a peaceable and effectual decision of all controversies arising among the parties," he wrote in 1829, "is not a Government, but a mere Treaty between independent nations, without any resort for terminating disputes but negotiation, and that failing, the sword." Two years later he affirmed the Supreme Court's appellate power over the state judiciaries, observing that the latter could "only be kept in their constitutional career by the control of the federal jurisdiction. Take the linch-pins from a carriage, and how soon would a wheel be off its axle; an emblem of the speedy fate of the federal system, were the parties to it loosened from the authority which confines them to their spheres." Similarly, in terms worthy of the chief justice himself, Madison asserted the supremacy of the federal judicial power as "a vital principle of the Constitution" and "a prominent feature in its text. A supremacy of the Constitution and laws of the Union, without a supremacy in the exposition and execution of them, would be as much a mockery as a scabbard put into the hand of a soldier without a sword in it." Near the close of his life, he professed his belief that the Supreme Court, "when happily filled," would "most engage the respect and reliance of the public as the surest expositor of the Constitution."[74]

With one exception, Madison confined his constitutional commentary in retirement to private correspondence. In 1830 he published a letter on nullification in the *North American Review*. Here he collected together all his views on this subject, including his defense of the federal judiciary. Although noting that there had "been occasional decisions from the bench which have incurred serious and extensive disapprobation," he acknowledged "that, with but few exceptions, the course of the judiciary has been hitherto sustained by the predominant sense of the nation." Chief Justice Marshall read this letter "with peculiar pleasure," adding that Madison was "himself again. He avows the opinions of his best days, and must be pardoned for his oblique insinuations that some of the opinions of our court are not approved."[75]

More than anyone else, John Marshall invented American constitutional law, a novel branch of law that brought constitutional interpretation into the ordinary task of adjudicating lawsuits.[76] So commonplace has judicial interpretation and application of the Constitution become in our own day that it is easy to miss the significance of this development. Yet it is this assimilation of constitutional exegesis to the methods of common law adjudication that may constitute Marshall's most enduring legacy. To be sure, his masterly opinions laid the foundations of our constitutional law and furnished a set of principles that continue to animate it. Still, the broader significance of his career may lie less in his particular interpretations of the Constitution as in his largely successful effort to infuse constitutional pronouncements with the qualities of an ordinary legal judgment. In this way he contributed immeasurably to the American people's ultimate acceptance of such pronouncements as so much *law*.

In the years preceding *Marbury*, American judicial review acquired its leading feature as enforcement of a written constitution. This development, however, did not significantly alter the original conception of judicial review. Written constitutions continued to be regarded as fundamental law, different in kind from ordinary law. They were understood as social contracts for organizing and limiting sovereign power, unlike ordinary law, which was concerned with restraining individual behavior. Enforcement of fundamental law was a political and moral, not a legal, responsibility; enforcement of ordinary law was an exclusively legal function. In the earliest exercises of judicial review, American judges acted essentially in a political capacity, defending the fundamental law against its clear violation, reasserting first principles as a kind of judicial substitute for revolution. In undertaking this extraordinary political act, judges were enforcing an explicit social contract, not expounding or interpreting a legal text as they did in enforcing ordinary law.

Over the course of three decades of leadership on the highest court of the land, Chief Justice John Marshall carried judicial review beyond judicial defense of fundamental law toward the modern notion of judicial exposition of the constitutional text. He effected this change by applying the methods of statutory interpretation to the Constitution, an innovation he was largely responsible for introducing and sustaining. In a subtle, almost imperceptible way the chief justice succeeded in blurring the distinction between fundamental law and ordinary law to one of degree rather than kind. He "legalized" the Constitution, made it amenable to routine judicial exposition and implementation. The Constitution, in short, became "supreme ordinary law," operating as a legal restraint on sovereign power in a way analogous to the legal restraint of ordinary law on individuals.

The degree to which Marshall consciously conceived and carried out this transformation is difficult to ascertain, for he never gave any indication that he was doing anything novel or extraordinary in expounding the Constitution by the rules of statutory construction. No doubt he understood that the older notion of judicial review was becoming obsolete by the early nineteenth century. The Constitution itself had put an end to the notorious abuses of legislative power of the 1780s that had called forth the first tentative assertions of judicial review. If the practice was to survive in the United States, it would have to become something different from an extraordinary, rarely invoked defense of first principles in a quasi-revolutionary situation. Further, if this practice was to be a responsibility of judges, it would have to be accommodated as much as possible to their familiar role as interpreters of ordinary law. Having been trained in the great tradition of common law adjudication, the chief justice naturally turned to its methods as the only way he knew to revitalize judicial review. He exercised judicial review with a combination of boldness and restraint, employing it sparingly but often enough to make it a regular and continuously operating principle of the American constitutional system. Marshall surely did not grasp all the implications or foresee all the consequences of what he was doing. To acknowledge that he was not a fully conscious actor in the historical process, however, in no way diminishes the magnitude of his achievement as "the great chief justice."

NOTES

In citing reports of law cases, I have followed (with some modification) standard legal citation form. The name of the case is followed by the volume number and short title (usually the reporter's last name); the page number(s); and, if needed, the court and year within parentheses. For Supreme Court cases, I have not designated the court. For other cases I have given the name of the court in abbreviated form. For example, cases in the U.S. Circuit Court for Virginia are cited "U.S. Cir. Ct., Va." ("N.C.," for North Carolina). Cases in the Virginia Court of Appeals, Virginia General Court, and Virginia High Court of Chancery are abbreviated "Va. Ct. of App.," "Va. Gen. Ct.," "Va. High Ct. of Ch." Full titles of all reports cited in this book are given below.

Brockenbrough	John W. Brockenbrough, *Reports of Cases Decided by the Honourable John Marshall . . . in the Circuit Court of the United States for the District of Virginia and North Carolina, from 1802 to 1833,* 2 vols. (Philadelphia, 1837)
Call	Daniel Call, *Reports of Cases Argued and Adjudged in the Court of Appeals of Virginia,* 6 vols. (Richmond, Va., 1801–1833)
Cranch	William Cranch, *Reports of Cases Argued and Adjudged in the Supreme Court of the United States, 1801-1815,* 9 vols. (New York and Washington, D.C., 1804–1817)
Dallas	Alexander J. Dallas, *Reports of Cases Ruled and Adjudged in the Several Courts of the United States, and of Pennsylvania,* 4 vols. (Philadelphia, 1790–1807)

Fed. Cas.	*Federal Cases* (1789–1880), 30 vols. (St. Paul, Minn., 1894–1897)
H. and M.	William W. Hening and William Munford, *Reports of Cases Argued and Determined in the Supreme Court of Appeals of Virginia,* 4 vols. (Philadelphia, 1808–1811)
Haywood	John Haywood, *Cases Adjudged in the Superior Courts . . . of North Carolina,* 2 vols. (Halifax and Raleigh, N.C., 1799–1806)
Peters	Richard Peters, Jr., *Reports of Cases Argued and Adjudged in the Supreme Court of the United States, from 1828 to 1843, Inclusive,* 17 vols. (Philadelphia, 1828–1843)
Va. Cas.	William Brockenbrough, *A Collection of Cases Decided by the General Court of Virginia,* 2 vols. (Philadelphia and Richmond, 1815–1826)
Washington	Bushrod Washington, *Reports of Cases Argued and Determined in the Court of Appeals of Virginia,* 2 vols. (Richmond, 1798–1799)
Wheaton	Henry Wheaton, *Reports of Cases Argued and Adjudged in the Supreme Court, 1816-1827,* 12 vols. (Philadelphia, 1816–1827)
Wythe	George Wythe, *Decisions of Cases in Virginia by the High Court of Chancery* (1852; Charlottesville, Va., 1900 reprint)

PREFACE

1. Marshall's literary output also includes one formal work of history, *The Life of George Washington,* published in five volumes between 1804 and 1807. In this work, Marshall occasionally paused from his relentless narrative to offer his reflections on political developments in the early republic. Such passages, all too rare, provide revealing clues to his political thought.

2. The quotation is from Madison to Spencer Roane, September 2, 1819, in Marvin Meyers, ed., *The Mind of the Founder: Sources of the Political Thought of James Madison,* rev. ed. (Hanover, N.H., 1981), 359. Madison was here expressing his disapproval of the Supreme Court's reasoning in McCulloch v. Maryland.

3. *Federalist* No. 10 (Madison), in Clinton Rossiter, ed., *The Federalist Papers* (New York, 1961), 84; Gordon S. Wood, *The Radicalism of the American Revolution* (New York, 1992), 323.

4. Wood elaborates this theme in *Radicalism of the American Revolution.*

5. William M. Wiecek, *Liberty Under Law: The Supreme Court in American Life* (Baltimore, 1988), 32–33.

Chapter 1. Republican Revolutionary

1. John Stokes Adams, ed., *An Autobiographical Sketch by John Marshall* (Ann Arbor, Mich., 1937), 3–4.

2. Ibid., 4. On Campbell and Thomson, see William Meade, *Old Churches, Ministers, and Families of Virginia,* 2 vols. (Baltimore, 1966; orig. pub., 1857), 2:159–62, 219.

3. Charles S. Sydnor, *American Revolutionaries in the Making: Political Practices in Washington's Virginia* (New York, 1965; originally published as *Gentleman Freeholders*).

4. Adams, ed., *Autobiographical Sketch,* 8.

5. Ibid., 11.

6. Herbert A. Johnson et al., eds., *The Papers of John Marshall,* vol. 1 (Chapel Hill, N.C., 1974), 276–77.

7. Adams, ed., *Autobiographical Sketch,* 14; Charles T. Cullen and Herbert A. Johnson, eds., *The Papers of John Marshall,* vol. 2 (Chapel Hill, N.C., 1977), 201–7, 221–28, 231–38, 238–47.

8. Adams, ed., *Autobiographical Sketch,* 19.

9. Ibid., 22.

10. Ibid., 30.

11. Felix Frankfurter, "John Marshall and the Judicial Function," in *James Bradley Thayer, Oliver Wendell Holmes, and Felix Frankfurter on John Marshall,* (Chicago, 1967), 145.

12. For an excellent brief account of Marshall's chief justiceship, see R. Kent Newmyer, *The Supreme Court under Marshall and Taney* (Arlington Heights, Ill., 1968). The Marshall Court is also covered by two volumes in *The Oliver Wendell Holmes Devise History of the Supreme Court of the United States,* George Lee Haskins and Herbert A. Johnson, *Foundations of Power: John Marshall, 1801–15* (New York, 1981), and G. Edward White, *The Marshall Court and Cultural Change, 1815–35* (New York, 1988).

13. Marshall to Edward Everett, November 3, 1830, Everett Papers, Massachusetts Historical Society; Marshall to Thomas S. Grimké, October 6, 1832, Library of Virginia; Marshall to Joseph Story, September 22, 1832, Story Papers, Massachusetts Historical Society.

14. Marshall to Joseph Story, September 30, 1829, Story Papers, Massachusetts Historical Society; Marshall to Story, November 26, 1826, in William W. Story, ed., *Life and Letters of Joseph Story* (Boston, 1851), 1:505–6.

15. Speech in the Virginia Convention, December 11, 1829, in *Proceedings and Debates of the Virginia State Convention, of 1829–30* (Richmond, Va.), 616.

16. Marshall to James Monroe, June 25, 1812, in Charles F. Hobson et al., eds., *The Papers of John Marshall,* Vol. 7 (Chapel Hill, N.C., 1993), 333.

17. Chester Harding, *My Egotistigraphy* (Cambridge, Mass., 1866), 144, as quoted in Andrew Oliver, *The Portraits of John Marshall* (Charlottesville, Va., 1977), 74.

18. George Wythe Munford, *The Two Parsons; Cupid's Sports; the Dream; and the Jewels of Virginia* (Richmond, Va., 1884), 333.

19. Jefferson to James Madison, November 26, 1795, quoted in Donald O. Dewey, *Marshall Versus Jefferson: The Political Background of Marbury v. Madison* (New York, 1970), 37.

20. Josiah Quincy, *Figures of the Past from the Leaves of Old Journals* (Boston, 1888), 189–90.

21. Joseph Story, "A Discourse upon the Life, Character, and Services of the Honorable John Marshall," in John F. Dillon, ed., *John Marshall: Life, Character, and Judicial Services* (Chicago, 1903), 3:377.

22. William Wirt, *Letters of a British Spy* (Richmond, Va., 1803), 119; Story, "Discourse," in Dillon, ed., *Life, Character, and Judicial Services,* 3:370.

23. Story, "Discourse," in Dillon, ed., *Life, Character, and Judicial Services,* 3:376–77.

24. Gustavus Schmidt, "Reminiscences of the Late Chief Justice," *Louisiana Law Journal* 1 (1841): 82; Story, "Discourse," in Dillon, ed., *Life, Character, and Judicial Services,* 3:377.

25. Story, "Discourse," in Dillon, ed., *Life, Character, and Judicial Services,* 3:373.

26. Ibid., 375.

27. Marshall to Joseph Story, July 3, 1829, Story Papers, Massachusetts Historical Society.

28. John Marshall, *The Life of George Washington* (2d ed., Philadelphia, 1838), 2:206–7, 348–49.

29. Ibid., 447.

30. Drew R. McCoy, *The Elusive Republic: Political Economy in Jeffersonian America* (Chapel Hill, N.C., 1980), 69–75, 77–80; Lance Banning, "Jeffersonian Ideology Revisited: Liberal and Classical Ideas in the New American Republic," *William and Mary Quarterly* 3d ser., 43 (1986): 3–19; idem, "Some Second Thoughts on Virtue and the Course of Revolutionary Thinking," in Terence Ball and J. G. A.

Pocock, eds., *Conceptual Change and the Constitution* (Lawrence, Kans., 1988), 194–212; Gordon S. Wood, "Ideology and the Origins of Liberal America," *William and Mary Quarterly* 3d ser., 44 (1987): 628–40. For a thorough study that subordinates Marshall's "republicanism" to his "liberalism," see Robert Kenneth Faulkner, *The Jurisprudence of John Marshall* (Princeton, N.J., 1968).

31. Adams, ed., *Autobiographical Sketch*, 9–10.

32. Story, "Discourse," in Dillon, ed., *Life, Character, and Judicial Services*, 3:368.

33. Madison to Jefferson, October 24, 1787, in Robert A. Rutland et al., eds., *The Papers of James Madison*, vol. 10 (Chicago, Ill., 1977), 212.

34. Marshall, *Life of Washington*, 2d ed., 2:117.

35. Marshall to Charles Simms, June 16, 1784; Marshall to Arthur Lee, March 5, 1787, in Johnson et al. eds., *Marshall Papers*, 1:124, 206.

36. Marshall, *Life of Washington*, 2d ed., 2:98–99, 103.

37. Marshall to James Wilkinson, January 5, 1787, in Johnson et al., eds., *Marshall Papers*, 1:201. See also Marshall, *Life of Washington*, 2d ed., 2:117.

38. Adams, ed., *Autobiographical Sketch*, 9.

39. Marshall to James Wilkinson, January 5, 1787, in Johnson et al., eds., *Marshall Papers*, 1:201; Marshall to Charles Cotesworth Pinckney, November 21, 1802, in Charles F. Hobson and Fredrika J. Teute, eds., *The Papers of John Marshall*, vol. 6 (Chapel Hill, N.C., 1990), 125.

40. For the struggle between "reason" and "passion," see Marshall, *Life of Washington*, 2d ed., 2:151, 209, 229. See also Marshall to Joseph Story, July 13, 1821, Story Papers, Massachusetts Historical Society; Marshall to Story, December 30, 1827, Clements Library, University of Michigan; Marshall to Martin Marshall, December 27, 1825, New York Public Library.

41. Speech in the Virginia Ratifying Convention, June 20, 1788, in Johnson et al, eds., *Marshall Papers*, 1:285. On "interest" as a check upon "the passions," see Albert O. Hirschman, *The Passions and the Interests: Political Arguments for Capitalism Before Its Triumph* (Princeton, N.J., 1977).

42. Speech in the Virginia Ratifying Convention, June 10, 1788, in Johnson et al., eds., *Marshall Papers*, 1:256.

43. Adams, ed., *Autobiographical Sketch*, 10.

44. Ogden v. Saunders, 12 Wheaton 354–55 (1827).

Chapter 2. The Common Law Background

1. Livingston v. Jefferson, 1 Brockenbrough 207 (U.S. Cir. Ct., Va., 1811); Charles F. Hobson, et al. eds., *The Papers of John Marshall*, vol. 7 (Chapel Hill, N.C. 1993), 282.

2. William Blackstone, *Commentaries on the Laws of England* (London, 1765), 1:69.

3. As quoted by Julius Goebel, "The Common Law and the Constitution," in W. Melville Jones, ed., *Chief Justice John Marshall: A Reappraisal* (Ithaca, N.Y., 1956), 109; C. H. S. Fifoot, *Lord Mansfield* (Oxford, 1936), 220–21.

4. Blackstone, *Commentaries*, 1:71.

5. B[everley] Tucker, *The Principles of Pleading* (Boston, 1846), 54, 55. See also Henry Hartwell, James Blair, and Edward Chilton, *The Present State of Virginia, and the College,* ed. Hunter Dickinson Farish (Charlottesville, Va., 1964), 44–48; Robert Beverley, *The History and Present State of Virginia,* ed. Louis B. Wright (Chapel Hill, N.C., 1947), 255; Stephen Botein, *Early American Law and Society* (New York, 1983), 35–38.

6. Tucker, *Principles of Pleading,* 54–56.

7. Ibid., 56–57; Henry Clay, "Memoir of the Author," in George Wythe, *Decisions of Cases in Virginia by the High Court of Chancery* (Richmond, Va., 1852), xxxiv.

8. This account of Marshall's practice is drawn from Charles F. Hobson et al., eds., *The Papers of John Marshall,* vol. 5 (Chapel Hill, N.C., 1987), xxviii, liii–lv, 3–6, 163–65, 259–63.

9. Ibid., 451–67.

10. On the common law as the "substratum," see Marshall's opinions in United States v. Burr, August 31 and September 3, 1807, ibid., 7:76, 120. For the Virginia "reception" statute and the laws abolishing entail and primogeniture, see William Waller Hening, *The Statutes at Large, Being a Collection of All the Laws of Virginia* (Richmond, Va., 1819–1823), 9:127, 226; 12:138.

11. Shermer v. Shermer, 1 Washington 267 (Va. Ct. of App., 1794); Hobson et al., eds., *Marshall Papers,* 5:90.

12. Fleming v. Willis, 2 Call 10 (Va. Ct. of App., 1799); Hobson et al., eds., *Marshall Papers,* 5:552.

13. Ross v. Poythress, 1 Washington 222 (Va. Ct. of App., 1792); Wilson v. Rucker, 1 Call 503–4 (Va. Ct. of App., 1799). The quotation is from Judge Roane's opinion in Baring v. Reeder, 1 H. and M. 162 (Va. Ct. of App., 1806).

14. Marbury v. Madison, 1 Cranch 176 (1803); Charles F. Hobson and Fredrika J. Teute, eds., *The Papers of John Marshall,* vol. 6 (Chapel Hill, N.C., 1990), 181.

15. Tucker, *Principles of Pleading,* 57–59; Daniel Call, "Biographical Sketches of the Judges," 4 Call vii–ix.

16. Blackstone, *Commentaries,* 1:70.

17. Benjamin N. Cardozo, *The Nature of the Judicial Process* (New Haven, Conn., 1921), 113.

18. Blackstone, *Commentaries,* 1:59–62, 87–91.

19. Fifoot, *Lord Mansfield,* 226–27.

20. Jefferson to Philip Mazzei, November 28, 1785; Jefferson to John Brown Cutting, October 2, 1788, in Julian P. Boyd, ed., *The Papers of Thomas Jefferson* (Princeton, N.J., 1950–), 9:71; 13:649.

21. Livingston v. Jefferson, 1 Brockenbrough 209 (U.S. Cir. Ct., Va., 1811; Hobson et. al., eds., *Marshall Papers*, 7:284.

22. Gordon S. Wood, *The Creation of the American Republic, 1776–1787* (Chapel Hill, N.C., 1969), 291–305.

23. Jefferson to Edmund Pendleton, August 26, 1776, in Boyd, ed., *Jefferson Papers*, 1:505.

24. Jefferson to Mazzei, November 28, 1785, in Boyd, ed., *Jefferson Papers*, 9:71; Jefferson, "Whether Christianity Is Part of the Common Law?" published as an appendix to Jefferson, *Reports of Cases Determined in the General Court of Virginia* (1829; Buffalo, N.Y., 1981 reprint), 139. Jefferson called the incorporation of Christianity into the common law "the most remarkable instance of Judicial legislation, that has ever occurred in English jurisprudence" (ibid., vi).

25. Wood, *Creation of the American Republic*, 302.

26. Randolph to James Madison, March 27 and May 19, 1789, in Charles F. Hobson and Robert A. Rutland., eds., *The Papers of James Madison*, vol. 12 (Charlottesville, Va., 1979), 32, 168. This law fundamentally altered common law rules by providing for equal division of intestates' estates.

27. Wood, *Creation of the American Republic*, 295–96.

28. Aylett v. Minnis, Wythe 225, 232, 233 (Va. High Ct. of Ch., 1793).

29. Kennon v. McRoberts, 1 Washington 102 (Va. Ct. of App., 1792); Shermer v. Shermer, 1 Wash. 272 (Va. Ct. of App., 1794).

30. Hobson et al., eds., *Marshall Papers*, 5:508–9; White v. Atkinson, 2 Wash. 104 (Va. Ct. of App., 1795).

31. Page v. Pendleton, Wythe 212–13 (Va. High Ct. of Ch., 1793).

32. On the case of Pleasants v. Pleasants, see Hobson et al., eds., *Marshall Papers*, 5:541–44.

33. Kennon v. McRoberts, 1 Washington 99 (Va. Ct. of App., 1792).

34. Osborn v. Bank of the United States, 9 Wheaton 866 (1824).

35. Marbury v. Madison, 1 Cranch 170 (1803); Hobson and Teute, eds., *Marshall Papers*, 6:177. On the Marshall Court's attempt to separate law and politics, see William E. Nelson, "The Eighteenth-Century Background of Marshall's Constitutional Jurisprudence," *Michigan Law Review* 76 (1978): 893–960; George Lee Haskins and Herbert A. Johnson, *Foundations of Power: John Marshall, 1801–15* (New York, 1981), 7, 188–89, 193–95, 246, 399–400, 421, 648–51; G. Edward White, *The Marshall Court and Cultural Change, 1815–35* (New York, 1988), 4, 8, 196–200, 973; Jennifer Nedelsky, *Private Property and the Limits of American Constitutionalism: The Madisonian Framework and Its Legacy* (Chicago, 1990), 190–97.

36. Wood, *Creation of the American Republic,* 430–67.

37. Pendleton's opinion in Commonwealth v. Caton, as printed in David J. Mays, ed., *Letters and Papers of Edmund Pendleton,* Vol. 2 (Charlottesville, Va., 1967), 422.

38. Wythe's opinion in Commonwealth v. Caton, 4 Call 8 (Va. Ct. of App., 1782).

39. Pendleton's opinion in Case of the Judges, 4 Call 142, 146 (Va. Ct. of App., 1788).

40. Marbury v. Madison, 1 Cranch 178 (1803); Hobson and Teute, eds., *Marshall Papers,* 6:183.

41. Kamper v. Hawkins, 1 Virginia Cases 20 (Va. Gen. Ct., 1793). See the discussion of this case in H. Jefferson Powell, "The Uses of State Constitutional History: A Case Note," *Albany Law Review* 53 (1989): 283–95.

42. Roane's opinion in Kamper v. Hawkins, 1 Virginia Cases 40 (Va. Gen. Ct., 1793).

CHAPTER 3. THE PROVINCE OF THE JUDICIARY

1. Marbury v. Madison, 1 Cranch 154.

2. "Mandamus" is Latin for "we command." A writ of mandamus was a common law remedy to compel a government officer to perform some ministerial act or duty imposed by law.

3. Charles Warren, *The Supreme Court in United States History* (Boston, 1926), 1:241–56.

4. See, for example, Donald O. Dewey, *Marshall Versus Jefferson: The Political Background of Marbury v. Madison* (New York, 1970).

5. Elizabeth McCaughey, "*Marbury* v. *Madison:* Have We Missed the Real Meaning?" *Presidential Studies Quarterly* 19 (1989): 491–528.

6. "Report on the Virginia Resolutions," in Marvin Meyers, ed., *The Mind of the Founder: Sources of the Political Thought of James Madison* (Hanover, N.H., 1981), 244–45, 252.

7. Warren, *Supreme Court in United States History,* 1:165.

8. "To a Freeholder," September 20, 1798, in William C. Stinchcombe and Charles T. Cullen, eds., *The Papers of John Marshall,* vol. 3 (Chapel Hill, N.C., 1979), 505–6; Marshall to St. George Tucker, November 27, 1800; editorial note, in Charles F. Hobson and Fredrika J. Teute., eds., *The Papers of John Marshall,* vol. 6 (Chapel Hill, N.C., 1990), 23, 144.

9. Marshall to William Paterson, April 19, 1802, May 3, 1802, in Hobson and Teute, eds., *Marshall Papers,* 6:108–9, 117. The Supreme Court formally ratified this decision to acquiesce in the repeal in Stuart v. Laird, decided at the same term as Marbury v. Madison (1 Cranch 299).

10. Marshall to James M. Marshall, March 18, 1801, in Hobson and Teute, eds., *Marshall Papers*, 6:90.

11. G. Edward White, *The American Judicial Tradition: Profiles of Leading American Judges* (New York, 1988), 25–34.

12. 1 Cranch 170.

13. Speech, March 7, 1800, in Charles T. Cullen, ed., *The Papers of John Marshall*, vol.4 (Chapel Hill, N.C., 1984), 95.

14. 1 Cranch 162.

15. 1 Cranch 165–66.

16. 1 Cranch 166.

17. 1 Cranch 167.

18. 1 Cranch 169–70.

19. 1 Cranch 170.

20. 1 Cranch 163.

21. *The Public Statutes at Large of the United States of America, 1789–1873* (Boston, 1845), 1:81.

22. For convenience, the term "judicial review" will be used to describe this doctrine or power, though Marshall and his contemporaries never used it themselves. The phrase implies a broader power than that advocated by Marshall. The noted constitutional scholar Edward S. Corwin apparently coined the phrase in an article published in 1910. See Robert Lowry Clinton, *Marbury v. Madison and Judicial Review* (Lawrence, Kans., 1989), 7.

23. 1 Cranch 176.

24. 1 Cranch 177.

25. Ibid.

26. 1 Cranch 178.

27. Ibid.

28. 1 Cranch 178–80.

29. Dr. Bonham's Case, as quoted in Charles Grove Haines, *The American Doctrine of Judicial Supremacy* (New York, 1973), 33.

30. William Blackstone, *Commentaries on the Laws of England*, (London, 1765), 1:91. On Coke's dictum, see Edward S. Corwin, *The Doctrine of Judicial Review* (Princeton, N.J., 1914), 68–69; Samuel E. Thorne, "Dr. Bonham's Case," in S. E. Thorne, *Essays in English Legal History* (London, 1985), 269–78.

31. As quoted in Thomas Grey, "Origins of the Unwritten Constitution: Fundamental Law in American Revolutionary Thought," *Stanford Law Review* 30 (1978): 869.

32. Leslie Friedman Goldstein, "Popular Sovereignty, the Origins of Judicial Review, and the Revival of Unwritten Law," *Journal of Politics* 48 (1986): 51–71; McCaughey, "*Marbury v. Madison*," 494–97.

33. Gordon S. Wood, *The Creation of the American Republic, 1776-1787*, (Chapel Hill, N.C., 1969), 393–429.

34. R. R. Palmer, *The Age of the Democratic Revolution: A Political History of Europe and America, 1760-1800,* 2 vols. (Princeton, N.J., 1959–1964), 1:214–15.

35. Wood, *Creation of the American Republic,* 446–63.

36. Haines, *American Doctrine of Judicial Supremacy,* 98–104.

37. Ibid., 109–12.

38. Ibid., 115–17.

39. *Federalist* No. 78, in Clinton Rossiter, ed., *The Federalist Papers* (New York, 1961), 468.

40. Goldstein, "Popular Sovereignty," 63–69; McCaughey, "*Marbury v. Madison,*" 516–20.

41. Herbert A. Johnson et al., eds., *The Papers of John Marshall,* vol. 1 (Chapel Hill, N.C., 1974), 277.

42. 4 Call 5 (Va. Ct. of App., 1782). Marshall, who was then in Richmond for the General Assembly session, almost certainly attended arguments or participated in the out-of-doors discussion of this case, which generated a great deal of public interest. See William T. Hutchinson and William M. E. Rachal, eds., *The Papers of James Madison,* vol. 5 (Chicago, 1967), 217–19, 230, 261.

43. Tucker's brief is in the Tucker-Coleman Papers, Special Collections, Swem Library, College of William and Mary. Just a few months after the hearing of *Caton,* Marshall, then a member of the state executive council, confronted a constitutional question involving the power of the council to remove a county court justice of the peace. Although a state law authorized the council upon inquiry to remove magistrates for misconduct, negligence, or malpractice, Marshall signed an opinion of council advising that this law was "repugnant to the Act of Government, contrary to the fundamental principles of our constitution and directly opposite to the general tenor of our Laws." No reasons were given, but evidently the law violated separation of powers by authorizing the executive to conduct a judicial inquiry (Johnson et al., eds., *Marshall Papers,* 1:96–97).

44. 1 Va. Cas. 20 (Va. Gen. Ct., 1793). The case attracted public attention beyond Virginia, a full report having been published (along with the 1788 "remonstrance" of the judges) as a pamphlet in Philadelphia in 1794. See Lyon G. Tyler, *The Letters and Times of the Tylers* (New York, 1970), 1:182 and n.

45. 1 Va. Cas. 36, 74.

46. 1 Va. Cas. 78.

47. 1 Va. Cas. 32; compare with Marshall in Marbury, 1 Cranch 177.

48. 1 Va. Cas. 38; compare with Marshall's denial that "courts must close their eyes on the constitution, and see only the law" (1 Cranch 178).

49. 1 Va. Cas. 79; compare with Marshall, 1 Cranch 179–80.

50. 1 Va. Cas. 39–40, 87. See H. Jefferson Powell, "The Uses of State Constitutional History: A Case Note," *Albany Law Review* 53 (1989): 283–95.

51. Kermit L. Hall, *The Supreme Court and Judicial Review in American History* (Washington, D.C., 1985), 1–17.

52. James Bradley Thayer, "The Origin and Scope of the American Doctrine of Constitutional Law," *Harvard Law Review* 7 (1893): 138–42; Sanford Byron Gabin, "Judicial Review, James Bradley Thayer, and the 'Reasonable Doubt' Test," *Hastings Constitutional Law Quarterly* 3 (1976): 961–1014.

53. 6 Cranch 128; 4 Wheaton 625; 12 Wheaton 436-37. See also Ex parte Randolph, 2 Brockenbrough 478–79 (U.S. Cir. Ct., Va., 1833).

54. Thayer, "Origin and Scope," 143–44.

55. Marshall to Paterson, April 19, 1802, in Hobson and Teute, eds., *Marshall Papers*, 6:108.

56. Alexis de Tocqueville, *Democracy in America* (New York, 1994), 1:280.

CHAPTER 4. PROPERTY RIGHTS AND THE CONTRACT CLAUSE

1. 6 Cranch 137–38.

2. Benjamin Fletcher Wright, Jr., *The Contract Clause of the Constitution* (Cambridge, Mass., 1938), 26.

3. See, for example, Joseph Lynch, "*Fletcher* v. *Peck:* The Nature of the Contract Clause," *Seton Hall Law Review* 13 (1982): 120.

4. Bruce A. Campbell, "John Marshall, the Virginia Political Economy, and the *Dartmouth College* Decision," *American Journal of Legal History* 19 (1975): 40-65.

5. Samuel Shepherd, *The Statutes at Large of Virginia* (1835; New York, 1979 reprint), 2:22–23. See Charles F. Hobson, ed., *The Papers of John Marshall* (Chapel Hill, N.C., 1995), 8:109–10.

6. H. Jefferson Powell, "The Original Understanding of Original Intent," *Harvard Law Review* 98 (1985): 885–948 (esp. 942–44). On the dangers of inferring constitutional meaning from "extrinsic circumstances," see Sturges v. Crowninshield, 4 Wheaton 202 (1819).

7. Max Farrand, ed., *The Records of the Federal Convention of 1787* (New Haven, Conn., 1966), 2:439–40; Wright, *Contract Clause*, 6–12.

8. The evidence from the Federal Convention of 1787 and the state ratifying conventions is summarized in Wright, *Contract Clause*, 8–16. For an argument that Marshall faithfully carried out the framers' intentions regarding the contract clause, see Wallace Mendelson, "B. F. Wright on the Contract Clause: A Progressive Misreading of the Marshall-Taney Era," *Western Political Quarterly* 38 (1985): 262–75.

9. Madison to Thomas Jefferson, October 24, 1787, in Robert A. Rutland et al., eds., *The Papers of James Madison*, vol. 10 (Chicago, 1977), 212.

10. Charles F. Hobson, "The Negative on State Laws: James Madison, the Constitution, and the Crisis of Republican Government," *William and Mary Quarterly* 3d ser., 36 (1979): 215–35.

11. *Federalist* No. 44, in Clinton Rossiter, ed., *The Federalist Papers* (New York, 1961), 282–83. Since bills of attainder and ex post facto laws relate to criminal law, "Publius" had the contract clause principally in mind in making these remarks.

12. Marshall, in Fletcher v. Peck, 6 Cranch 139 (1810); Justice Paterson, in Van Horne's Lessee v. Dorrance, 2 Dallas 310 (U.S. Cir. Ct., Pa., 1795); Justice Chase, in Calder v. Bull, 3 Dallas 388 (1798).

13. Edward S. Corwin, "The Basic Doctrine of American Constitutional Law," in Alpheus T. Mason and Gerald Garvey, eds., *American Constitutional History: Essays by Edward S. Corwin* (New York, 1964), 25–45.

14. Van Horne's Lessee v. Dorrance, 2 Dallas 310 (U.S. Cir. Ct., Pa., 1795).

15. Calder v. Bull, 3 Dallas 388 (1798).

16. Calder v. Bull, 3 Dallas 387–88 (Chase), 399 (Iredell). See Elizabeth McCaughey, "*Marbury* v. *Madison*: Have We Missed the Real Meaning?" *Presidential Studies Quarterly* 19 (1989): 506–9.

17. Suzanna Sherry, "The Founders' Unwritten Constitution," *University of Chicago Law Review* 54 (1987): 1127–77.

18. G. Edward White, *The Marshall Court and Cultural Change, 1815–35* (New York, 1988), 627–28.

19. Ogden v. Witherspoon, 2 Haywood 227–29 (U.S. Cir. Ct., N.C., 1803). The correct title of the case is Ogden v. Blackledge. See Charles F. Hobson and Fredrika J. Teute, eds., *The Papers of John Marshall*, Vol. 6 (Chapel Hill, N.C., 1990), 147–48; Ogden v. Blackledge, 2 Cranch 272–79 (1804).

20. Corwin, "Basic Doctrine of American Constitutional Law," 37–38; McCaughey, "*Marbury* v. *Madison*," 508.

21. C. Peter Magrath, *Yazoo: Law and Politics in the New Republic: The Case of Fletcher v. Peck* (Providence, R.I., 1966), 54–55, 65–69; George Lee Haskins and Herbert A. Johnson, *Foundations of Power: John Marshall, 1801–15* (New York, 1981), 343–45.

22. Fletcher v. Peck, 6 Cranch 128.

23. 6 Cranch 130–31.

24. 6 Cranch 133–34.

25. 6 Cranch 135–36.

26. 6 Cranch 136–38.

27. 6 Cranch 139.

28. Horace H. Hagan, "Fletcher vs. Peck," *Georgetown Law Journal* 16 (1927): 26. See also Charles Warren, *The Supreme Court in United States History* (Boston, 1926), 1:396; Robert L. Hale, "The Supreme Court and the Contract Clause,"

pt. 2, *Harvard Law Review* 57 (1944): 633–35; Christopher Wolfe, *The Rise of Modern Judicial Review* (New York, 1986), 112–13.

29. David P. Currie, *The Constitution in the Supreme Court: The First Hundred Years, 1789–1888* (Chicago, 1985), 128–32; Sylvia Snowiss, *Judicial Review and the Law of the Constitution* (New Haven, Conn., 1990), 126–30.

30. White, *Marshall Court and Cultural Change,* 604–6.

31. Joseph M. Lynch, "*Fletcher* v. *Peck:* The Nature of the Contract Clause," *Seton Hall Law Review* 13 (1982): 15–20 (quotation at 17).

32. 6 Cranch 143, 144.

33. Warren B. Hunting, *The Obligation of the Contracts Clause of the United States Constitution* (Baltimore, 1919), 25–38.

34. On Wilson, see ibid., 36–37. For Paterson's opinion, see Vanhorne's Lessee v. Dorrance, 2 Dallas 304, 320 (U.S. Cir. Ct., Pa.). In an 1805 Supreme Court opinion Marshall, referring to a state law providing for the sale of lands, said, "This is a contract, and although a state is a party, it ought to be construed according to those well established principles which regulate contracts generally" (Huidekoper's Lessee v. Douglas, 3 Cranch 70).

35. As quoted in Wright, *Contract Clause,* 22.

36. New Jersey v. Wilson, 7 Cranch 164–67 (1812).

37. See Francis N. Stites, *Private Interest and Public Gain: The Dartmouth College Case, 1819* (Amherst, Mass., 1972).

38. The nominal defendant, William H. Woodward, had been secretary-treasurer of the college but was now loyal to the university.

39. Timothy Farrar, *Report of the Case of the Trustees of Dartmouth College Against William H. Woodward* (Portsmouth, N.H., 1819), 229; Stites, *Private Interest and Public Gain,* 52–54.

40. For Webster's argument in Dartmouth College v. Woodward, see 4 Wheaton 551–600.

41. Webster to Jeremiah Mason, April 28, 1818, in Fletcher Webster, ed., *The Private Correspondence of Daniel Webster* (Boston, 1857), 1: 282–83; Stites, *Private Interest and Public Gain,* 89–95.

42. Duvall silently dissented, Washington and Story wrote separate concurring opinions, Johnson joined Marshall, and Livingston concurred with Marshall, Washington, and Story (4 Wheaton 666, 713).

43. White, *Marshall Court and Cultural Change,* 622–28.

44. Webster to Jeremiah Mason, February 2, 1819, quoted in Warren, *Supreme Court in United States History,* 1:483; Hopkinson to Francis Brown, February 2, 1819, in Webster, ed., *Private Correspondence of Daniel Webster,* 1:301.

45. 4 Wheaton 625.

46. Hunting, *Obligation of Contracts Clause,* 64–93; Stites, *Private Interest and Public Gain,* 78–79.

47. 4 Wheaton 629.

48. 4 Wheaton 635, 636.

49. 4 Wheaton 638, 640.

50. 4 Wheaton 641–42.

51. 4 Wheaton 641.

52. 4 Wheaton 642, 643–44.

53. 4 Wheaton 644.

54. 4 Wheaton 645

55. R. Kent Newmyer, *The Supreme Court Under Marshall and Taney* (Arlington Heights, Ill., 1968), 77–79; Stites, *Private Interest and Public Gain,* 99–100.

56. Stites, *Private Interest and Public Gain,* 112–13; Bruce A. Campbell, "*Dartmouth College* as a Civil Liberties Case: The Formation of Constitutional Policy," *Kentucky Law Journal* 70 (1981–1982): 643–706.

57. Bracken v. College of William and Mary, 3 Call 579–81, 591–99 (Va. Ct. of App., 1790); Charles T. Cullen and Herbert A. Johnson, eds., *The Papers of John Marshall,* vol. 2 (Chapel Hill, N.C., 1977), 72–81.

58. Hunting, *Obligation of Contracts Clause,* 72–75; Stites, *Private Interest and Public Gain,* 83–86; Campbell, "*Dartmouth College* as a Civil Liberties Case," 661–66.

59. A federal bankruptcy statute was in force between 1800 and 1803, Marshall having served on the committee that prepared the bill (Charles T. Cullen, ed., *The Papers of John Marshall,* vol. 4 [Chapel Hill, N.C., 1984], 52).

60. Golden v. Prince, 10 Fed. Cas. 542, 544, 545 (U.S. Cir. Ct., Pa., 1814).

61. Adams v. Storey, 1 Fed. Cas. 141 (U.S. Cir. Ct., N.Y., 1814).

62. Peter J. Coleman, *Debtors and Creditors in America: Insolvency, Imprisonment for Debt, and Bankruptcy, 1607–1900* (Madison, Wis., 1974), 6–15, 31–36.

63. Sturges v. Crowninshield, 4 Wheaton 194.

64. Marshall to Bushrod Washington, April 19, 1814, in Hobson, ed., *Marshall Papers,* 8:34–35.

65. Gerald T. Dunne, *Justice Joseph Story and the Rise of the Supreme Court* (New York, 1970), 158; Coleman, *Debtors and Creditors,* 32–33. The case was argued February 8 and 9; Marshall delivered the Court's opinion on February 17.

66. 4 Wheaton 193.

67. 4 Wheaton 195–96.

68. White, *Marshall Court and Cultural Change,* 635–36.

69. 4 Wheaton 197.

70. 4 Wheaton 202.

71. 4 Wheaton 205, 206.

72. Ogden v. Saunders, 12 Wheaton 272–73.

73. 4 Wheaton 209.

74. 12 Wheaton 213.

75. 12 Wheaton 270, 294.

76. 12 Wheaton 332.

77. For an argument that Marshall paid only lip service to the reasonable doubt rule, see Snowiss, *Judicial Review and the Law of the Constitution*, 157–58.

78. 12 Wheaton 332.

79. The quotation is from Justice Johnson's opinion at 12 Wheaton 286.

80. 12 Wheaton 334.

81. 12 Wheaton 335.

82. 12 Wheaton 336.

83. 12 Wheaton 343.

84. Ibid.

85. 12 Wheaton 345.

86. 12 Wheaton 346–47.

87. 12 Wheaton 347. He did not identify these authors or their writings but undoubtedly had in mind the works of Grotius, Vattel, and others mentioned in argument (see Daniel Webster's argument at 12 Wheaton 240).

88. 12 Wheaton 291.

89. 12 Wheaton 348–49.

90. 12 Wheaton 287.

91. 12 Wheaton 349.

92. 12 Wheaton 352.

93. 12 Wheaton 354, 355.

94. 12 Wheaton 335.

95. Gozler v. Georgetown, 6 Wheaton 593 (1821).

96. 4 Peters 514, 561, 562, 563.

97. Newmyer, *Supreme Court under Marshall and Taney*, 81–88; White, *Marshall Court and Cultural Change*, 655–56, 668–73.

98. 7 Peters 243.

99. 7 Peters 247–49.

100. 7 Peters 249–50.

101. William Winslow Crosskey, *Politics and the Constitution in the History of the United States* (Chicago, 1953), 2:1056-82. Crosskey's tortured reading of *Barron* is typical of his entire book: prodigious scholarship in support of an untenable thesis. His work still has its modern adherents. See Thomas C. Shevory, *John Marshall's Law: Interpretation, Ideology, and Interest* (Westport, Conn., 1994), 62–65. For a more balanced discussion, see White, *Marshall Court and Cultural Change*, 589–93.

Chapter 5. National Supremacy and States' Rights

1. Edward S. Corwin, *John Marshall and the Constitution* (New Haven, Conn., 1920), 173.

2. R. Kent Newmyer, *The Supreme Court Under Marshall and Taney* (Arlington Heights, Ill., 1968), 54.

3. G. Edward White, *The Marshall Court and Cultural Change, 1815–35* (New York, 1988), 2, 486–87. On the limited scope of Marshall's "nationalism," see also William E. Nelson, "The Eighteenth-Century Background of John Marshall's Constitutional Jurisprudence," *Michigan Law Review* 76 (1978): 895–97; Robert Lowry Clinton, *Marbury v. Madison and Judicial Review* (Lawrence, Kans., 1989), 194–99.

4. Andrew C. McLaughlin, *A Constitutional History of the United States* (New York, 1935), 383.

5. Albert J. Beveridge, *The Life of John Marshall* (Boston, 1919), 4:289, 308; Charles Grove Haines, *The Role of the Supreme Court in American Government and Politics, 1789–1835* (New York, 1973), 354. See also Newmyer, *Supreme Court Under Marshall and Taney,* 44.

6. Corwin, *John Marshall and the Constitution,* 122; Beveridge, *Life of Marshall,* 4:308; Newmyer, *Supreme Court under Marshall and Taney,* 44.

7. William Draper Lewis, "John Marshall," in William Draper Lewis, ed., *Great American Lawyers* (Philadelphia, 1907), 2:372–75. Lewis's observation came to my attention by way of George L. Haskins, "Marshall and the Commerce Clause of the Constitution," in W. Melville Jones, ed., *Chief Justice John Marshall: A Reappraisal* (Ithaca, N.Y., 1956), 166–67.

8. Marshall purchased seventeen shares of stock in the bank in 1817 but sold them early in 1819, before the decision in McCulloch v. Maryland. The chief justice reportedly chose not "to remain a stockholder in that institution, as questions would come before the Supreme Court . . . in which the bank might be concerned." See Charles F. Hobson, ed., *The Papers of John Marshall,* vol. 8 (Chapel Hill, N.C., 1995), 402.

9. McCulloch v. Maryland, 4 Wheaton 401.

10. Charles Warren, *The Supreme Court in United States History* (Boston, Mass., 1926), 1:499–507; Haines, *Role of the Supreme Court in American Government and Politics,* 351–53.

11. 4 Wheaton 400.

12. 4 Wheaton 404–5.

13. 4 Wheaton 406, 407. See Robert Kenneth Faulkner, *The Jurisprudence of John Marshall* (Princeton, N.J., 1968), 197; A. I. L. Campbell, "'It is *a constitution* we are expounding': Chief Justice Marshall and the 'Necessary and Proper' Clause," *Journal of Legal History* 12 (1991): 204–5. "A constitution, from its na-

ture, deals in generals, not in detail," Marshall wrote in an 1809 opinion. "Its framers cannot perceive minute distinctions which arise in the progress of the nation, and therefore confine it to the establishment of broad and general principles" (Bank of the U.S. v. Deveaux, 5 Cranch 87).

14. 4 Wheaton 408.

15. 4 Wheaton 415. See Christopher Wolfe, *The Rise of Modern Judicial Review: From Constitutional Interpretation to Judge-Made Law* (New York, 1986), 40–41; Campbell, "'It is *a constitution* we are expounding,'" 205–6.

16. 4 Wheaton 420, 421.

17. 4 Wheaton 425, 428–29.

18. 4 Wheaton 429–30.

19. 4 Wheaton 430–31, 432–33.

20. 2 Peters 449.

21. 2 Peters 466.

22. Lewis, "John Marshall," in Lewis, ed., *Great American Lawyers*, 2:391.

23. Marshall to Timothy Pickering, March 18, 1828, Pickering Papers, Massachusetts Historical Society. See also Marshall to James Monroe, June 13, 1822, Monroe Papers, Library of Congress.

24. Martin v. Hunter's Lessee, 1 Wheaton 304. Years later Story wrote that Marshall "concurred in every word" of his opinion (Story to George Ticknor, January 22, 1831, in William W. Story, ed., *Life and Letters of Joseph Story* [Boston, 1851], 2:48–49).

25. Gerald Gunther, ed., *John Marshall's Defense of McCulloch v. Maryland* (Stanford, Calif., 1969). See also Hobson, ed., *Marshall Papers*, 8:282–87.

26. "A Friend of the Constitution," No. 1, in Gunther, ed., *Marshall's Defense*, 155–56; Hobson, ed., *Marshall Papers*, 8:318.

27. Marshall to Story, April 28, May 27, 1819, in Hobson, ed., *Marshall Papers*, 8:309, 314; "Hampden," No. 4, in Gunther, ed., *Marshall's Defense*, 146.

28. "Hampden," No. 4, in Gunther, ed., *Marshall's Defense*, 138–54.

29. "A Friend of the Constitution," Nos. 8, 9, ibid., 202–3, 211–12; Hobson, ed., *Marshall Papers*, 8:354–55, 356, 361–62.

30. "A Friend of the Constitution," Nos. 8, 9, in Gunther, ed., *Marshall's Defense*, 204, 213–14; Hobson, ed., *Marshall Papers*, 8:356, 362–63.

31. Haines, *Role of Supreme Court in American Government and Politics*, 428–31; White, *Marshall Court and Cultural Change*, 504–5.

32. Cohens v. Virginia, 6 Wheaton 302–3 (1821).

33. 6 Wheaton 379–80.

34. 6 Wheaton 380.

35. 6 Wheaton 380.

36. 6 Wheaton 384.

37. 6 Wheaton 387, 389–90.

38. 6 Wheaton 393.

39. 6 Wheaton 399.

40. 6 Wheaton 407.

41. 6 Wheaton 413–14.

42. 6 Wheaton 416, 418.

43. 6 Wheaton 427, 429.

44. Warren, *Supreme Court in United States History,* 1:552–64. This time Marshall confined his reaction to private correspondence.

45. 6 Wheaton 404. See similar passages in Bank of the U.S. v. Deveaux, 5 Cranch 87 (1809); Lessor of Fisher v. Cockerell, 5 Peters 259 (1831).

46. Warren, *Supreme Court in United States History,* 1:528–30, 533–38; Haines, *Role of the Supreme Court in American Government and Politics,* 471–80 (quotation at 479–80).

47. Osborn v. Bank of the United States, 9 Wheaton 818–19.

48. 9 Wheaton 820, 821.

49. 9 Wheaton 823, 824–25.

50. 9 Wheaton 846, 847–48.

51. 9 Wheaton 857.

52. 9 Wheaton 867.

53. 9 Wheaton 865–66.

54. Benjamin N. Cardozo, *The Nature of the Judicial Process* (New Haven, Conn., 1921), 169–70. See also Arthur S. Miller and Ronald F. Howell, "The Myth of Neutrality in Constitutional Adjudication," in Leonard W. Levy, *Judicial Review and the Supreme Court: Selected Essays* (New York, 1967), 217, 239; Wolfe, *Rise of Modern Judicial Review,* 40–41.

55. U.S. v. Burr (U.S. Cir. Ct., Va., June 13, 1807), in Charles F. Hobson et al., eds., *The Papers of John Marshall,* vol. 7 (Chapel Hill, N.C., 1993), 43. See Robert Kenneth Faulkner, *The Jurisprudence of John Marshall* (Princeton, N.J., 1968), 66–68; Gary J. Jacobsohn, *The Supreme Court and the Decline of Constitutional Aspiration* (Totowa, N.J., 1986), 63.

56. For a brief but thorough account of the case in its political, legal, and economic dimensions, see Maurice G. Baxter, *The Steamboat Monopoly: Gibbons v. Ogden, 1824* (New York, 1972).

57. Gibbons v. Ogden, 9 Wheaton 187, 188–89.

58. 9 Wheaton 189–93. Marshall had previously maintained on circuit that commerce embraced navigation. See Brig Wilson v. U.S., 1 Brockenbrough 431–32 (U.S. Cir. Ct., Va., 1820): "From the adoption of the Constitution, till this time, the universal sense of America has been, that the word commerce, as used in that instrument, is to be considered a generic term, comprehending navigation, or, that a control over navigation is necessarily incidental to the power to regulate commerce."

59. 9 Wheaton 194, 195.

60. 9 Wheaton 196, 197.

61. 9 Wheaton 203.

62. 9 Wheaton 204, 205.

63. 9 Wheaton 209.

64. 9 Wheaton 211–14.

65. 9 Wheaton 219.

66. 9 Wheaton 220, 221.67. Newmyer, *Supreme Court under Marshall and Taney*, 50.

68. Baxter, *Steamboat Monopoly*, 61–62; White, *Marshall Court and Cultural Change*, 578–80.

69. This phrase is from Marshall's opinion in Sturges v. Crowninshield, 4 Wheaton 196 (1819).

70. See John R. Schmidhauser, *The Supreme Court as Final Arbiter in Federal-State Relations, 1789–1957* (Westport, Conn., 1973); McCulloch v. Maryland, 4 Wheaton 400–401 (1809).

71. 4 Wheaton 193, 196.

72. Sturges v. Crowninshield, 4 Wheaton 194–95.

73. Gibbons v. Ogden, 9 Wheaton 210.

74. 2 Peters 245, 252 (1829).

75. Sturges v. Crowninshield, 4 Wheaton 193.

76. In addition to *Gibbons* and *Willson*, the Marshall Court decided one other commerce clause case, *Brown* v. *Maryland* (1827). The decision invalidated a state law imposing a license tax on importers and wholesalers of imports. The Court construed this tax as in effect a tax on imports, which the Constitution expressly prohibited. The law was also considered to be in violation of Congress's power to regulate foreign commerce. But here the conflict was not with the Constitution but with an actual exercise of legislation, namely, the tariff laws (12 Wheaton 419, 445–49).

77. 9 Wheaton 222.

CHAPTER 6. THE LIMITS OF JUDICIAL POWER

1. Marbury v. Madison, 1 Cranch 170.

2. Speech, March 7, 1800, in Charles T. Cullen, ed., *The Papers of John Marshall*, vol. 4 (Chapel Hill, N.C., 1984), 95–96. The Supreme Court underscored this point from the beginning by refusing to render advisory opinions. See Charles Warren, *The Supreme Court in United States History* (Boston, 1926), 1:108–11.

3. George Lee Haskins and Herbert A. Johnson, *Foundations of Power: John Marshall, 1801–15* (New York, 1981), 654–64; G. Edward White, *The Marshall Court and Cultural Change,* 1815–35 (New York, 1988), 978–79.

4. Foster and Elam v. Neilson, 2 Peters 307 (1829).

5. Robert Kenneth Faulkner, *The Jurisprudence of John Marshall* (Princeton, N.J., 1968), 79, quoting Marshall's opinions in Dartmouth College v. Woodward, 4 Wheaton 630, and Ogden v. Saunders, 12 Wheaton 334.

6. Charles F. Hobson, "The Recovery of British Debts in the Federal Circuit Court of Virginia, 1790 to 1797," *Virginia Magazine of History and Biography* 91 (April 1984): 190.

7. Speech, March 7, 1800, in Cullen, ed., *Marshall Papers,* 4:95, 103–4. See also U.S. v. Brig Diana (U.S. Cir. Ct., Va., 1811), in Charles F. Hobson et al., eds., *The Papers of John Marshall,* vol. 7 (Chapel Hill, N.C., 1993), 272.

8. U.S. v. Schooner Peggy, 1 Cranch 103, 107, 110 (1801).

9. Schooner Exchange v. McFaddon, 7 Cranch 135, 145–46 (1812).

10. Brown v. U.S., 8 Cranch 128–29 (1814). See also The Nereide, 9 Cranch 422–23 (1815).

11. U.S. v. Palmer, 3 Wheaton 634, 635 (1818).

12. 2 Peters 307, 309.

13. 2 Peters 314.

14. Of 1,235 reported opinions of the Marshall Court between 1801 and 1835, only 97 fall into the category of constitutional law. See Haskins and Johnson, *Foundations of Power,* 652, 662; White, *Marshall Court and Cultural Change,* 746n.

15. U.S. v. Burr (U.S. Cir. Ct., Va., August 31, 1807), in Hobson et al., eds., *Marshall Papers,* 7:115; Cohens v. Virginia, 6 Wheaton 404 (1821). See also Bank of the U.S. v. Deveaux, 5 Cranch 87 (1809); Lessor of Fisher v. Cockerell, 5 Peters 259.

16. U.S. v. Burr (U.S. Cir. Ct., Va., June 13, 1807), in Hobson et al., eds., *Marshall Papers,* 7:42.

17. U.S. v. Burr, ibid., 47, 48.

18. A "libel" was a pleading filed by the complainant bringing an action in a court of admiralty.

19. U.S. v. Brig Diana (U.S. Cir. Ct., N.C., 1811), in Hobson et al., eds., *Marshall Papers,* 7:272–73, 320–21.

20. Brown v. U.S., 8 Cranch 128–29 (1814).

21. Little v. Barreme, 2 Cranch 179 (1804). See also Murray v. Schooner Charming Betsey, 2 Cranch 115–25 (1804).

22. Dickson v. U.S. (U.S. Cir. Ct., Va., 1811), in Hobson et al., eds., *Marshall Papers,* 7:294. See also U.S. v. Gordon and Shepherd (U.S. Cir. Ct., Va., 1811), ibid., 300–301.

23. Ex parte Randolph, 2 Brockenbrough 487 (U.S. Cir. Ct., Va., 1833).

24. After specifying the cases in which the Supreme Court shall have original jurisdiction, the Constitution (Art. III, sec. 2) states that in all other cases the Court "shall have appellate Jurisdiction . . . with such Exceptions, and under such Regulations as the Congress shall make."

25. U.S. v. Fisher, 2 Cranch 396 (1805).

26. On Marshall's disgust with the embargo policy, see Marshall to Charles Cotesworth Pinckney, September 21, 1808; Marshall to Timothy Pickering, December 19, 1808, in Hobson et al., eds., *Marshall Papers*, 7:183, 188.

27. Dickson v. U.S. (U.S. Cir. Ct., Va., 1811), ibid., 7:289–90.

28. McCulloch v. Maryland, 4 Wheaton 421, 423 (1819).

29. 4 Wheaton 415.

30. 4 Wheaton 423. For other reminders, see U.S. v. Fisher, 2 Cranch 396 (1805); Dartmouth College v. Woodward, 4 Wheaton 625 (1819); Bank of Hamilton v. Dudley's Lessee, 2 Peters 524 (1829). Marshall never wavered in his belief that the Constitution imposed this duty on the judiciary. In a private letter to Henry Clay, he wrote, "It is I think difficult to read that instrument attentively without feeling the conviction that it intends to provide a tribunal for every case of collision between itself and a law, so far as such case can assume a form for judicial enquiry" (Marshall to Clay, December 22, 1823, Gilder Lehrman Collection, Pierpont Morgan Library, New York City).

31. U.S. v. Gordon and Shepherd (U.S. Cir. Ct., Va., 1811); Ship Adventure (U.S. Cir. Ct., Va., 1812), in Hobson et al., eds., *Marshall Papers*, 7:301, 351.

32. U.S. v. Wiltberger, 5 Wheaton 95 (1820).

33. U.S. v. Logwood (U.S. Cir. Ct., Va., 1804), in Charles F. Hobson and Fredrika J. Teute, eds., *The Papers of John Marshall*, vol. 6 (Chapel Hill, N.C., 1990), 290–91; U.S. v. Burr (U.S. Cir. Ct., Va., September 14, 1807), in Hobson et al., eds, *Marshall Papers*, 7:136–37; U.S. v. Palmer, 3 Wheaton 626–35 (1818); U.S. v. Wiltberger, 5 Wheaton, 93–105. For cases arising under the embargo and nonintercourse laws, see Dickson v. U.S. (U.S. Cir. Ct., Va., 1811); U.S. v. Gordon and Shepherd (U.S. Cir. Ct., Va., 1811); U.S. v. Brig Diana (U.S. Cir. Ct., N.C., 1812); U.S. v. [Anonymous] (U.S. Cir. Ct., Va. 1812); Ship Adventure (U.S. Cir. Ct., Va., 1812), in Hobson et al., eds., *Marshall Papers*, 7:288–95, 299–301, 320–21, 344–48, 350–54.

34. U.S. v. Burr (U.S. Cir. Ct., Va., September 14, 1807); Ship Adventure (U.S. Cir. Ct., Va., 1812), in Hobson et al., eds., *Marshall Papers*, 7:136, 351; U.S. v. Wiltberger, 5 Wheaton 95 (1820).

35. The Venus, 8 Cranch 297 (1814). See also Talbot v. Seeman, 1 Cranch 44 (1801); Murray v. Schooner Charming Betsey, 2 Cranch 118 (1804); Meade v. Deputy Marshall of Virginia District, 1 Brockenbrough 328 (U.S. Cir. Ct., Va., 1815).

36. Murray v. Schooner Charming Betsey, 2 Cranch 118.

37. Brown v. U.S., 8 Cranch 125 (1814); The Nereide, 9 Cranch 423 (1815).

38. Evans v. Jordan and Morehead, 1 Brockenbrough 251 (U.S. Cir. Ct., Va., 1813).

39. U.S. v. Fisher, 2 Cranch 390 (1805).

40. Evans v. Jordan and Morehead, 1 Brockenbrough 252–53.

41. The Nereide, 9 Cranch 422–23 (1815).

42. The Antelope, 10 Wheaton 120 (1825).

43. Sallie E. Marshall Hardy, "John Marshall, third Chief Justice of the United States . . . ," *Green Bag* 8 (1896): 488 (quoting Harriet Martineau). Marshall's views on slavery are well summarized in Faulkner, *Jurisprudence of John Marshall,* 49–51; Francis N. Stites, *John Marshall: Defender of the Constitution* (Boston, 1981), 145–48.

44. Marshall to unknown correspondent, undated, quoted in Faulkner, *Jurisprudence of John Marshall,* 51–52n; Marshall to Timothy Pickering, March 20, 1826, in Massachusetts Historical Society, *Proceedings* 2d ser., 14 (1900): 321–22; Marshall to R. R. Gurley, December 14, 1831, in American Colonization Society, *Annual Report* 15 (1832): vi–viii. Privately, Marshall appears to have regarded colonization "as being merely a palliative, and slavery incurable but by convulsion" (Hardy, "John Marshall, third Chief Justice of the United States . . . ," 488 [quoting Harriet Martineau]).

45. Charles F. Hobson et al., eds., *The Papers of John Marshall,* vol. 5 (Chapel Hill, N.C., 1987), 541–46 (quotation at 545).

46. Scott v. Negro London, 3 Cranch 329 (1806); Scott v. Negro Ben, 6 Cranch 1 (1810); Wood v. Davis, 7 Cranch 271 (1812); Mima Queen v. Hepburn, 7 Cranch 293 (1813); Henry v. Ball, 1 Wheaton 1 (1816).

47. Mima Queen v. Hepburn, 7 Cranch 293–98.

48. Brig Caroline v. U.S., 1 Brockenbrough 384. Brockenbrough mistakenly reported this case as occurring on the Virginia circuit in 1819. In fact, the opinion was prepared for a case decided in the Supreme Court in 1813. See Charles F. Hobson, ed., *The Papers of John Marshall,* vol. 8 (Chapel Hill, N.C., 1995), 404.

49. The Antelope, 10 Wheaton 67–69. For a comprehensive study of this case, see John T. Noonan, Jr., *The Antelope: The Ordeal of the Recaptured Africans in the Administrations of James Monroe and John Quincy Adams* (Berkeley, Calif., 1977).

50. The Constitution, Art. 1., sec. 9, prevented Congress from prohibiting the importation of slaves until 1808. In 1807 Congress enacted legislation prohibiting the importation of slaves, effective January 1, 1808. Subsequent laws were adopted in 1818, 1819, and 1820 (*The Public Statutes at Large of the United States of America, 1789–1873* [Boston, 1845–73], 2:426; 3:450, 532, 600).

51. 10 Wheaton 114.

52. See Robert M. Cover, *Justice Accused: Antislavery and the Judicial Process* (New Haven, Conn., 1975), 102–4.

53. 10 Wheaton 115–16.

54. 10 Wheaton 118–20.

55. 10 Wheaton 120–21.

56. 10 Wheaton 121–23.

57. 10 Wheaton 130.

58. See Joseph C. Burke, "The Cherokee Cases: A Study in Law, Politics, and Morality," *Stanford Law Review* 21 (1969): 500–531.

59. 5 Peters 1 (1831).

60. 8 Wheaton 543. Marshall also briefly discussed the nature of Indian title in Fletcher v. Peck, 6 Cranch 141–43 (1810).

61. 8 Wheaton 592.

62. 8 Wheaton 572.

63. 8 Wheaton 573–74.

64. 8 Wheaton 588.

65. 8 Wheaton 590, 591–92.

66. 8 Wheaton 593.

67. Milner S. Ball, "Constitution, Court, Indian Tribes," *American Bar Foundation Research Journal* 1 (1987): 23–29.

68. Marshall to Joseph Story, October 29, 1828, Story Papers, Massachusetts Historical Society.

69. Burke, "Cherokee Cases," 512–13.

70. 5 Peters 15 (1831).

71. 5 Peters 16.

72. 5 Peters 17.

73. 5 Peters 20.

74. Marshall to Richard Peters, May 19, 1831, Peters Papers, Historical Society of Pennsylvania.

75. 6 Peters 536 (1832).

76. 6 Peters 542.

77. 6 Peters 543.

78. 6 Peters 544, 544–45, 546.

79. 6 Peters 552.

80. 6 Peters 559.

81. 6 Peters 561–63.

82. For the origins of this alleged remark, see Warren, *Supreme Court in United States History,* 1:759 and n.

83. Burke, "Cherokee Cases," 524–32.

84. Story to Sarah W. Story, March 4, 1832, in William W. Story, ed., *Life and Letters of Joseph Story* (Boston, 1851), 2:87.

Chapter 7. Principle, Precedent, and Interpretation

1. See, generally, Sylvia Snowiss, *Judicial Review and the Law of the Constitution* (New Haven, Conn., 1990).

2. William M. Wiecek, *Liberty Under Law: The Supreme Court in American Life* (Baltimore, 1988), 32–33. See also David P. Currie, *The Constitution in the Supreme Court: The First Hundred Years, 1789–1888* (Chicago, 1985), 89, 196.

3. 9 Wheaton 851 (1824).

4. Joseph Story, "A Discourse upon the Life, Character, and Services of the Honorable John Marshall," in John F. Dillon, ed., *John Marshall: Life, Character, and Judicial Services* (Chicago, 1903), 3:377.

5. For examples of the distinction in Supreme Court opinions, see U.S. v. Grundy and Thornburgh, 3 Cranch 351 (1806); Rose v. Himely, 4 Cranch 269–70 (1808); Alexander v. Baltimore Insurance Co., 4 Cranch 376 (1808); Schooner Exchange v. McFaddon, 7 Cranch 136 (1812); The Venus, 8 Cranch 298 (1814); The Commercen, 1 Wheaton 404 (1816); Hughes v. Union Insurance Co., 3 Wheaton 164 (1818); Blight's Lessee v. Rochester, 7 Wheaton 550 (1822). See also the following circuit opinions: Blane v. Drummond (U.S. Cir. Ct., Va., 1803), in Charles F. Hobson and Fredrika J. Teute, eds., *The Papers of John Marshall*, vol. 6 (Chapel Hill, N.C., 1990), 216; U.S. v. Burr (U.S. Cir. Ct., Va., May 28, 1807), in Charles F. Hobson et al., eds., *The Papers of John Marshall*, vol. 7 (Chapel Hill, N.C., 1993), 29; Mutter's Executors v. Munford (U.S. Cir. Ct., Va., 1814), in Charles F. Hobson, ed., *The Papers of John Marshall*, vol. 8 (Chapel Hill, N.C., 1995), 56.

6. Murdock v. Hunter (U.S. Cir. Ct., Va., 1809), in Hobson et al., eds, *Marshall Papers*, 7:209–10, 211. See also Livingston v. Jefferson (U.S. Cir. Ct., Va., 1811), ibid., 284.

7. Short v. Skipwith (U.S. Cir. Ct., Va., 1806), in Hobson and Teute, eds., *Marshall Papers*, 6:458–59. For another circuit case in which he adhered to a line of English decisions, this time in preference to a decision of the U.S. Supreme Court, see U.S. v. Nelson and Myers, 2 Brockenbrough 73–75 (U.S. Cir. Ct., Va., 1822).

8. Mutter's Executors v. Munford (U.S. Cir. Ct., Va., 1814), in Hobson, ed., *Marshall Papers*, 8:57.

9. U.S. v. Burr (U.S. Cir. Ct., Va., May 28, 1807), in Hobson et al., eds., *Marshall Papers*, 7:29.

10. Lidderdale v. Robinson, 2 Brockenbrough 129 (U.S. Cir. Ct., Va., 1824).

11. Livingston v. Jefferson (U.S. Cir. Ct., Va., 1811), in Hobson et al., eds., *Marshall Papers*, 7:284, 285.

12. Elmendorf v. Taylor, 10 Wheaton 159–60 (1825). Marshall went on to say that by the same principle other courts must accept as definitive the Supreme

Court's interpretation of the Constitution and laws of the United States. See, in this context, Marshall to Dudley Chase, February 7, 1817, in Hobson, ed., *Marshall Papers*, 8:148–49. For other cases affirming the rule that federal courts must adopt state judicial constructions of local law, see M'Keen v. DeLancy's Lessee, 5 Cranch 32 (1809); Polk's Lessee v. Wendell, 9 Cranch 98 (1815); Thatcher v. Powell, 6 Wheaton 127 (1821); Backhouse's Administrator v. Jett's Administrator, 1 Brockenbrough 515 (U.S. Cir. Ct., Va., 1821).

13. Backhouse's Administrator v. Jett's Administrator, 1 Brockenbrough 515 (U.S. Cir. Ct., Va., 1821).

14. Graves and Barnewall v. Boston Marine Insurance Co., 2 Cranch 442 (1805); U.S. v. Feely (U.S. Cir. Ct., Va., 1813), in Hobson et al., eds., *Marshall Papers*, 7:393, 394; Backhouse's Administrator v. Jett's Administrator, 1 Brockenbrough 512, 513 (U.S. Cir. Ct., Va., 1821); Garnett v. Macon, 2 Brockenbrough 242, 246–47 (U.S. Cir. Ct., Va., 1825); Hamilton, Donaldson and Co. v. Cunningham, 2 Brockenbrough 350 (U.S. Cir. Ct., Va., 1828). See also Murdock v. Hunter (U.S. Cir. Ct., Va., 1809), in Hobson et al., eds., *Marshall Papers*, 7:210.

15. Wilson v. Codman's Executor, 3 Cranch 209 (1805); Bond v. Ross (U.S. Cir. Ct., Va., 1805), in Hobson and Teute, eds., *Marshall Papers*, 6:418–19; Furniss v. Ellis and Allan, 2 Brockenbrough 16 (U.S. Cir. Ct., Va., 1822).

16. For examples, see Calloway v. Dobson (U.S. Cir. Ct., Va., 1807), in Hobson et al., eds., *Marshall Papers*, 7:34–35; Alexander v. Harris, 4 Cranch 302 (1808); Hughes v. Union Insurance Co., 3 Wheaton 166 (1818); Garnett v. Macon, 2 Brockenbrough 214 (U.S. Cir. Ct., Va., 1825).

17. Alexander v. Baltimore Insurance Co., 4 Cranch 377 (1808); Scriba v. Deane (U.S. Cir. Ct., Va., 1810), in Hobson et al., eds., *Marshall Papers*, 7:264; Mutter's Executors v. Munford (U.S. Cir. Ct., Va., 1814), in Hobson, ed., *Marshall Papers*, 8:56; Bayley v. Greenleaf, 7 Wheaton 56–57 (1822); Bank of the U.S. v. Dandridge, 12 Wheaton 107 (1827). See also Olivera v. Union Insurance Co., 3 Wheaton 190, 191 (1818).

18. U.S. v. Burr (U.S. Cir. Ct., Va., August 31, 1807), in Hobson et al., eds., *Marshall Papers*, 7:87–88.

19. Cohens v. Virginia, 6 Wheaton 399–400 (1821). For other cases in which he reiterated this maxim, see Corbet v. Johnson (U.S. Cir. Ct., Va., 1805), in Hobson and Teute, eds., *Marshall Papers*, 6:386; The Venus, 8 Cranch 307–8 (1814); Handly's Lessee v. Anthony, 5 Wheaton 381 (1820); Brooks v. Marbury, 11 Wheaton 90 (1826).

20. Alexander v. Baltimore Insurance Co., 4 Cranch 379, 380 (1808).

21. Scriba v. Deane (U.S. Cir. Ct., Va., 1810), in Hobson et al., eds., *Marshall Papers*, 7:266.

22. U.S. v. Nelson and Myers, 2 Brockenbrough 71–72 (U.S. Cir. Ct., Va., 1822); Brooks v. Marbury, 11 Wheaton 90–92 (1826).

23. U.S. v. Burr (U.S. Cir. Ct., Va., August 31, 1807), in Hobson et al., eds., *Marshall Papers,* 7:104–6.

24. The Venus, 8 Cranch 298–99, 314, 315 (1814).

25. Hopkirk v. Randolph, 2 Brockenbrough 138–44 (U.S. Cir. Ct., Va., 1824 [quotations at 138, 141, 144]).

26. Hamilton, Donaldson and Co. v. Cunningham, 2 Brockenbrough 370 (U.S. Cir. Ct., Va., 1828).

27. Story, "Discourse," in Dillon, ed., *John Marshall: Life, Character, and Judicial Services,* 3:370.

28. King v. Delaware Insurance Co., 6 Cranch 80 (1810). For other references to the imperfection of language, see U.S. v. Burr (U.S. Cir. Ct., Va., June 13, 1807), in Hobson et al., eds., *Marshall Papers,* 7:40; Shore's Executor v. Jones (U.S. Cir. Ct., Va., 1814), in Hobson, ed., *Marshall Papers,* 8:44.

29. Turner v. Fendall, 1 Cranch 131 (1801); U.S. v. Willing and Francis, 4 Cranch 56 (1807); U.S. v. Burr (U.S. Cir. Ct., Va., June 13, 1807), in Hobson et al., eds., *Marshall Papers,* 7:40; Peisch v. Ware, 4 Cranch 363 (1808); Rutherford v. Green's Heirs, 2 Wheaton 201 (1817); Chirac v. Chirac, 2 Wheaton 271 (1817); Postmaster General v. Early, 12 Wheaton 150 (1827).

30. "A Friend to the Union," No. 2, in Gerald Gunther, ed., *John Marshall's Defense of McCulloch v. Maryland* (Stanford, Calif., 1969), 92; Hobson, ed., *Marshall Papers,* 8:299.

31. Coates v. Muse, 1 Brockenbrough 545 (U.S. Cir. Ct., Va., 1822); Kirkpatrick v. Gibson, 2 Brockenbrough 390 (U.S. Cir. Ct., Va., 1828).

32. See U.S. v. Fisher, 2 Cranch 386 (1805): "As the enacting clause in this case, would plainly give the United States the preference they claim, it is incumbent on those who oppose that preference, to shew an intent varying from that which the words import."

33. Schooner Patriot v. U.S., 1 Brockenbrough 412 (U.S. Cir. Ct., Va., 1820).

34. Coates v. Muse, 1 Brockenbrough 545 (U.S. Cir. Ct., Va., 1822).

35. Pennington v. Coxe, 2 Cranch 52 (1804); Postmaster General v. Early, 12 Wheaton 152 (1827). See also similar statements in U.S. v. Fisher, 2 Cranch 386 (1805); Alexander v. Mayor and Commonalty of Alexandria, 5 Cranch 7–8 (1809); The Mary Ann, 8 Wheaton 387 (1823); U.S. v. Burr (U.S. Cir. Ct., Va., September 18, 1807); Strode v. Stafford Justices (U.S. Cir. Ct., Va., 1810), U.S. v. Twitty (U.S. Cir. Ct. N.C., 1811), in Hobson et al., eds., *Marshall Papers,* 7:144, 260, 275; Shore's Executor v. Jones (U.S. Cir. Ct., Va., 1814), in Hobson, ed., *Marshall Papers,* 8:44.

36. U.S. v. Burr (U.S. Cir. Ct., Va., September 18, 1807), in Hobson et al., eds., *Marshall Papers,* 7:144; Adams v. Woods, 2 Cranch 341 (1805). See also Alexander v. Mayor and Commonalty of Alexandria, 5 Cranch 7–8 (1809); The Mary Ann, 8 Wheaton 387 (1823).

37. The Brig Wilson v. U.S., 1 Brockenbrough 434 (U.S. Cir. Ct., Va., 1820); Oneale v. Thornton, 6 Cranch 68 (1810).

38. Pennington v. Coxe, 2 Cranch 51–64 (quotations at 54, 55, 62).

39. 2 Cranch 386.

40. 3 Wheaton 630–31.

41. 5 Wheaton 93–105 (quotations at 96, 105). See also U.S. v. Bevans, 3 Wheaton 386–91 (1818).

42. Huidekoper's Lessee v. Douglas, 3 Cranch 66 (1805).

43. Durosseau v. U.S., 6 Cranch 314 (1810).

44. William Blackstone, *Commentaries on the Laws of England* (London, 1765), 1:88.

45. Hodgson v. Butts, 3 Cranch 156–58 (1805).

46. Bond v. Ross (U.S. Cir. Ct., Va., 1815), in Hobson, ed., *Marshall Papers,* 8:101–6 (quotations at 103, 105, 106).

47. Gallego v. U.S., 1 Brockenbrough 443 (U.S. Cir. Ct., Va., 1820).

48. Postmaster General v. Early, 12 Wheaton 150–52 (1827).

49. Adams's comment is quoted in Charles Warren, *The Supreme Court in United States History* (Boston, 1926), 1:578n. See also Story's comment on Marshall's opinion in U.S. v. Bevans (William W. Story, ed., *Life and Letters of Joseph Story* [Boston, 1851], 1:305).

50. Schooner Paulina v. U.S., 7 Cranch 61 (1812).

51. "A Friend of the Constitution," No. 3, in Gunther, ed., *Marshall's Defense,* 168–69; Hobson, ed., *Marshall Papers,* 8:328.

52. Speech in the Virginia Convention, January 13, 1830, in *Proceedings and Debates of the Virginia State Convention, of 1829–30* (Richmond, Va., 1830), 872.

53. On Marshall's understanding of intent, see H. Jefferson Powell, "The Original Understanding of Original Intent," *Harvard Law Review* 98 (1985): 885–948 (esp. 942–44); Leslie Friedman Goldstein, *In Defense of the Text: Democracy and Constitutional Theory* (Savage, Md., 1991), 7–12. The literature on "original intent" is voluminous. A useful anthology is Jack Rakove, ed., *Interpreting the Constitution: The Debate over Original Intent* (Boston, 1990).

54. Brown v. Maryland, 12 Wheaton 437 (1827); Sturges v. Crowninshield, 4 Wheaton 202 (1819).

55. Sturges v. Crowninshield, 4 Wheaton 202–3 (1819).

56. Dartmouth College v. Woodward, 4 Cranch 629 (1819).

57. Ogden v. Saunders, 12 Wheaton 332 (1827); Dartmouth College v. Woodward, 4 Wheaton 627–28 (1819).

58. Craig v. Missouri, 4 Peters 433–34 (1830).

59. Brown v. Maryland, 12 Wheaton 437–38, 441 (1827).

60. McCulloch v. Maryland, 4 Wheaton 407, 412 (1819).

61. 4 Wheaton 413–20 (quotations at 413, 415, 419, 420).

62. "A Friend to the Union," No. 2, in Gunther, ed., *Marshall's Defense,* 97; Hobson, ed., *Marshall Papers,* 8:303.

63. "A Friend of the Constitution," No. 3, in Gunther, ed., *Marshall's Defense,* 169; Hobson, ed., *Marshall Papers,* 8:328; Gibbons v. Ogden, 9 Wheaton 188 (1824).

64. "A Friend of the Constitution," Nos. 2, 3, in Gunther, ed., *Marshall's Defense,* 166, 169–71; Hobson, ed., *Marshall Papers,* 8:326–30.

65. Gibbons v. Ogden, 9 Wheaton 222 (1824); "A Friend to the Union," No. 2, in Gunther, ed., *Marshall's Defense,* 99; Hobson, ed., *Marshall Papers,* 8:304.

66. "A Friend of the Constitution," No. 1, in Gunther, ed., *Marshall's Defense,* 155; Hobson, ed., *Marshall Papers,* 8:318.

67. Marshall to John Quincy Adams, October 3, 1831, Adams Papers, Massachusetts Historical Society.

68. Madison also corresponded with Roane in 1821 in the wake of Cohens v. Virginia, but his comments on that occasion were more a critique of Roane than of the Court. See Madison to Roane, September 2, 1819, May 6, 1821, June 29, 1821, in Marvin Meyers, ed., *The Mind of the Founder: Sources of the Political Thought of James Madison,* rev. ed. (Hanover, N.H., 1981), 359–69.

69. Madison to Roane, September 2, 1819, ibid., 359–61.

70. For a discriminating reading of Madison's critique of the Marshall Court, see Drew R. McCoy, *The Last of the Fathers: James Madison and the Republican Legacy* (New York, 1989), 99–103.

71. Madison to Roane, September 2, 1819, in Meyers, ed., *Mind of the Founder,* 361–62.

72. Madison to Roane, May 6, 1821, ibid., 366; Madison to Jefferson, June 27, 1823, in [William C. Rives and Philip R. Fendall, eds.], *Letters and Other Writings of James Madison,* 4 vols. (Philadelphia, 1865), 3:325, 326.

73. See McCoy, *Last of the Fathers,* 130–36.

74. Madison to Joseph C. Cabell, September 7, 1829, September 16, 1831; Madison to N. P. Trist, December 1831; Madison to Unknown, 1834, in [Rives and Fendall, eds.], *Letters and Other Writings,* 4:47, 196, 210–11, 350.

75. Madison to Edward Everett, August 1830, *Letters and Other Writings,* 4:100; Marshall to Joseph Story, October 15, 1830, Story Papers, Massachusetts Historical Society. In 1834 Story offered this comment on the two elder statesmen in a published sketch of Marshall: "Many have witnessed, with no ordinary emotions, the pleasure with which both of these gentlemen look back upon their cooperation at that period [the 1780s], and the sentiments of profound respect with which they habitually regard each other" (see "John Marshall, LL.D., Chief justice of the United States," in James Herring and James B. Longacre, eds., *National Portrait Gallery of Distinguished Americans* [Philadelphia, 1837], 1:6).

76. This and the following paragraphs draw heavily from Snowiss, *Judicial Review and the Law of the Constitution,* especially 1–12, 113–21.

BIBLIOGRAPHICAL ESSAY

PRIMARY SOURCES

The foundation of this study is the writings of John Marshall, principally those prepared as official legal judgments. Like other statesmen of the founding era, Marshall is the subject of a comprehensive annotated edition of "papers." To date, eight volumes of *The Papers of John Marshall* (Chapel Hill, N.C., 1974–) have been published (under the successive editorships of Herbert A. Johnson, Charles T. Cullen, and Charles F. Hobson), documenting Marshall's life and career through 1819. This edition brings together correspondence, judicial opinions, speeches, newspaper essays, and miscellaneous writings and will eventually supersede previously published collections of source material. Legal papers constitute by far the largest portion of Marshall's surviving literary output. His correspondence is disappointingly meager, particularly when compared with the rich collections of his fellow Virginians George Washington, Thomas Jefferson, and James Madison. Unlike them Marshall evidently made no attempt to preserve his private papers. Nearly all of his extant letters are to be found in the papers of his correspondents or in scattered autograph collections. The most valuable of these are letters he wrote to his Supreme Court colleagues Joseph Story and Bushrod Washington.

Pending completion of the *Marshall Papers*, still useful printed collections of correspondence include Charles C. Smith, ed., "Letters of

Chief Justice Marshall," *Proceedings of the Massachusetts Historical Society* 2d ser., 14 (1900): 320–60, and Charles Warren, "The Story-Marshall Correspondence (1819–1831)," *William and Mary Quarterly* 2d ser., 21 (1941): 1–26. Marshall's autobiographical letter to Story, written in 1827, has been separately published in John Stokes Adams, ed., *An Autobiographical Sketch by John Marshall* (Ann Arbor, Mich., 1937). Besides a modest collection of correspondence, other nonjudicial sources of Marshall's thought consist of reported speeches and polemical newspaper essays. His speeches at the Virginia ratifying convention of 1788 and in Congress in 1799 and 1800 (including that defending the Adams administration in the Jonathan Robbins affair) are available in the Marshall Papers edition.

The same is true of his newspaper pieces of the 1790s and those written in 1819 in defense of *McCulloch* v. *Maryland*. The latter have also been conveniently brought together, along with the text of the decision and the essays by William Brockenbrough and Spencer Roane attacking the decision, in Gerald Gunther, ed., *John Marshall's Defense of McCulloch v. Maryland* (Stanford, Calif., 1969). As an elder statesman at the Virginia constitutional convention of 1829–1830, Marshall delivered several speeches (including a notable defense of an independent judiciary), which are printed in *Proceedings and Debates of the Virginia State Convention, of 1829–30* (Richmond, Va., 1830). John Edward Oster, *The Political and Economic Doctrines of John Marshall* (New York, 1914) is an ill-organized, inaccurate collection of correspondence, excerpts of speeches, opinions, and other writings, some of which are not readily accessible elsewhere. An invaluable guide to Marshall documents is Irwin S. Rhodes, *The Papers of John Marshall: A Descriptive Calendar,* 2 vols. (Norman, Okla., 1969).

Soon after his appointment as chief justice, Marshall began work on *The Life of George Washington,* 5 vols. (Philadelphia, 1804–1807), an essential source for the author's political ideas. The first volume was subsequently published separately as *A History of the Colonies* (Philadelphia, 1824). The other volumes of the *Life* were compressed into a two-volume revised edition (Philadelphia, 1832), which was reprinted several times and can be found on the shelves of most libraries.

Perhaps this is the place to request future scholars to refrain from attributing to Marshall authorship of the *Address of the Minority in the Virginia Legislature* (Richmond, Va., 1799), drawn up in defense of the

Alien and Sedition Laws. This attribution is based entirely on the unsupported assertion of biographer Albert J. Beveridge. There is no positive evidence of Marshall's authorship of the address, and there are good reasons for concluding that he was not the writer. The probable author was Henry Lee, who was actually a member of the Virginia legislature at the time and who reported the address to that body.

Of necessity, an inquiry into Marshall's political and constitutional thought must be confined largely to his voluminous legal writings. The chief justice wrote more than six hundred opinions, including those given on circuit. The *Marshall Papers* is reprinting complete texts of all the constitutional decisions and a highly selective number of nonconstitutional opinions delivered on the Supreme Court. The somewhat less accessible circuit opinions are also presented in full in this edition. Marshall's Supreme Court opinions were originally published in the reports of William Cranch, Henry Wheaton, and Richard Peters, Jr., which were later incorporated into the ongoing official series of *United States Reports*. His circuit opinions were first published in John W. Brockenbrough, *Reports of Cases Decided by the Honourable John Marshall*, 2 vols. (Philadelphia, 1837). The circuit opinions in the 1807 treason and misdemeanor trials of Aaron Burr were published in David Robertson, *Reports of the Trials of Colonel Aaron Burr*, 2 vols. (1808; New York, 1969 reprint) and Thomas Carpenter, *The Trial of Col. Aaron Burr*, 3 vols. (Washington, D.C., 1807–1808). All of the circuit opinions were subsequently reprinted in the alphabetically arranged *Federal Cases*, 30 vols. (St. Paul, Minn., 1894–1897). Among numerous anthologies of Marshall's principal opinions, the most comprehensive is Joseph P. Cotton, Jr., ed., *The Constitutional Decisions of John Marshall*, 2 vols. (1905; New York, 1969 reprint).

SECONDARY SOURCES

My reading of Marshall has been shaped and informed by a vast body of scholarship dealing broadly with the formative era of the American federal republic and more particularly with the jurist's life and thought. The following brief survey includes only those works that have been most directly relevant to my enterprise of explicating Marshall's legal and political ideas.

Political Thought of the Founding Generation

The immense outpouring of studies on the founding era during the last thirty years forms the essential framework and point of departure for examining Marshall's thought. A predominant theme of this literature is the emergence of a "republican" ideology based on the concept of civic virtue and its subsequent eclipse (at some point between the Constitution and the election of Andrew Jackson) by a "liberal" ideology based on the concept of individual self-interest. My understanding of this development has been profoundly influenced by the seminal scholarship of Gordon S. Wood, notably, *The Creation of the American Republic, 1776–1787* (Chapel Hill, N.C., 1969), and *The Radicalism of the American Revolution* (New York, 1992). Wood has supplied a convenient summary and spirited defense of his work in "Ideology and the Origins of Liberal America," *William and Mary Quarterly* 3d ser., 44 (1987): 628–40. My short list of other titles that illuminate this topic includes Drew R. McCoy, *The Elusive Republic: Political Economy in Jeffersonian America* (Chapel Hill, N.C., 1980); idem, *The Last of the Fathers: James Madison and the Republican Legacy* (New York, 1989); Lance Banning, "Jeffersonian Ideology Revisited: Liberal and Classical Ideas in the New American Republic," *William and Mary Quarterly* 3d ser., 43 (1986): 3–19; Banning, "Some Second Thoughts on Virtue and the Course of Revolutionary Thinking," in Terence Ball and J. G. A. Pocock, eds., *Conceptual Change and the Constitution* (Lawrence, Kans., 1988), 194–212.

Although Banning's major study of James Madison's thought, *The Sacred Fire of Liberty: James Madison and the Founding of the Federal Republic* (Ithaca, N.Y., 1995), appeared too late for consideration, some of the author's arguments and themes have been sketched out in previously published articles. For an excellent historiographical overview, see Peter S. Onuf, "Reflections on the Founding: Constitutional Historiography in Bicentennial Perspective," *William and Mary Quarterly* 3d. ser., 46 (1989): 341–75.

The Common Law Tradition

The political thought of the founders, comprising in varying degrees both "republican" and "liberal" elements, supplies useful analytical categories for interpreting Marshall's jurisprudence (see below). Still, an underlying premise of this study is that an equally if not more important source of his juristic thought was the tradition of English common law and equity as manifested in the provincial setting of eighteenth-century Virginia. To understand the legal culture that formed Marshall the lawyer, one must first acquire a basic knowledge of English law. An excellent guide is J. H. Baker, *An Introduction to English Legal History* (London, 1971). S. F. C. Milsom, *Historical Foundations of the Common Law,* 2d ed. (Toronto, 1981), is a sophisticated treatment of its subject. The best entry into Marshall's legal world is through the text that he himself read: William Blackstone, *Commentaries on the Laws of England,* 4 vols. (London, 1765–69). Better still, because it combines Blackstone with developments in American and Virginia law, is St. George Tucker, *Blackstone's Commentaries: With Notes of Reference to the Constitution and Laws, of the Federal Government of the United States; and of the Commonwealth of Virginia,* 5 vols. (Philadelphia, 1803). For a description of the Virginia legal system in which Marshall practiced law, see the introductory essay in Charles F. Hobson et al., eds., *The Papers of John Marshall,* vol. 5 (Chapel Hill, N.C., 1987), xxiii–lx. An exemplary essay that demonstrates Marshall's solid grounding in common law learning is Julius Goebel, Jr., "The Common Law and the Constitution," in W. Melville Jones, ed., *Chief Justice John Marshall: A Reappraisal* (Ithaca, N.Y., 1956). C. H. S. Fifoot's superb study of Marshall's great English counterpart, *Lord Mansfield* (Oxford, 1936), has been a model for the present undertaking.

Biographies

Among works focusing specifically on Marshall, biographies are a convenient place to begin. Albert J. Beveridge, *The Life of John Marshall,* 4 vols. (Boston, 1916–1919), is woefully dated but remains the classic life and times, portraying its subject as an almost mythological hero and symbol of American nationality. Leonard Baker, *John Marshall: A Life in Law* (New York, 1974), the only major biography to appear since Beveridge, is a competent account by a journalist. An excellent short biography by a seasoned historian is Francis N. Stites, *John Marshall: Defender of the Constitution* (Boston, 1981). A new full-length life of Marshall by Jean Edward Smith, a professor of political science at the University of

Toronto, is scheduled for publication in 1996. Historian R. Kent Newmyer, biographer of Joseph Story, is also writing a Marshall biography. Still valuable for their insights into Marshall's juridical thought are brief biographical treatments by two distinguished legal scholars of an earlier generation: James B. Thayer, *John Marshall* (Boston, 1901), and Edward S. Corwin, *John Marshall and the Constitution* (New Haven, Conn., 1920). The former has been reprinted, along with Oliver Wendell Holmes's iconoclastic 1901 address on Marshall and Felix Frankfurter's 1955 essay, "John Marshall and the Judicial Function," as *James Bradley Thayer, Oliver Wendell Holmes, and Felix Frankfurter on John Marshall* (Chicago, 1967). Still unsurpassed for its portrait of Marshall's mind is Joseph Story, "A Discourse upon the Life, Character, and Services of the Honorable John Marshall," in John F. Dillon, ed., *John Marshall: Life, Character, and Judicial Services,* 3 vols. (Chicago, 1903), 3:327–80.

The Marshall Court

The Supreme Court under Chief Justice Marshall is covered in two massive volumes in *The Oliver Wendell Holmes Devise History of the Supreme Court of the United States:* George Lee Haskins and Herbert A. Johnson, *Foundations of Power: John Marshall, 1801–15* (New York, 1981), and G. Edward White, *The Marshall Court and Cultural Change, 1815–35* (New York, 1988). The former emphasizes the Court's largely successful effort to separate law and politics, while the latter is a noteworthy attempt to show how the Court's jurisprudence was shaped by republican ideology. Both volumes have generated critical commentary. See, for example, the following review essays: Jennifer Nedelsky, "Confining Democractic Politics: Anti-Federalists, Federalists, and the Constitution," *Harvard Law Review* 96 (1982): 340–60; Stephen A. Siegel, "The Marshall Court and Republicanism," *Texas Law Review* 67 (1989): 903–42; Herman Belz, "Book Review," *Constitutional Commentary* 8 (1991): 234–45. Two older histories are still useful, principally for their extensive quotations from contemporary sources: Charles Warren, *The Supreme Court in United States History,* rev. ed., 2 vols. (Boston, 1926), and Charles Grove Haines, *The Role of the Supreme Court in American Government and Politics, 1789–1835* (New York, 1973). The best brief surveys are R. Kent Newmyer, *The Supreme Court Under Marshall and Taney* (Arlington Heights, Ill., 1968), and the relevant chapters of Herman Belz's revision of a standard text: Alfred H. Kelly, Winfred A. Harbison, and Herman Belz, *The American Constitution: Its Origins and Development*, 6th ed. (New York, 1983).

Marshall's Jurisprudence

Most studies of Marshall's thought have been conducted by political scientists. Nearly forty years ago Morton J. Frisch offered a preliminary sketch, "John Marshall's Philosophy of Constitutional Republicanism," *The Review of Politics* 20 (1958): 34–45. A decade later, Robert Kenneth Faulkner published a path-breaking work, *The Jurisprudence of John Marshall* (Princeton, N.J., 1968), to which all students of Marshall are deeply indebted. From the chief justice's public and private writings, Faulkner extracted a coherent political philosophy of constitutional democracy that in many ways was representatively American. He placed Marshall squarely within the tradition of political and economic liberalism originating in John Locke and Adam Smith. Republicanism, he argued, was an important and "ennobling" strand in Marshall's jurisprudence, though subordinate to a liberalism that accorded highest value to the promotion of the individual's private interests. Faulkner's exhaustive inquiry, marked by an astute and discriminating reading of texts, effectively foreclosed scholarship for nearly a generation.

Recently there have been signs of renewed interest in Marshall as a thinker and jurist. Proceeding from Faulkner's conceptual framework, much of this newer work focuses on identifying the republican and liberal aspects of Marshall's jurisprudence. See Thomas C. Shevory, ed., *John Marshall's Achievement: Law Politics, and Constitutional Interpretations* (Westport, Conn., 1989), in particular the essays by Shevory, "John Marshall as Republican: Order and Conflict in American Political History," 75–93, and Richard A. Brisbin, Jr., "John Marshall on History, Virtue, and Legality," 95–115. See also Brisbin, "John Marshall and the Nature of Law in the Early Republic," *Virginia Magazine of History and Biography* 98 (1990): 57–80. Shevory's essay has been incorporated in his short book, *John Marshall's Law: Interpretation, Ideology, and Interest* (Westport, Conn., 1994), which is marred however by numerous errors and a presentism that reflects the author's interest in modern judicial interpretation rather than the historical John Marshall. Legal scholars have also turned their attention to Marshall. See, for example, William E. Nelson, "The Eighteenth-Century Background of Marshall's Constitutional Jurisprudence," *Michigan Law Review* 76 (1978): 893–960. Before undertaking their respective histories of the Marshall Court, Herbert A. Johnson and G. Edward White essayed the chief justice's jurisprudence. See Johnson, "John Marshall," in Leon Friedman and Fred Israel, eds., *The Justices of the Supreme Court, 1789–1969,* 4 vols. (New York, 1969), 1:285–304; White, *The American Judicial Tradition: Profiles of Leading American Judges,* rev. ed. (New York, 1988), 7–34. W. Melville Jones, ed., *Chief Justice John Marshall: A Reappraisal* (Ithaca, N.Y., 1956), a volume issuing out of the Marshall bicentennial, contains some useful essays by an older generation of scholars.

Judicial Review

Judicial review requires separate consideration because of Chief Justice Marshall's pivotal role in establishing this distinctively American judicial function. Although it has long been an entrenched institution of American constitutional democracy, judicial review has perennially provoked controversy over its nature and limits. The debate has spawned a voluminous literature, much of it normative and prescriptive, that is, addressed to modern concerns about how courts should exercise this prerogative. In general, political scientists and lawyers have shown greater scholarly interest in this topic than have historians. An exception, of course, is Gordon S. Wood, whose *Creation of the American Republic* provides the best account of the historical origins of judicial review. Wood later summarized his views in "The Origins of Judicial Review," *Suffolk University Law Review* 22 (1988): 1293–1307. Another recent historical survey, J. M. Sosin, *The Aristocracy of the Long Robe: The Origins of Judicial Review in America* (Westport, Ct., 1989), looks deeply into our English and colonial past and finds little precedent for the modern practice of judicial review. The best brief introduction is a pamphlet by Kermit L. Hall, *The Supreme Court and Judicial Review in American History* (Washington, D.C., 1985). Hall is also the editor and compiler of *Judicial Review in American History* (Hamden, Conn., 1987), a collection of twenty-five articles on the subject written during the past one hundred years. Elizabeth McCaughey, "*Marbury* v. *Madison*: Have We Missed the Real Meaning?" *Presidential Studies Quarterly* 19 (1989): 491–528, persuasively argues that this so-called landmark case was not a bold assertion of judicial power but a cautious retreat to a more limited and circumscribed role for courts in exercising review.

While pursuing avowedly normative purposes, political scientists have also performed some excellent historical recovery work on judicial review in recent years. See, for example, Christopher Wolfe, *The Rise of Modern Judicial Review: From Constitutional Interpretation to Judge-Made Law* (New York, 1986); Leslie Friedman Goldstein, "Popular Sovereignty, the Origins of Judicial Review, and the Revival of Unwritten Law," *Journal of Politics* 48 (1986): 51–71, reprinted in her book, *In Defense of the Text: Democracy and Constitutional Theory* (Savage, Md., 1991), 67–91; Robert Lowry Clinton, *Marbury v. Madison and Judicial Review* (Lawrence, Kans., 1989); and Sylvia Snowiss, *Judicial Review and the Law of the Constitution* (New Haven, Conn., 1990). In their various ways these scholars argue for a return to a more limited conception of judicial review, which they contend was endorsed by the founders and exemplified by Chief Justice Marshall. Professor Snowiss's contribution is particularly noteworthy for its cogently argued thesis and tone of dispassionate inquiry. Notwithstanding her sympathy for judicial restraint and admiration for Marshall, Snowiss devotes a major portion of her book to showing how the chief justice laid the groundwork for modern, expansive judicial review by "legalizing" the Constitution, transforming the instrument into "supreme ordinary law" by employing the techniques of judicial exposition. The author builds her case on too narrow an evidentiary base, and her insistence that modern judicial review sprang single-handedly from Marshall's "deliberate design," which the chief justice deviously contrived to keep concealed from public view, betrays an unrealistic understanding of a complex historical process. Still, she has produced an original and illuminating study of judicial review that is a model of disinterested scholarship.

Other scholars have conducted researches into our colonial and revolutionary past to validate a modern conception of judicial review as enforcing an "unwritten constitution" of fundamental principles not found in the text itself. In this scholarship Marshall is portrayed as abandoning natural law principles in favor of positivist, text-based review. See Thomas Grey, "Origins of the Unwritten Constitution: Fundamental Law in American Revolutionary Thought," *Stanford Law Review* 30 (1978): 843–93 (reprinted in Hall's compendium), and Suzanna Sherry, "The Founders' Unwritten Constitution," *University of Chicago Law Review* 54 (1987): 1127–77. All the arguments for a judicially enforceable "unwritten constitution" have not succeeded in overcoming the intractable historical fact that acceptance of judicial review in America occurred only because constitutions were reduced to writing.

Even the briefest survey of the literature of judicial review would be incomplete without mentioning the classic essays by James B. Thayer and Edward S. Corwin. See Thayer, "The Origin and Scope of the American Doctrine of Constitutional Law," *Harvard Law Review* 7 (1893): 129–56 (reprinted in Hall's compendium), and Corwin, *The Doctrine of Judicial Review* (Princeton, N.J., 1914).

INDEX